T0224077

Communications
in Computer and Information Science 507

Commenced Publication in 2007
Founding and Former Series Editors:
Alfredo Cuzzocrea, Dominik Ślęzak, and Xiaokang Yang

Editorial Board

More information about this series at http://www.springer.com/series/7899

Fernando S. Osório · Denis Fernando Wolf
Kalinka Castelo Branco · Valdir Grassi Jr.
Marcelo Becker · Roseli A. Francelin Romero (Eds.)

Robotics

Joint Conference on Robotics,
LARS 2014, SBR 2014, Robocontrol 2014
São Carlos, Brazil, October 18–23, 2014
Revised Selected Papers

 Springer

Editors

Fernando S. Osório
Universidade de São Paulo
São Carlos, São Paulo
Brazil

Valdir Grassi Jr.
Universidade de São Paulo
São Carlos, São Paulo
Brazil

Denis Fernando Wolf
Universidade de São Paulo
São Carlos, São Paulo
Brazil

Marcelo Becker
Universidade de São Paulo
São Carlos, São Paulo
Brazil

Kalinka Castelo Branco
Universidade de São Paulo
São Carlos, São Paulo
Brazil

Roseli A. Francelin Romero
Universidade de São Paulo
São Carlos, São Paulo
Brazil

ISSN 1865-0929   ISSN 1865-0937   (electronic)
Communications in Computer and Information Science
ISBN 978-3-662-48133-2   ISBN 978-3-662-48134-9   (eBook)
DOI 10.1007/978-3-662-48134-9

Library of Congress Control Number: 2015950459

Springer Heidelberg New York Dordrecht London

Printed on acid-free paper

Springer-Verlag GmbH Berlin Heidelberg is part of Springer Science+Business Media
(www.springer.com)

Preface

This volume on "Intelligent Robotics and Automation Systems" from the Springer *Communications in Computer and Information Science* series (Springer CCIS) consists of the best papers selected from the Joint Conference on Robotics 2014: 11th Latin-American Robotics Symposium, Second Brazilian Robotics Symposium, and 6th Workshop on Applied Robotics and Automation. The Joint Conference on Robotics and Intelligent Systems (JCRIS 2014) was held during October 18–23, 2014, at the University of São Paulo at São Carlos, Brazil. JCRIS 2014 was composed of several satellite events including artificial intelligence and computational intelligence conferences, robotics competitions, PhD and MSc Best Dissertation and Thesis Contest, and the most important Latin-American Robotic Conferences composed by three major joint events: LARS-SBR-Robocontrol.

The Joint Conference on Robotics 2014 was organized by the ICMC (Computer and Mathematics Sciences Institute from USP São Carlos), the EESC (São Carlos School of Engineering), and the CRob/USP-SC (Center for Robotics of USP São Carlos). The event was promoted jointly by the SBC (Brazilian Computer Society) and the SBA (Brazilian Automation Society), with support from FAPESP, CAPES, and CNPq. The joint conferences received more than 3,000 participants following the competitions, plenary talks with renowned international invited speakers, panels, posters, and oral presentations of papers.

We received 76 submissions (57 submissions to LARS/SBR and 19 submissions to Robocontrol) from eight countries, from which 45 papers were accepted for oral presentation at the SBR-LARS-Robocontrol conferences (37 papers accepted for LARS/SBR and eight papers accepted for Robocontrol). Each paper was reviewed by at least three experts. Our final decision on these submissions took into account mainly the potential of each paper to foster fruitful discussions and the future development of robotics in Latin America and Brazil. In some cases, an additional review was offered in order for a decision to be taken.

The best papers were selected considering the best scores obtained by the papers according to the reviewers. We selected the eight best papers from SBR-LARS-Robocontrol and also one paper as the Best PhD Thesis in 2014 from the PhD Thesis Contest in Robotics. Extended and improved versions of the best papers were requested from the authors of these nine papers. The submitted articles were reviewed again by selected Program Committee members of the conferences and, after corrections, the articles were accepted for publication in this volume of the CCIS series.

This book aims to bring together innovative results and new research trends in intelligent robotics and automation systems selected from the Joint Conference on Robotics 2014. Authors of selected best papers were invited to revise and extend their papers submitting their work to this special volume. We have also included in this book a chapter describing the awarded thesis work (first place) from the PhD Thesis Contest in Robotics presented by Douglas Macharet and Mario Campos (Advisor). The selected papers present a complete and solid reference of the state of the art in the intelligent robotics and automation research field, covering the following areas: autonomous mobile robots, tele-operated and telepresence robots, human–robot interaction, trajectory control for mobile robots, autonomous vehicles, service-oriented robotic systems, semantic mapping, environment mapping, visual odometry, applications of RGB-D sensors, humanoid and biped robots, Robocup Soccer robots, robot control, path planning, multiple vehicles, and teams of robots.

We hope that you will find these papers interesting and consider them a helpful reference in the future when addressing any of the aforementioned research areas.

May 2015

Fernando S. Osório
Denis Fernando Wolf
Kalinka Castelo Branco
Valdir Grassi Jr.
Marcelo Becker
Roseli A. Francelin Romero

Organization

JCRIS 2014 - *Joint Conference on Robotics and Intelligent Systems*

General Chair

Roseli A. Francelin Romero, USP/ICMC

SBR LARS 2014 – *Second Brazilian Conference on Robotics and 11th Latin American Robotics Symposium*

Program Chairs

Denis Fernando Wolf, USP/ICMC
Fernando Santos Osório, USP/ICMC
Kalinka Castelo Branco, USP/ICMC

Robocontrol 2014 – *6th Workshop on Applied Robotics and Automation*

Program Chairs

Valdir Grassi Jr., USP/EESC
Marcelo Becker, USP/EESC

SBR LARS 2014 – Program Committee

Alejandro Aceves-López	ITESM, Mexico
Alfredo Weitzenfeld	University of South Florida, USA
Andre Barczak	Massey University, New Zealand
Andre Possani	ITAM, Mexico
Andre Gustavo Scolari Conceicao	Federal University of Bahia – UFBA, Brazil
Angelica Munoz-Melendez	INAOE, Mexico
Anna Costa	Universidade de São Paulo – USP, Brazil
Arthur Miranda Neto	UNICAMP, Brazil
Arturo Forner Cordero	Universidade de São Paulo – USP, Brazil
Cairo Nascimento Jr.	Instituto Tecnológico de Aeronáutica – ITA, Brazil
Carlos Ribeiro	Instituto Tecnológico de Aeronáutica – ITA, Brazil
Carlos Eduardo Pereira	UFRGS, Brazil
Damian Lyons	Fordham Univesrity – New York, USA
Dante Elias	PUCP, Peru
Denis Wolf	Universidade de São Paulo, USP, Brazil

Martin Adams   Universidad de Chile, Chile
Milton Heinen   Universidade Federal do Pampa – UNIPAMPA, Brazil
Orides Morandin Junior   Universidade Federal de São Carlos – UFSCar, Brazil
Pablo Alsina   Universidade Federal do Rio Grande do Norte –
                                    UFRN, Brazil
Paulo Miyagi   Universidade de São Paulo – USP, Brazil
Rafael Aroca   Universidade Federal de São Carlos – UFSCar, Brazil
Reinaldo Bianchi   Centro Universitário da FEI, Brazil
Renato Tinos   Universidade de São Paulo – USP, Brazil
Rene Pegoraro   Universidade Estadual Paulista – UNESP, Brazil
Ricardo Gudwin   Universidade Estadual de Campinas – UNICAMP,
                                    Brazil
Rod Grupen   University of Massachusetts, USA
Rodrigo Calvo   Universidade Estadual de Maringá – UEM, Brazil
Ronald Arkin   Georgia Tech., USA
Roseli Francelin Romero   Universidade de São Paulo – USP, Brazil
Samuel Bueno   Centro de Tecnologia da Informação Renato
                                    Archer – CTI, Brazil
Sergio Campello Oliveira   Universidade de Pernambuco – UFPE, Brazil
Silvia Botelho   FURG, Brazil
Valdir Grassi Jr.   Universidade de São Paulo – USP, Brazil
Vitor Romano   UFRJ, Brazil
Walter Fetter Lages   UFRGS, Brazil
Yvan Tupac   Universidad Católica San pablo, Peru

SBR LARS 2014 – Additional Reviewers

Alejandro Aceves-López   ITESM, Mexico
Alessandro Marro   UFRN, Brazil
Alex Pinto   UNESP, Brazil
Alfredo Perez   Northern New Mexico College, USA
Andre Barczak   Massey University, New Zealand
Andre Possani   ITAM, México
Andre Gustavo Scolari   Federal University of Bahia – UFBA, Brazil
    Conceicao
Angelica Munoz-Melendez   INAOE, Mexico
Anna Costa   Escola Politécnica - University of São Paulo – USP,
                                    Brazil
Arthur Miranda Neto   UNICAMP, Brazil
Arturo Forner Cordero   Universidade de São Paulo – USP, Brazil
Bruno da Silva   Universidade Federal do Rio Grande do Norte –
                                    UFRN, Brazil
Cairo Nascimento Jr.   Instituto Tecnológico de Aeronáutica – ITA, Brazil
Carlos Ribeiro   ITA, Brazil
Claudio Rosales   Universidad Nacional de San Juan, Argentina
Damian Lyons   Fordham Univesrity – New York, USA

Daniel Sales	University of São Paulo – USP, Brazil
Dante Elias	PUCP, Peru
Denis Wolf	University of Sao Paulo – USP, Brazil
Dennis Barrios	Universidad Católica San Pablo, Peru
Edison Pignaton de Freitas	University of Halmstadt, Sweden
Edson De Pieri	Federal University of Santa Catarina – UFSC, Brazil
Edson Ferreira	Universidade Federal do Espírito Santo – UFES, Brazil
Eduardo Freire	Universidade Federal de Sergipe – UFS, Brazil
Eduardo Todt	Universidade Federal do Paraná – UFPR, Brazil
Eric Antonelo	Ghent University, Belgium
Fabricio de Franca	University of Campinas – UNICAMP, Brazil
Felipe Silva	University of Sao Paulo – USP, Brazil
Fernando Lizarralde	Universidade Federal do Rio de Janeiro – UFRJ, Brazil
Fernando Osorio	Universidade de Sao Paulo – USP, Brazil
Fernando Von Zuben	University of Campinas – UNICAMP, Brazil
Flavio Tonidandel	Centro Universitario da FEI, Brazil
Gerardo Reyes-Salgado	CENIDET, Mexico
Glauco A.P. Caurin	USP, Brazil
Guilherme Barreto	Universidade Federal do Ceará – UFC, Brazil
Guilherme Pereira	Universidade Federal de Minas Gerais – UFMG, Brazil
Guillem Alenyà	CSIC-UPC, Spain
Guillermo Rafael-Valdivia	Universidad Católica San Pablo, Peru
Gustavo Pessin	Universidade de São Paulo – USP, Brazil
Gustavo Teodoro Laureano	Federal University of Goiás – UFG, Brazil
Hugo Vieira Neto	Universidade Tecnológica Federal do Paraná – UFTPR, Brazil
Humberto Ferasoli Filho	Universidade Estadual Paulista – UNESP, Brazil
Ivan Muller	Universidade Federal do Rio Grande do Sul – UFRGS, Brazil
Ivan Nunes da Silva	USP/EESC/SEL, Brazil
Jean Michel Winter	Universidade Federal do Rio Grande do Sul – UFRGS, Brazil
Jefferson Souza	Universidade de São Paulo – USP, Brazil
Jes Cerqueira	Universidade Federal da Bahia – UFBA, Brazil
Jochen Steil	Bielefeld University, Germany
Jorge Dias	Universidade de Coimbra, Portugal
José Eduardo Ochoa Luna	Universidad Católica San Pablo, Peru
José Tenreiro Machado	Institute of Engineering, Polytechnic of Porto, Portugal
José Luiz Pio	Universidade Federal do Amazonas – UFAM, Brazil
José Reginaldo Hughes Carvalho	ICOMP/UFAM, Brazil
Josue Junior G. Ramos	CTI - Centro de Tecnologia da Informação Renato Archer, Brazil
Juan Calderon	University of South Florida, USA
Jun Okamoto	USP, Brazil
Kalinka Castelo Branco	ICMC – USP, Brazil

Leonardo Garrido	Tecnológico de Monterrey, Campus Monterrey, Mexico
Luis Gomes	Universidade Nova de Lisboa, Portugal
Luis Paulo Reis	Universidade do Minho/LIACC, Portugal
Luiz Chaimowicz	Universidade Federal de Minas Gerais – UFMG, Brazil
Luiz Mirisola	Instituto Tecnologico de Aeronáutica – ITA, Brazil
Manfred Huber	University of Texas at Arlington, USA
Marcelo Franchin	DEE/FE/UNESP Campus de Bauru – SP, Brazil
Mario Sarcinelli Filho	UFES, Brazil
Mauricio Dias	University of São Paulo – USP, Brazil
Milton Heinen	Universidade Federal do Pampa – UNIPAMPA, Brazil
Natássya Silva	Universidade de São Paulo – USP, Brazil
Orides Morandin Junior	UFSCar, Brazil
Pablo Alsina	Universidade Federal do Rio Grande do Norte – UFRN, Brazil
Paulo Miyagi	Escola Politecnica - University of São Paulo – USP, Brazil
Rafael Aroca	Universidade Federal de São Carlos – UFSCar, Brazil
Reinaldo Bianchi	Centro Universitário da FEI, Brazil
Renato Tinós	USP, Brazil
Rene Pegoraro	UNESP - Campus de Bauru, Brazil
Ricardo Gudwin	UNICAMP, Brazil
Rod Grupen	University of Massachusetts, USA

ROBOCONTROL 2014 – Program Committee

Antonio Carlos Sementille	Universidade Estadual Paulista – UNESP, Brazil
Arturo Forner Cordero	Universidade de São Paulo – USP, Brazil
Denis Wolf	Universidade de São Paulo – USP, Brazil
Didier Dumur	École Supérieure d'Électricité, France
Edson De Pieri	Universidade Federal de Santa Catarina – UFSC, Brazil
Fernando Lizarralde	Universidade Federal do Rio de Janeiro – UFRJ, Brazil
Fernando Osorio	Universidade de Sao Paulo – USP, Brazil
Flavio Tonidandel	Centro Universitario da FEI, Brazil
Guilherme Pereira	Universidade Federal de Minas Gerais – UFMG, Brazil
Humberto Ferasoli Filho	Universidade Estadual Paulista – UNESP, Brazil
Ivan Guilherme	Universidade Estadual Paulista – UNESP, Brazil
Ivan Nunes da Silva	Universidade de São Paulo – USP, Brazil
Joao Perea Martins	Universidade Estadual Paulista – UNESP, Brazil
José Tenreiro Machado	Instituto Politécnico do Porto, Portugal
José Eduardo Castanho	Universidade Estadual Paulista – UNESP, Brazil
Jun Okamoto	Universidade de São Paulo – USP, Brazil
Kalinka Castelo Branco	Universidade de São Paulo – USP, Brazil
Liu Hsu	Coppe/Universidade Federal do Rio de Janeiro – UFRJ, Brazil
Luiz Chaimowicz	Universidade Federal de Minas Gerais – UFMG, Brazil

Luiz Gonçalves	Universidade Federal do Rio Grande do Norte – UFRN, Brazil
Marcelo Becker	Universidade de São Paulo – USP, Brazil
Marcelo Franchin	Universidade Estadual Paulista – UNESP, Brazil
Marco Terra	Universidade de São Paulo – USP, Brazil
Marco Antônio Corbucci Caldeira	Universidade Estadual Paulista – UNESP, Brazil
Marilza Lemos	Universidade Estadual Paulista – UNESP, Brazil
Mario Sarcinelli Filho	Universidade Federal do Espírito Santo – UFES, Brazil
Mario Eduardo Bordon	Universidade Estadual Paulista – UNESP, Brazil
Mario Fernando Campos	Universidade Federal de Minas Gerais – UFMG, Brazil
Paulo Kurka	Universidade Estadual de Campinas – UNICAMP, Brazil
Reinaldo Bianchi	Centro Universitario da FEI, Brazil
Renato Henriques	Universidade Federal do Rio Grande do Sul – UFRGS, Brazil
Rene Pegoraro	Universidade Estadual Paulista – UNESP, Brazil
Ricardo Gudwin	Universidade Estadual de Campinas – UNICAMP, Brazil
Roseli Francelin Romero	Universidade de São Paulo – USP, Brazil
Sadek Absi Alfaro	Universidade de Brasilia – UnB, Brazil
Silas Alves	Universidade de São Paulo – USP, Brazil
Tatiana Pazelli	Universidade Federal de São Carlos – UFSCar, Brazil
Teodiano F. Bastos	Universidade Federal do Espírito Santo – UFES, Brazil
Valdir Grassi Jr.	Universidade de São Paulo – USP, Brazil
Vitor Romano	Universidade Federal do Rio de Janeiro – UFRJ, Brazil
Walter Fetter Lages	Universidade Federal do Rio Grande do Sul – UFRGS, Brazil

ROBOCONTROL 2014 – Additional Reviewers

Antonio Carlos Sementille	Universidade Estadual Paulista – UNESP, Brazil
Arturo Forner Cordero	Universidade de São Paulo – USP, Brazil
Cassius Resende	Universidade Federal do Espírito Santo – UFES, Brazil
Didier Dumur	SUPELEC, France
Douglas Macharet	Universidade Federal De Minas Gerais – UFMG, Brazil
Edson De Pieri	Federal University of Santa Catarina – UFSC, Brazil
Fernando Lizarralde	Universidade Federal do Rio de Janeiro – UFRJ, Brazil
Fernando Osorio	Universidade de Sao Paulo – USP, Brazil
Flavio Tonidandel	Centro Universitario da FEI, Brazil
Guilherme Pereira	Universidade Federal de Minas Gerais – UFMG, Brazil
Humberto Ferasoli Filho	Universidade Estadual Paulista – UNESP, Brazil
Ivan Guilherme	UNESP, Brazil
Ivan Nunes da Silva	USP São Carlos, Brazil

Joao Perea Martins	UNESP, Brazil
José Tenreiro Machado	Institute of Engineering, Polytechnic of Porto, Portugal
José Eduardo Castanho	UNESP, Brazil
Jose Reginaldo Carvalho	Universidade Federal do Amazonas – UFAM, Brazil
Jun Okamoto	USP, Brazil
Luis Filipe Rossi	USP, Brazil
Luiz Chaimowicz	Universidade Federal de Minas Gerais – UFMG, Brazil
Marcelo Becker	Escola de Engenharia de São Carlos – USP, Brazil
Marcelo Franchin	DEE/FE/UNESP Campus de Bauru – SP, Brazil
Marco Terra	USP, Brazil
Marco Antônio Corbucci Caldeira	UNESP - Campus de Bauru – SP, Brazil
Marilza Lemos	Universidade Estadual Paulista Julio de Mesquita Filho – UNESP, Brazil
Mario Sarcinelli Filho	UFES, Brazil
Mario Eduardo Bordon	Sao Paulo State University – UNESP, Brazil
Mario Fernando Campos	UFMG, Brazil
Paulo Kurka	DPM/FEM/UNICAMP, Brazil
Reinaldo Bianchi	Centro Universitario da FEI, Brazil
Renato Henriques	UFRGS, Brazil
Rene Pegoraro	UNESP - Campus de Bauru, Brazil
Ricardo Gudwin	UNICAMP, Brazil
Roseli Francelin Romero	USP – Campus de São Carlos, Brazil
Silas Alves	Universidade de São Paulo – USP, Brazil
Tatiana Pazelli	Federal University of Sao Carlos – UFSCAR, Brazil
Teodiano F. Bastos	Universidade Federal do Espírito Santo – UFES, Brazil
Valdir Grassi Jr.	University of São Paulo – USP, Brazil
Vitor Romano	UFRJ, Brazil
Walter Fetter Lages	UFRGS, Brazil

Best PhD Thesis Contest in Robotics – Program Chairs

Silvia Silva da Costa Botelho	Universidade Federal do Rio Grande – FURG, Brazil
Guilherme de Alencar Barreto	Universidade Federal do Ceará – UFC, Brazil

SBR LARS Robocontrol 2014

Support Organizations

USP/SC - Universidade de São Paulo/Campus of São Carlos, Brazil
CROB - Center for Robotics of USP São Carlos, Brazil
ICMC - Institute of Mathematics and Computer Science of USP São Carlos, Brazil
EESC - São Carlos School of Engineering/USP São Carlos, Brazil

Publicity

SBC - Brazilian Computer Society
CER SBC - Robotics Council of SBC/Special Interest Group on Robotics (CER)
SBA - Brazilian Automation Society

SOCIEDADE BRASILEIRA DE AUTOMÁTICA

Financial Support and Special Sponsors

CNPq - National Council for Scientific and Technological Development
FAPESP - São Paulo Research Foundation
Google Brazil
SOMAI Education Brazil

Contents

Searching for Regions Out of Normal Conditions Using a Team of Robots

David Saldaña[✉], Luiz Chaimowicz, and Mario F.M. Campos

Computer Vision and Robotics Laboratory (VeRLab), Computer Science Department, Universidade Federal de Minas Gerais, Belo Horizonte, MG, Brazil
{saldana,chaimo,mario}@dcc.ufmg.br

Abstract. Searching for regions in abnormal conditions is a priority in environments susceptible to catastrophes (*e.g.* forest fires or oil spills). Those disasters usually begin with an small anomaly that may became unsustainable if it is not detected at an early stage. We propose a probabilistic technique to coordinate multiple robots in perimeter searching and tracking, which are fundamental tasks if they are to detect and follow anomalies in an environment. The proposed method is based on a particle filter technique, which uses multiple robots to fuse distributed sensor information and estimate the shape of an anomaly. Complementary sensor fusion is used to coordinate robot navigation and reduce detection time when an anomaly arises. Validation of our approach is obtained both in simulation and with real robots. Five different scenarios were designed to evaluate and compare the efficiency in both exploration and tracking tasks. The results have demonstrated that when compared to state-of-the art methods in the literature, the proposed method is able to search anomalies under uncertainty and reduce the detection time by automatically increasing the number of robots.

Keywords: Multi-robot systems · Robotic sensor networks · Particle filter · Perimeter detection · Level-curve tracking

1 Introduction

Real-time monitoring is paramount in environments where disasters may occur at any moment and when human or animal lives are in danger. Disasters are usually initiated by anomalies which were not timely detected and possibly corrected or even reported. In most cases it would be highly desirable to not only detect, but also to identify the affected area, whose perimeter may change over time. A typical example is the monitoring of a forest, where not only the identification of the increase in temperature, possibly due to a fire is of utmost importance, but also to be able to determine the affected area in real time, which would be

---

F.M. Campos—The authors thanks to Professor Renato Asunção for his advises and contribution in the proposal. The authors also gratefully acknowledge the support of CAPES, CNPq and FAPEMIG.

© Springer-Verlag Berlin Heidelberg 2015
F.S. Osório et al. (Eds.): LARS/SBR/Robocontrol 2014, CCIS 507, pp. 1–15, 2015.
DOI: 10.1007/978-3-662-48134-9_1

of great relevance to firefighters. Similarly, detecting and tracking anomalies are important tasks in several domains such as: oil spills in water bodies, radiation leaks from nuclear power plants, and algae bloom in lakes.

Systems composed of cameras or multiple static sensors dispersed in the environment may be used for detection, but their capabilities are constrained when dynamic anomalies need to be tracked. Therefore, one feasible approach is to spread multiple mobile robots in the environment, which may be coordinated to navigate and to dynamically monitor changing anomalies in the environment. Complementary sensor fusion may be readily applied to estimate the sensed phenomenon based on the information acquired by the multiple robots, taking advantage of any additional information that may become available to provide a better partial observation. Such mobile robots, which are usually equipped with processors, wireless communication, and several sensors, constitute what has been known in the literature as Robotic Sensor Networks (RSN) [4,21]. Their locomotion system enables them to cover large areas and to adjust their location based on the environmental dynamics or other natural occurrences. In addition, RSNs have a great advantage over other monitoring techniques, such as wireless sensor networks or multiple static monitoring cameras, since they are able to dynamically modify their actions over time, which enables them to sense, detect, and also track anomalies in the monitored environment.

We use the term *anomaly* to designate an area in the environment where the value of a given physical variable is out of its typical range. An *anomaly* can be modeled as a gradient [8] or a (gradient-free) binary surface [12]. For instance, a gradient is generated by a physical phenomenon like temperature or light, which typically decay with distance. In this case, a robot would follow an iso-temperature or iso-illumination level-curve. In the gradient-free case, a robot would just identify if it is within or without the affected area and then proceed to identify the boundary of the sensed anomaly.

In this paper, we propose a probabilistic technique based on particle filters, to search, detect and track multiple dynamic anomalies. A group of anomalies can be seen as a multi-modal probabilistic distribution, and the mobile robots in the RSN move about in the environment while estimating this distribution by combining the information acquired from their sensors.

The rest of this paper is organized as follows: Sect. 2 describes the main techniques in the literature for perimeter detection and tracking. Section 3 presents the proposed model. Section 4 details the implementation used to validate the proposed model and its results. Finally, Sect. 5 discusses the main findings, the conclusions and indicates directions for further investigation.

2   Related Works

Bruemer et al. [4] developed one of the first studies on perimeter detection and tracking, a bio-inspired approach based on swarm intelligence to detect gradient-free chemicals. In their work, a robotic swarm detects the chemicals and communicates capturing and generating sounds. The prototype runs on low-cost robots deployed on a physical environment. With an uncoordinated method, those robots were able to detect multiple anomalies within the environment without using any tracking systems nor wireless communication.

Bachmayer and Leonard [1] proposed a bio-inspired technique for navigating on gradients with underwater robots in the ocean. Each robot behaves like a individual of a school of fish to find the most dense source of food by individually responding not only to local perception but also integrating shared information from its nearest neighbors. The authors further improved their work to enable tracking on gradients [7,8]. Their robots worked in pairs to determine their movement via an algorithm which used the measured potential between both robots. Their algorithm applies a planning technique to explore the underwater environment in three dimensions and defined virtual leaders to follow the defined path or to track the contour of the anomalies. Leadership was allowed to change depending on the position or actions while executing a specific plan [17,18].

Marthaler et al. [14,15] proposed a method based on the well-known computer vision deformable contour technique *snake* which was modified to detect gradient-free anomalies. Their method was defined as a kind of edge search algorithm by a group of autonomous mobile robots, which required local communication and interaction among them. In a subsequent work, the authors proposed an algorithm to detect and track gradient-free substances, known as UUV-Gas [10,12], where tests are performed with a single vehicle for evaluating and comparing the classical *bang-bang* algorithm performance [2]. The algorithm *Page's cumulative sum* (CUSUM) also integrates *bang-bang* algorithm and additionally includes a filter to increase the turning points by improving the accuracy of the sensing data. In 2009, J. Abhijeet [11] implemented the CUSUM algorithm on low-cost robots and subsequently Jin and Bertozzi refined this technique to create *improved CUSUM* [3].

Clark and Fierro [5,6] proposed a biologically inspired, hierarchical architecture for decentralized control and coordination that allows a robot swarm to locate and track a dynamic perimeter. One of their main features is a software architecture based on behavior-focused fault tolerant cooperative control. Their architecture defines two types of agents: Sensor agents, whose role is to sample environmental data and communicate useful information wirelessly with their robot neighbors and groupal agents in charge of receiving and processing all related information about the environment and located perimeters. The agent control is a model based on modes, which are represented by a hierarchical state machine. The hierarchical architecture that consists of four drivers that act according to the robots state. A main controller integrates three sub-controllers for: random coverage by spiral exploration; point attraction by potential field; and tracking. The strengths of that work are the following: the algorithm covers the entire process of anomaly detection (exploration, attraction and tracking), their model is tested through simulation and real prototype ground robots. Those sub-controllers internally also include collision avoidance. Their architecture is scalable and robust mainly due to the major states that are defined for the detection and tracking process, as well as different connections to change control status. Although their architecture is robust and defines some links to state control, the finite state machine may generate unnecessary state changes due to noisy sensors or small changes in the conditions in the environment.

3 A Model for Searching and Tracking

The problem of searching for anomalies with multiple robots can be stated as follows. Consider a team $\mathcal{R}$ of n robots, located in an environment defined in the Euclidean space $\mathbb{R}^2$. Let $\mathcal{W}$ be the robot's workspace in the environment. The problem is focused on detecting and tracking the perimeter that surrounds a dynamic shape $\mathcal{A}$, with $\mathcal{A} \subset \mathcal{W}$. $\mathcal{A}$ is the representation of a single or multiple anomalies. The size, form and position of each anomaly may dynamically change over time.

Each robot $r \in \mathcal{R}$ has sensing capabilities to identify the anomaly in time t. The measured value z_t represents the binary sensor's output, which determines if the area sensed by the robot is located inside the area of the anomaly location $loc(r) \subset \mathcal{A}$ for binary anomalies or if the sensed value is greater than the reference value of the level-curve. $Z_t = [z_t^{[r_1]}, z_t^{[r_2]}, ..., z_t^{[r_n]}]$ is the set of all measurements performed by each robot at time t. Each robot r can gather its global location, and the uncertainty of its measurements is known *a priori* (*e.g.* by sensor calibration). Additionally, a communication network allows any robot to send and receive messages from other robots. Every robot $r \in \mathcal{R}$ can communicate its sensed value $Z_t^{[r]}$ in time t.

As described in the previous section, searching, attraction and tracking are behaviors performed with a high level control for this problem. In this work, robot navigation and coordination are based on the uncertainty of the anomaly; every robot tries to visit the nearest spot with highest likelihood of being an anomaly. The shape of an anomaly can be seen as a multi-modal distribution, and our method attempts to estimate this distribution using *particle filter* technique. Searching and tracking are the main robot behaviors, but attraction is implicit in the searching process in order to avoid erroneous motions due to noisy data. Our approach also supports multiple anomalies and robot coordination with concurrent exploration and tracking.

3.1 Particle Filter for Anomaly Estimation

The particle filter technique has many applications since it offers a probabilistic method that converge to multi-modal probability distributions. In robotics this technique has been thoroughly applied in localization, mapping, target tracking, and many other tasks [22]. In our specific scenario, we want to identify the anomaly shape by using multiple robots. There are three relevant reasons for using particle filter in this context. (1) If an anomaly exists in the environment, exploration with multiple robots leads the particles to converge to the shape of the anomaly, otherwise the robots will continue to explore the environment which tends to reduce the uncertainty of the occurrence of an anomaly along the

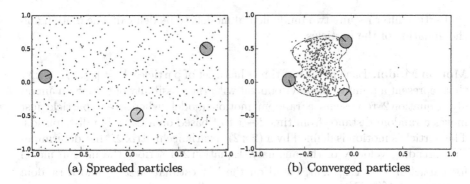

(a) Spreaded particles   (b) Converged particles

Fig. 1. Particle representation for the yellow robot. The other robots of the team are represented as gray circles, blue points for particles, and the perimeter of the anomaly is a non-continuous black line (Color figure online).

traversed path. (2) Each robot has an independent representation of the updated map, based on the robot's measurements and the communicated information from other robots. The set of particles offer a representation of the areas in the map which have been recently covered, incorporating the uncertainty in the non-visited zones and reducing the belief of the sensed path in time. This updating process could be modeled as a complex geometric process, but under this approach, it can be computed with simple arithmetic operations on the particle's motion. (3) The natural, randomized movement of the anomaly is incorporated in the particle's motion. Any additional information on the anomaly can be added as *a priori* data in order to improve the estimation updating of the map.

In [16], a particle filter approach was used to track a target with multiple robots. In the initial state, when robots start searching without previous knowledge about the anomaly existence, an anomaly can be seen as a target. We assume that the map of the environment has been provided *a priori* and a global localization system is available. Therefore, our goal is to estimate the probability distribution of the anomaly x_t at time t, based on the estimated belief on x_t (Eq. 1) given the robots measurements $Z_{1:t}$ and the estimated anomaly motion $u_{1:t}$ in time.

$$Bel(x_t) = P(x_t|Z_{1:t}, u_{1:t}). \tag{1}$$

Every particle can be depicted as a point on map, and it represents the possibility of having an anomaly or apart of it, thereof, in that location. The objective of this technique is to dynamically converge the particles to the anomaly's shape. In the initial state, without a previous estimation of the anomaly, the particles are spreaded along the environment (Fig. 1a). The objective is concentrating the largest number of accumulated particles (blue points) within the perimeter of the anomaly, as illustrated in Fig. 1b. As each robot has its own particles, particles represents the robot's belief about the existence of an anomaly in the environment.

Particle filter require two fundamental models to be defined: The motion and the updating of the particles.

Motion Model. Each robot r at time t has a set of particles $\mathcal{X}_t = [x_t^1, x_t^2, ..., x_t^m]$, that represent a point in the environment with the possibility of having an anomaly. Equation 2 represents a random motion model, when every particle just moves a random distance from time $t-1$ to t based on a Gaussian distribution. The particle's motion is defined by a (2×2) covariance matrix Σ that determines the spreading velocity of the anomaly. Equation 2 describes the motion model for particle i, $i = 1, 2, ..., m$, based on the last estimation $x_{t-1}^{[i]}$ and a random motion $u_t = \mathcal{N}(0, \Sigma^2)$:

$$p(x_t^{[i]} | u_t, x_{t-1}) \sim \mathcal{N}(x_{t-1}^{[i]}, \Sigma^2). \tag{2}$$

This model is applied when there is no additional information about the anomaly behavior, then a random motion is assumed. Having information *a priory* about the anomaly may help to enhance the exploration process as long as particles simulate that behavior. For example, a fire in a forest normally has a random movement, but if the fire is pushed by the wind, and we know the wind's strength and orientation, then a better estimation about the position of the anomaly can be predicted.

Updating Model. Estimation about the anomaly's distribution is iteratively updated by using each robot's sensor readings. In each iteration, every particle is re-sampled based on weights. Each particle begins with a normalized weight, and depending on its position and the robot's sensed values, that weight may be modified. Equation 3 determines how the weight of a particle i is updated based on sensor observations.

$$w_t^{[i]} = \begin{cases} a, & \text{if } z_t = 0 \\ b, & \text{if } z_t > 0 \\ 1/m, & \text{outside sensor range} \\ 0, & \text{outside the map,} \end{cases} \tag{3}$$

where the constant a is a small value that represents a low probability of the existence of an anomaly in the sensed area when no anomaly is identified by the robot's sensors ($z_t = 0$); b is a value ≥ 1 used to increase the particle's weight given that an anomaly has been detected and c is an intermediate value to represent the uncertainty of a non sensed area at time t. In the experiments we used $a = 0.1$, and $b = 1.3$.

When every particle has its own weight, the group of particles is re-sampled [9] to randomly clone particles proportionally to their updated weight. After several iterations, the result is an accumulation of particles in places with more possibility of the existence of an anomaly. When no anomaly is detected in the environment, robots will try to navigate towards the areas with particle accumulations in order to visit the most probable spots with anomalies.

3.2 Searching for Anomalies

Each robot running the navigating and searching processes must attain the following objectives: (1) maximize the number of visited particles, giving priority to the nearest one, (2) maximize the distance to other robots, (3) maximize the distances to obstacles and map borders. To fulfill these requirements, a few techniques could be applied like Partially Observable Markov Decision Processes (POMDPs) and potential fields in a discretized map [16]. In both cases, a map discretization is required to create a grid. For large cells, the robot will move through cell centers, whereas for small cells, complex motions for non-holonomic robots are likely to be generated, especially when the best target cell is adjacent to the current robot cell, and the path's orientation is different from the current orientation of the robot.

In our approach, we assume that navigation is based on the potential field technique in a continuous space. This well known technique is based on the physical model of electrical charges, assuming that a robot is a positive electrical charge which is attracted by all the negative charges (particles generated by the defined filter in the previous section). Other robots and obstacles are also modeled as positive charges that repel the robot. Therefore, the robot's velocity and orientation are computed as the vector sum of all forces involved.

As the number of particles must be large (more than thousand) for good approximations, similar particles may be grouped into a small number of clusters, where each cluster is represented by a centroid. We have used the *k-means* clustering method to group the particles. However, one difficult issue with this method is defining k, the number of groups. In our approach, we computed $k = 3|\mathcal{R}|$ in order to give three choices for each robot.

The force generated by a centroid $c \in \mathcal{C}$ is proportional to the number of particles in the cluster and it is computed based on Coulomb's law (Eq. 4):

$$|F_c| = \alpha \frac{|q_r||q_c|}{d^2}, \tag{4}$$

where α is a constant; $|q_r|$ is the robot's charge, defined as a unitary charge $|q_r| = 1$; $|q_c| = m_c/k$ is the cluster's charge, which is proportional to the total of particles in the cluster m_c; and d is the distance between the robot r and the cluster's centroid c. Finally, the resultant force that acts on each robot F_r is computed based on the attraction force by the clusters and repealed forces F_s generated by each of the other robots, Eq. 5:

$$F_T = \sum_{c \in \mathcal{C}} F_c - \sum_{s \in \mathcal{R}-\{r\}} F_s - \sum_{o \in Obs} F_o \tag{5}$$

The force vector $F_T = \langle \rho, \phi \rangle$ may be decomposed into its magnitude ρ and orientation ϕ. The robot navigates with constant linear speed $v = K_v$ in the direction of the resultant force. Angular speed is defined by a *Proportional-Derivative (PD)* controller as described by Eq. 6,

$$\omega = K_1 \phi + K_2 \dot{\phi}, \tag{6}$$

where K_1, and K_2 are the *PD* constants.

3.3   Tracking an Anomaly

The tracking process starts when a robot detects an anomaly and then it starts to border the whole boundary to estimate its shape. In a previous work [20], a PID (Proportional, Integrative, and Derivative) control was used for tracking gradients. It used an analog sensor such as a thermometer or light-meter. We have extended that approach for a different kind of sensor – a RGB camera –, which makes it possible to track binary anomalies running a PID controller on the angular velocity ω. Meanwhile, linear velocity v is constant.

The control of the linear speed is based on the distance to other robots in order to avoid collisions (Eq. 7) and the angular speed is computed based on the gradient of the anomaly concentration, ∇c_r in the area (Eq. 8). This gradient can be estimated by the time series of values acquired from a punctual sensor measurements or by employing multiple spatially distributed sensors [13].

$$v = v_{track} - \frac{K_{track}}{d(r,r')}, \tag{7}$$

$$\omega = K_3(\nabla c_r - \tau) + K_4 \nabla \dot{c}_r, \tag{8}$$

where K_3 and K_4 are *PD* control constants, v_{track} is the maximum linear speed, K_{track} is a proportionality constant, and r' is the robot in front of robot r. In anomaly tracking, one of the most used methods is the *bang-bang* [3,11], which can be emulated with the model of Eq. 8 and setting $K_4 = 0$. However, by sintonizing K_4, oscillations and convergence time is reduced. The linear velocity v is just proportional to the closest robot or obstacle in front of it.

3.4   Coordination

Each robot has its own particle set to update its beliefs about the world. The communication is based on broadcasted messages but their contents is very small (*e.g.* a few bytes). Every robot broadcasts its position and the sensed values. Sensor fusion is distributed and complementary, and for this purpose a robot does not depend on the others, but it can combine its current sensed data, historical measurements and all the information received from other robots. For example, if one value is missing (*e.g.* $z_t^{[r_i]}$), the algorithm can still proceed with the other measurements ($Z_t - \{z_t^{[r_i]}\}$).

4   Experiments and Results

A previous work in the literature [6] has been chosen as baseline since it is a robust distributed architecture that includes exploration, tracking, collision avoidance, and potential attraction. Additionally, our method has been tested on virtual and real robots. We implemented our method and the baseline in the Robot Operating System platform (ROS) [19].

Initially, we implemented and tested on the ROS-Gazebo 3D simulator and subsequently on physical robots in the laboratory. Each real and virtual robot

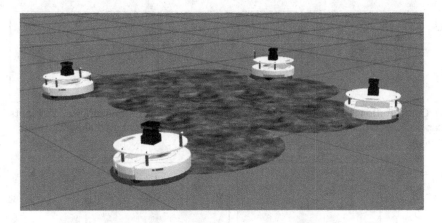

Fig. 2. Simulated environment with four robots tracking an anomaly.

Fig. 3. Physical robots tracking an anomaly.

is equipped with the same components: Onboard-computer for processing and communication by IEEE 802.3.11 (WIFI); one RGB camera, which is used as the anomaly sensor, and the *iCreate* base as differential mobile platform. Figure 2 shows the Gazebo environment with four robots, and those that are tracking the anomaly (represented by a rug with a texture of fire). In this simulated environment, robot localization is obtained from a gazebo service.

Figure 3 shows four real robots with localization tags. For localization purposes, we use Dragonfly CCD Firewire cameras with a wide-angle lenses mounted on the ceiling. A localization computer server is connected to the cameras and runs the software *AR-Alvar-Track* to determine the localization of each robot based on the markers placed on the top of each one of them. In the

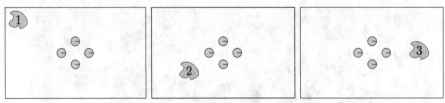

(a) Configuration 1: robots near to the center of the map.   (b) Configuration 2: robots distributed along the map.   (c) Configuration 2: robots distributed along the map.

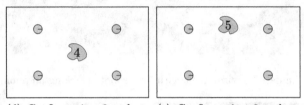

(d) Configuration 2: robots distributed along the map.   (e) Configuration 2: robots distributed along the map.

Fig. 4. Scenarios for validation and comparison

accompanying video sample [http://youtu.be/wG8WdsW_JiM] can be seen results from simulation and real robots.

We have defined two configurations for the four robots and five different cases of anomaly positions. Figure 4a shows a common configuration where robots start near to a central area. In Fig. 4e, the map is divided in four parts and each robot occupies their respective centers, which is the best configuration for spiral exploration (*e.g.* the exploration method of the baseline), because it reduces the redundancy of explored spaces in the map. Figure 5a and b show the robot paths in the detection and tracking tasks for the baseline and the proposed method, respectively. Spiral exploration is simple and fast. It can be considered as a greedy algorithm, but it is not complete, since it does not explore every spot in map, inasmuch as an anomaly may appear anywhere. For that reason, the five anomalies in Fig. 5a are located in covered places by at least one of the spiral lines. In Fig. 5b it can be seen that the robot paths are more stochastic in nature than those in the baseline (Fig. 5a); however, on average, the traveled distance until boundary detection is shorter for our method (proposal = 8.7 m and baseline = 10.7 m). A more detailed comparison and analysis is presented in the next section. Both techniques were executed at least ten times for each anomaly case and two metrics were defined for comparison: detection time and tracking time.

4.1   Results for Detection Time

Detection time is measured from the moment the robots starts in the initial positions (Fig. 4a and e) until one or more robots detect an anomaly. This

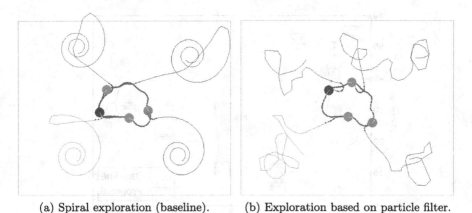

(a) Spiral exploration (baseline).   (b) Exploration based on particle filter.

Fig. 5. Robot paths for exploration and tracking in scenario 4

measurement is an indication of the efficiency to explore the environment since the anomaly may be located in any of the five places represented in Fig. 5b.

Figure 6 shows a box-plot to compare the baseline and our method in the exploration process. We assume an error distributed normally and represent the confidences interval as notches. The spiral exploration method (baseline) finds the anomaly with standard deviation between 1.0 and 2.0 s. It has a small variation of 2.8 % because the detection is almost always at the same point of the spiral. In contrast, our method has standard deviation between 5.5 and 13.1 s, since robot navigation is associated with the particles random movement. However, our method detects anomalies approximately two times faster than the baseline, on average. Cases 3 and 5 are the cases, where the methods are similar based on a *t-test*. Although cases 4 and 5 are most favorable for the baseline, the spiral exploration require many iterations to arrive to anomaly 4 and the detection time increases (Fig. 7).

4.2   Results for Tracking Time

Tracking time is measured since an anomaly is detected until its perimeter is completely defined by one or more robots. The perimeter identification can be reduced when some robots border the anomaly in different sections, that is why our method works better for cases 1,2, and 3. One robot detects the anomaly and the others continue exploring the environment where there is a possibility of anomaly. Robots navigate attempting to follow the uncertainty. Baseline has a different behavior, when a robot detects an anomaly all the other robots go to the identified point. This generates redundancy, since robots explore the same detected point and, additionally, it becomes a possible point of collision. On the one hand, only in cases 4 and 5, for which the redundant method works better because there is an anomaly between the robot and the detected point, the robots cover the anomaly by different sections. On the other hand, cases 1,2,

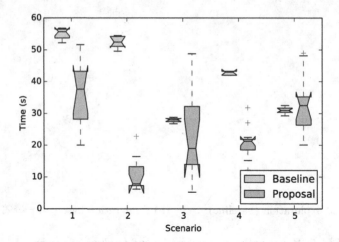

Fig. 6. Comparison for detection time in 5 anomaly cases.

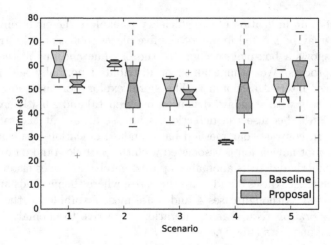

Fig. 7. Comparison for time to surround an anomaly in 5 anomaly cases.

and 3 are the most common, because the anomaly may appear at any time and the robots may not be in the optimal position.

4.3   Results for the Number of Robots

Now we want to analyze the behavior of the proposal when the number of robots increase. In the baseline, the spiral behavior does not improve the value of the metrics because more robots only increase the redundancy on the same visited places.

In our approach, the robots try maximize the places that were not visited before and also maximize the distance among the other robots. By this reason, when there are more robots in the exploration process, the time for detection

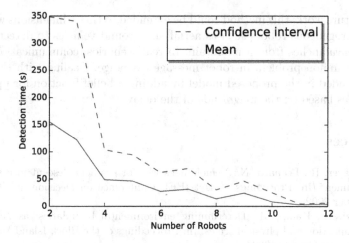

Fig. 8. Detection time by increasing the number of robots.

is reduced. Figure 8 shows the results for the scenario 1, where the experiments where replicated 85 times. We can see that the detection time reduces exponentially with the number of robots. The limit is estimated as the confidence interval in one direction with a confidence of 95 %. The oscillatory behavior of the descent curves for confidence interval and mean is related to the initial configuration of the robots. When a new robot is added, it reduces the detection time if it is located near to the anomaly, in other case, the impact of the new robot influences with less impact.

Therefore, in an ambient of dimensions $80\,m^2$, an anomaly is detected in less than 6.6 s with 12 robots (confidence of 95 %).

5   Conclusions and Future Work

In this article, we proposed a probabilistic distributed coordination method for multiple robots used in the task of anomaly detection and tracking. We have experimentally shown, both in simulation and with real robots, that it improves the searching and coordination processes by taking advantage of the particle filter technique. Experimental results demonstrated efficiency in exploration and tracking for most of the cases. Furthermore, it offers additional advantages such as: Support for multiple anomalies, fully environmental exploration, and predictions for dynamic anomalies.

On the one hand, in the implementation, the ROS platform offered a very useful development environment to implement programs for robots; it works well regardless if robots are simulated or real. On the other hand, in a real deployment, parameter configuration for the proposed model has shown to be critical, since a poor parametrization may generate collision among robots or even induce navigation outside the map.

As a future work, this method could be extended to three dimensions with the use of heterogeneous robots such as aerial and ground vehicles to detect falling rocks and avalanches from a mountain. In real scenarios, communication delay is a very common problem in robot message exchange. Dealing with this issue can be included in the proposed model by adding a belief function for updating the particles based on the magnitude of the delay.

References

1. Bachmayer, R., Leonard, N.: Vehicle networks for gradient descent in a sampled environment. In: Procedings of 41st IEEE Conference on Decision and Control, December 2002
2. Bertozzi, A., Kemp, M.: Determining environmental boundaries: asynchronous communication and physical scales. In: Proceedings of the Block Island Workshop Cooperative Control (2004)
3. Bertozzi, A.L.: Environmental boundary tracking and estimation using multiple autonomous vehicles. In: 2007 46th IEEE Conference on Decision and Control, pp. 4918–4923 (2007)
4. Bruemmer, D.: A robotic swarm for spill finding and perimeter formation. In: Spectrum: International Conference on Nuclear and Hazardous Waste Management (2002)
5. Clark, J., Fierro, R.: Cooperative hybrid control of robotic sensors for perimeter detection and tracking. In: Proceedings of the 2005, American Control Conference, pp. 3500–3505 (2005)
6. Clark, J., Fierro, R.: Mobile robotic sensors for perimeter detection and tracking. ISA Trans. **46**(1), 3–13 (2007)
7. Fiorelli, E., Bhatta, P., Leonard, N.E.: Adaptive sampling using feedback control of an autonomous underwater glider fleet. In: Aerospace Engineering, August 2003
8. Fiorelli, E., Leonard, N.E.: Exploring scalar fields using multiple sensor platforms: tracking level curves. In: 2007 46th IEEE Conference on Decision and Control, pp. 3579–3584 (2007)
9. Hol, J.D., Schon, T.B., Gustafsson, F.: On resampling algorithms for particle filters. In: 2006 IEEE Nonlinear Statistical Signal Processing Workshop, pp. 79–82. IEEE (2006)
10. Hsieh, C., Marthaler, D., Nguyen, B., Tung, D., Bertozzi, A.L., Murray, R.: Experimental validation of an algorithm for cooperative boundary tracking. In: Proceedings of the 2005, American Control Conference, pp. 1078–1083 (2005)
11. Joshi, A., Ashley, T., Huang, Y.R., Bertozzi, A.L.: Experimental validation of cooperative environmental boundary tracking with on-board sensors. In: Control, pp. 2630–2635 (2009)
12. Kemp, M., Bertozzi, A., Marthaler, D.: Multi-UUV perimeter surveillance. In: IEEE OES Workshop on Multiple AUV Operations (2004)
13. Li, S., Guo, Y., Bingham, B.: Multi-robot cooperative control for monitoring and tracking dynamic plumes. In: IEEE International Conference on Robotics and Automation, Proceedings, ICRA 2014. IEEE (2014)
14. Marthaler, D., Bertozzi, A.: Collective motion algorithms for determining environmental boundaries. In: SIAM Conference on Applications of Dynamical Systems (2003)

15. Marthaler, D., Bertozzi, A.: Tracking environmental level sets with autonomous vehicles. J. Electrochem. Soc. **129**, 2865 (2003)
16. Mottaghi, R., Vaughan, R.: An integrated particle filter and potential field method for cooperative robot target tracking. In: IEEE International Conference on Robotics and Automation, ICRA 2006. IEEE (2006)
17. Ogren, P., Fiorelli, E., Leonard, N.: Cooperative control of mobile sensor networks: adaptive gradient climbing in a distributed environment. IEEE Trans. Autom. Control **49**(8), 1292–1302 (2004)
18. Ogren, P., Fiorelli, E., Leonard, N.E.: Formations with a mission: stable coordination of vehicle group maneuvers. In: Symposium on Mathematical Theory of Networks and Systems (2002)
19. Quigley, M., Conley, K., Gerkey, B., Faust, J., Foote, T., Leibs, J., Wheeler, R., Ng, A.Y.: ROS: an open-source robot operating system. In: ICRA Workshop on Open Source Software (2009)
20. Saldana, D., Ovalle, D., Montoya, A.: Improved algorithm for perimeter tracking in robotic sensor networks. In: XXXVIII Latin American Conference on Informatics (CLEI), pp. 1–7. IEEE (2012)
21. Sibley, G., Rahimi, M., Sukhatme, G.: Robomote: a tiny mobile robot platform for large-scale ad-hoc sensor networks. In: IEEE International Conference on Robotics and Automation, Proceedings, ICRA 2002, vol. 2, pp. 1143–1148. IEEE (2002)
22. Thrun, S.: Probabilistic robotics. Commun. ACM **45**(3), 52–57 (2002)

Visual Odometry and Mapping for Indoor Environments Using RGB-D Cameras

Bruno M.F. Silva[✉] and Luiz M.G. Gonçalves

Department of Computer Engineering and Automation,
Federal University of Rio Grande do Norte Natal, Natal, Brazil
{brunomfs,lmarcos}@dca.ufrn.br

Abstract. RGB-D cameras (e.g. Microsoft Kinect) offer several sensing capabilities that can be suitable for Computer Vision and Robotics. Low cost, ease of deployment and video rate appearance and depth streams are examples of the most appealing features found on this class of devices. One major application that directly benefits from these sensors is Visual Odometry, a class of algorithms responsible to estimate the position and orientation of a moving agent at the same time that a map representation of the sensed environment is built. Aiming to compute 6DOF camera poses for robots in a fast and efficient way, a Visual Odometry system for RGB-D sensors is designed and proposed that allows real-time position estimation despite the fact that no specialized hardware such as modern GPUs is employed. Through a set of experiments carried out on publicly available benchmark and datasets, we show that the proposed system achieves localization accuracy and computational performance superior to the state-of-the-art RGB-D SLAM algorithm. Results are presented for a thorough evaluation of the algorithm, which involves processing over 6, 5 GB of data corresponding to more than 9000 RGB-D frames.

Keywords: Visual odometry · RGB-D cameras · 3D reconstruction

1 Introduction

Recently, low cost depth sensing devices were introduced into the market designed for entertainment purposes. One such sensor is the RGB-D camera called Microsoft Kinect [20], which is capable to deliver synchronized color and depth data at 30 Hz and VGA resolution. Although initially designed for gesture based interfaces, RGB-D cameras are now being employed in scientific applications as for example object recognition [1] and 3D modeling [6]. Previously inaccessible data (range sensing) and hard to solve problems (color and depth registration) are now available and consolidated with RGB-D sensors, enabling sophisticated algorithms for Robotics and for one of its most studied research topics, SLAM (*Simultaneous Localization and Mapping*).

Due to the particularities involved in the process of estimating depth measurements from images, SLAM with pure visual sensors (Visual SLAM) can be considered a nontrivial problem. However, systems relying on Visual SLAM are

© Springer-Verlag Berlin Heidelberg 2015
F.S. Osório et al. (Eds.): LARS/SBR/Robocontrol 2014, CCIS 507, pp. 16–31, 2015.
DOI: 10.1007/978-3-662-48134-9_2

very efficient in dealing with issues such as data association (by tracking visual features between different images) and loop closing (by detecting previously visited locations using image similarity). Since RGB-D cameras employ accurate depth estimation techniques (e.g. structured light stereo used in the Microsoft Kinect), SLAM can benefit from both visual data and range sensing.

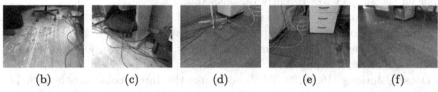

(b)   (c)   (d)   (e)   (f)

Fig. 1. (a) Top view of the resulting 3D map of the sequence *FR1 floor*, obtained by concatenating the RGB-D data of each frame in a single point cloud. The resulting map can be used for robot navigation and obstacle avoidance, despite the fact that no SLAM techniques were used in the reconstruction process. (b–f) Some sample images used to build the map are also shown.

The problem of map building and localization can also be solved by Visual Odometry [9,28]. In contrast to Visual SLAM, that allows long term localization by associating visual data with a global map, Visual Odometry systems incrementally estimate frame to frame pose transformations. Consequently, faster computation times are prioritized over localization accuracy. In light of this, mapping and localization with RGB-D sensors can be designed to be both fast and accurate.

In this work, a Visual Odometry solution for RGB-D sensors is proposed for indoor mobile robots. By tracking and detecting visual salient features across consecutive frames, the pose (position and orientation) of a moving sensor can be computed in a fast and robust manner with RANSAC [8]. Also, by registering RGB-D data utilizing the respective estimated transformation, a map of the environment is built, as illustrated in Fig. 1. The system is evaluated through a set of experiments carried out on public RGB-D datasets [32] to demonstrate the accuracy and computation performance of the method.

In the remaining text, Sect. 2 lists the related works on Visual SLAM and Odometry based on RGB-D sensors. Section 3 describes the inner workings of the proposed system, while the experiments and results are discussed on Sect. 4. Finally, we close the paper in Sect. 5.

2   Related Work

Robot localization is a well studied problem with solutions emerging from research in Simultaneous Localization and Mapping (SLAM). Successful strategies are being achieved with range sensors such as lasers [21] or Time of Flight cameras [19]. Solutions with perspective cameras are also employed in monocular [5] and stereo [13] configurations. The work of Nistér et al. [22] introduces the "Visual Odometry" terminology, which refers to systems that employ cameras to estimate the position and orientation of a moving agent. This class of systems is generally formed by incremental *Structure from Motion* [11] approaches that estimate frame to frame pose transformations instead of finding the position relative to a global map (which is the general definition of SLAM). A tutorial paper on the subject was recently pusblished [9,28].

Once unaffordable, depth measurement devices are now being employed in solutions to the localization and mapping problem with the advent of consumer grade RGB-D sensors. These solutions are either dense [16,25,30,35] or feature based [7,12,14,26,31] approaches.

Dense solutions [16,25,30,35] directly use the input color/depth data i.e. they do not rely on the extraction and matching of visual features. Steinbruecker et al. [30] propose a method to compute camera motion by estimating the warping transformation between adjacent frames under the assumption of constant image brightness. This work is later complemented [16] to support probabilistic motion models and robust estimators in the transformation estimation, resulting in a system more resilient to moving objects in the scene. Whelan et al. [35] extend the solution of Steinbruecker et al. with a GPU implementation of the algorithm and the incorporation of feature based visual front-ends to the pose estimation process. Osteen et al. [25] take an innovative direction proposing a Visual Odometry algorithm that works by computing correlations between the frequency domain representations of the scene normals.

Alternatively, feature based solutions work by matching extracted features between sequential pair of images and then estimating the corresponding transformation through sets of three point matches and RANSAC [8] and/or *Iterative Closest Point* (ICP) [2]. Henry et al. [12] detect and match FAST [27] features using Calonder descriptors [4] and optimize an error function with RANSAC and a non-linear version of ICP. After detecting loop closures, Bundle Adjustment [33] or graph optimization [10] is executed to ensure global pose consistency. Paton and Kosecka [26] and Hu et al. [14] propose a similar system, although the latter has a strategy to switch between the algorithm of Henry et al. and a

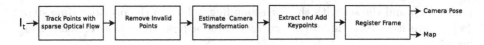

Fig. 2. The proposed Visual Odometry method.

pure monocular Visual Odometry algorithm. This strategy is employed to deal with situations in which the available depth data is not sufficient. The detection and extraction of sparse visual features was also the direction taken by Endres et al. When designing RGB-D SLAM [7], which works by extracting SIFT features [18] on a GPU implementation and optimizing the pose graph with g2o [17]. Finally, Stückler and Benhke [31] employ a surfel representation of the scene containing depth and color statistics which are later matched and registered in a multi-resolution scheme.

Our work relies on sparse visual features and incremental pose estimation between adjacent frames. However, in contrast to all mentioned solutions of this class, we do not employ *tracking by detection* in frame to frame matching. Instead of extracting keypoints and matching them using their descriptors, we track features using a short baseline optical flow tracker. As evidenced by the experiments, the system can rapidly estimate accurate camera poses without the need of using state-of-the-art GPUs.

3   Proposed System

3.1   Overview

Our goal is to estimate the pose (position and orientation) of a moving sensor (a Kinect style RGB-D camera) using only the captured color and depth information. Camera poses are estimated relative to the first RGB-D frame (the origin reference frame). A map consisting of all registered RGB-D frames is also computed at each time step.

The proposed system tracks visually salient features across consecutive image pairs I_{t-1}, I_t, adds keypoints on an as-needed basis and then robustly estimates the camera pose $[R_t|t_t]$ using the feature points. Each step of the algorithm, depicted on Fig. 2, is explained as follows.

3.2   Tracking Visual Features

At the initial time step (frame I_0), Shi-Tomasi corners [29] are extracted and invalid keypoints (points without a depth measurement) are removed. The remaining points form the initial set of features $\{\hat{\mathbf{x}}\}_0$, with $\hat{\mathbf{x}} = [x, y, d]^t$, where d is the depth of the point at image coordinates x, y. Then, for each frame I_t with $t > 0$, the points of the set $\{\hat{\mathbf{x}}\}_t$ are tracked through sparse multiscale optical flow [3], assuming a small capture interval between I_{t-1} and I_t and image brightness held constant. Since a point can become lost (or invalid) after tracking, invalid points are removed once again. Then, the resulting set of tracked points $\{\mathbf{x}\}_t$ and the set with the corresponding points on the previous time step $\{\mathbf{x}\}_{t-1}$ are used to estimate the current camera pose $[R_t|\mathbf{t}_t]$, as explained in Sect. 3.3.

We proceed with the following strategy for the management of keypoints being currently tracked. Instead of detecting and adding keypoints only when the number of tracked keypoints is below a threshold, we extract Shi-Tomasi corners at every frame, although each keypoint is only added to the tracker if two conditions are met: the current number of active keypoints is below a threshold τ and the keypoint lies in a region in the image without any tracked point.

To accomplish this, every point $\hat{\mathbf{p}}$ of the set of newly extracted points $\{\hat{\mathbf{p}}\}_t$ is checked to test whether it lies inside any of the rectangular perimeter W_j centered around each tracked point $\mathbf{x}_j$ of the set $\{\mathbf{x}\}_t$. If $\hat{\mathbf{p}}$ is not inside any rectangular region, it is added to the tracker in the set $\{\mathbf{p}\}_t$. Note that it can only be used to estimate the camera pose on the next frame, since it does not have a correspondence at $t-1$ yet. Points with invalid depth measurements once again discarded. This process is illustrated in Fig. 3.

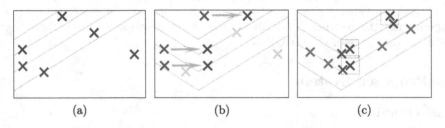

| (a) | (b) | (c) |

Fig. 3. Feature tracking strategy: (a) At I_0, the initial set of features $\{\hat{\mathbf{x}}\}_0$ (blue crosses) is extracted. (b) At I_t with $t > 0$, $\{\hat{\mathbf{x}}\}_t$ (gray crosses) is tracked into $\{\mathbf{x}\}_t$ (blue crosses). Keypoints that could not be tracked are shown in yellow. (c) The set of added keypoints $\{\mathbf{p}\}_t$ is shown with green crosses, whereas the rejected points, which are within the rectangular perimeter (dashed rectangles) of the tracked points, are shown with red crosses (Color figure online).

By varying the maximum number of active points τ and the size of the rectangular windows W_j, different configurations of the algorithm can be achieved, allowing tuning based on application requirements (such as accuracy or performance).

3.3   Frame to Frame Motion Estimation

The sets containing all tracked points in the current $\{\mathbf{x}\}_t$ and in the previous frame $\{\mathbf{x}\}_{t-1}$ are used to estimate the camera pose $[R_t|\mathbf{t}_t]$. For this, points are reprojected to 3D as

$$\begin{bmatrix} X \\ Y \\ Z \end{bmatrix} = \begin{bmatrix} d(x - c_x)/f_x \\ d(y - c_y)/f_y \\ d \end{bmatrix},$$

resulting in the sets $\{\mathbf{X}\}_t$ and $\{\mathbf{X}\}_{t-1}$ of 3D points referenced in the camera frames of I_t and I_{t-1} respectively. The terms f_x, f_y, c_x, c_y are the intrinsic parameters of the Kinect RGB sensor. The current camera pose can be estimated by finding the rigid transformation $[R^*|\mathbf{t}^*]$ that minimizes in the least squares sense the alignment error in 3D space between the two point sets, as shows Eq. 1. We proceed with the method proposed by Umeyama [34] which uses Singular Value Decomposition to solve for the transformation parameters.

$$R^*, \mathbf{t}^* = \underset{R,\mathbf{t}}{\operatorname{argmin}} \sum_i ||\mathbf{X}_{t-1}^i - (R\mathbf{X}_t^i + \mathbf{t})||^2 \tag{1}$$

Since point correspondences $\mathbf{X}_t^i, \mathbf{X}_{t-1}^i$ can be falsely estimated (due to occlusions, bad lighting conditions, the aperture problem inherent to optical flow, etc.), a robust pose estimator should be employed to compute the desired transformation. The RANSAC [8] algorithm accomplishes this function. RANSAC works by sampling a minimal set of data to estimate a model, which in our case are point correspondences and a camera transformation respectively. For a given number of iterations, minimal sets of three point matches are randomly chosen to estimate a hypothesis pose by minimizing Eq. 1. All other point correspondences are then used to count the number of inliers (correspondences with alignment error below a specified threshold ϵ). The hypothesis with the largest number of inliers is elected as the winner transformation. Using all the inliers corresponding to the winner solution, a new least squares transformation is computed, resulting in the sought $[R_t|\mathbf{t}_t]$. This last step results in camera poses significantly better than simply taking the R and $\mathbf{t}$ related to the winner transformation and the performance penalty is negligible.

The RANSAC algorithm can run faster by using an adaptive termination of the procedure that takes into account an estimate of the fraction of inlier correspondences [8]. Hence, by updating this fraction with the largest ratio found after each iteration of the algorithm, a significant speedup is achieved.

The last step in our algorithm involves registering the RGB-D frame I_t with that of I_{t-1}. The estimated pose is used to transform the 3D points in the current camera frame to the reference frame relative to the previous camera by applying the $[R_t|\mathbf{t}_t]$ to each point of $\{\mathbf{X}\}_t$. By doing so, the current transformation is always estimated relative to the origin reference frame and a map formed by all registered RGB-D frames until time step t is computed.

3.4   Algorithm Parameterization

In the current implementation, all rectangular regions W_j of the tracked points have a fixed size. All experiments of Sect. 4 are executed with maximum number of tracked points $\tau = 1000$ and window W_j with size 30×30.

RANSAC parameters are set with a correspondence error threshold ϵ of 8 mm (which automatically rejects the imprecise measurements for features with large depth) and a maximum of 10000 iterations. The reported values for all parameters were found after running the algorithm through several initial experiments.

4   Experiments and Results

4.1   Methodology

The proposed Visual Odometry system is evaluated with respect to its local-ization accuracy and computational performance. All experiments were carried out on a desktop PC with an Intel Core i5 3470 3.2 GHz processor and 8 GB of RAM running on Ubuntu Linux 12.04. The system is implemented in C++ using Point Cloud Library [23] and OpenCV [24]. We note that the OpenCV library provides a parallelized implementation of the optical flow algorithm based on Threading Building Blocks [15], a multithread library that was key to achieve the reported performance of the algorithm.

We resort to the datasets and benchmark proposed by Sturm et al. [32] to evaluate our system. Using the provided RGB-D data (with synchronized ground truth collected by a motion capture system), we assess the localization accuracy of the proposed system by estimating the translational and rotational *Relative Positioning Error* (RPE). The RPE is a performance metric suitable to Visual Odometry systems since it gives a measure of the drift (accumulated error) per unit of time. Accordingly, we report the Root Mean Square Error (RMSE) between all possible pairs of consecutive frames I_i, I_{i+1}, provinding thus a robust statistic of all estimated trajectories. The same error statistics are also computed for the RGB-D SLAM system [7] to clarify how the proposed system compares against state-of-the-art algorithms in RGB-D localization. The results from RGB-D SLAM are available at the website from the authors of the benchmark used in the experiments[1].

A total of eight datasets having different characteristics such as linear and angular camera velocities, total trajectory length and number of input frames on different scenes were selected for the experiments. All of the chosen image sequences were captured by a sensor hand-held by a moving person and have plenty of texture from which visual features can be extracted. The details about the image sequences are shown in Table 1.

4.2   Accuracy

Exploiting the fact that the RPE gives independent measurements for the trans-lational and rotational motion estimation, the results after executing the algo-rithm on each image sequence are presented on two different tables, Tables 2 and 3. The RMSE and maximum translational and rotational error accumula-tion per frame are shown for both the proposed system and RGB-D SLAM.

The proposed Visual Odometry system shows superior or equivalent accuracy regarding the RMSE translational and rotational drifts per frame compared to RGB-D SLAM. Error reductions in the translational RMSE varies between 0.3 mm (on *FR1 XYZ*) to 14.4 mm (*FR1 plant*), which represents respectively an

---

[1] https://svncvpr.in.tum.de/cvpr-ros-pkg/trunk/rgbd_benchmark/rgbd_benchmark_tools/data/rgbdslam/.

Table 1. Details of the datasets used in the experiments.

Sequence	Length	Frames	Avg. Transl. Vel	Avg. Ang. Vel
FR1 desk	9.236 m	573	0.413 m/s	23.327°/s
FR1 desk2	10.161 m	620	0.426 m/s	29.308°/s
FR1 room	15.989 m	1352	0.334 m/s	29.882°/s
FR1 floor	12.569 m	979	0.258 m/s	15.071°/s
FR1 XYZ	7.029 m	792	0.058 m/s	8.920°/s
FR2 desk	18.880 m	2893	0.193 m/s	6.338°/s
FR1 plant	14.795 m	1126	0.365 m/s	27.891°/s
FR1 teddy	15.709 m	1401	0.315 m/s	21.320°/s

Table 2. Comparison between the proposed system and the state-of-the-art implementation of RGB-D SLAM. Shown are the RMSE and maximum translational Relative Positioning Error, which gives the resulting drift in meters per frame. Best results are in boldface.

Translational relative positioning error (m/frame)				
Sequence	Prop. System		RGB-D SLAM		Improvement
FR1 desk	**0.0105 m**	**(0.0476 m)**	0.0117 m	(0.0630 m)	10.2 %
FR1 desk2	**0.0101 m**	**(0.0508 m)**	0.0175 m	(0.2183 m)	42.2 %
FR1 room	**0.0096 m**	**(0.1100 m)**	0.0137 m	(0.1590 m)	29.9 %
FR1 floor	**0.0030 m**	**(0.0141 m)**	0.0037 m	(0.0271 m)	18.9 %
FR1 XYZ	**0.0054 m**	**(0.0203 m)**	0.0057 m	(0.0212 m)	5.2 %
FR2 desk	**0.0039 m**	**(0.0164 m)**	0.0047 m	(0.0685 m)	17.0 %
FR1 plant	**0.0063 m**	**(0.0715 m)**	0.0207 m	(0.1210 m)	69.5 %
FR1 teddy	**0.0194 m**	(0.1836 m)	0.0254 m	**(0.1094 m)**	23.6 %

Table 3. Comparison between the proposed system and the state-of-the-art implementation of RGB-D SLAM. Shown are the RMSE and maximum rotational Relative Positioning Error, which gives the resulting drift in degrees per frame. Best results are in boldface.

Rotational relative positioning error (°/frame)				
Sequence	Prop. System		RGB-D SLAM		Improvement
FR1 desk	**0.5378**	**2.0777**	0.7309	6.8548	26.4 %
FR1 desk2	**0.5464**	**3.1128**	1.0665	9.6320	48.7 %
FR1 room	**0.4057**	**1.9463**	0.6319	5.1501	35.7 %
FR1 floor	**0.2418**	**1.7575**	0.2833	1.9288	14.6 %
FR1 XYZ	**0.3380**	**1.0935**	0.3529	1.6332	4.2 %
FR2 desk	**0.2712**	**1.2527**	0.2999	2.4685	9.5 %
FR1 plant	**0.3592**	**2.1466**	1.2550	4.1202	71.3 %
FR1 teddy	**0.5900**	**4.6240**	1.4490	7.2330	59.2 %

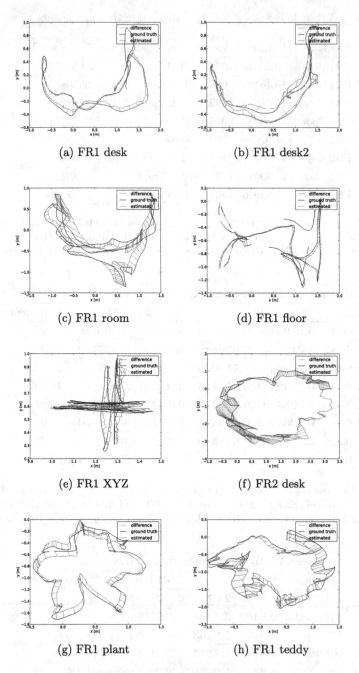

(a) FR1 desk   (b) FR1 desk2

(c) FR1 room   (d) FR1 floor

(e) FR1 XYZ   (f) FR2 desk

(g) FR1 plant   (h) FR1 teddy

Fig. 4. Camera path computed by the proposed Visual Odometry algorithm (shown in blue) in comparison to the ground truth trajectory (shown in black). The red lines are the distance between the computed and ground truth positions for corresponding time steps, which were equally sample at every 10 frames (Color figure online).

improvement of 5.2 % and 69.5 % over the compared algorithm. Similar results also hold for the rotational error, with improvements ranging from 4.2 % (on *FR1 XYZ*) up to 71.3 % (on *FR1 plant*). On average, the RMSE translational and rotational RPEs are 8.5 mm/frame and 0.411°/frame for the proposed system and 12.8 mm/frame and 0.758°/frame for RGB-D SLAM, although loop closures and drift minimization are not employed as does RGB-D SLAM. Figure 4 shows the resulting camera trajectory computed by the proposed system along with the ground truth trajectory and positional error for equally sampled time steps.

Remarkably, the proposed system shows accurate localization on several adverse situations. The camera pose can be computed with good accuracy on image sequences with high speed camera movement (and thus considerable amounts of motion blur) and even on sequences consisting on a large number of frames and traveled distances.

4.3   Computational Performance

The performance of the proposed algorithm is assessed by collecting the total time spent on the execution of each RGB-D frame. The average, standard deviation and maximum time per frame are shown in Table 4. Figure 5 depicts the running time of each image sequence used in the experiments.

The resulting running times for the proposed algorithm stays in an stable margin during most of the time, as can be noticed from the reported running times and standard deviations. Despite the fact that no specialized hardware (e.g. modern GPUs) is used by our system, the camera pose can be computed at more than 36 Hz, as evidenced by the computed average over all sequences (27.346 ms per frame). The slowest time spent on a single frame (∼170 ms) is still faster than the reported average of RGB-D SLAM (330/350 ms without/with global optimization respectively) [7] and is still fast enough for doing real-time

Table 4. Performance of the proposed RGB-D Visual Odometry system. Shown are the average, standard deviation and maximum running times computed over all frames of each sequence.

Sequence	Avg	Std. dev	Max
FR1 desk	25.041 ms	4.988 ms	101.109 ms
FR1 desk2	25.642 ms	9.558 ms	137.624 ms
FR1 room	24.304 ms	4.072 ms	66.056 ms
FR1 floor	34.217 ms	8.548 ms	103.023 ms
FR1 XYZ	22.573 ms	1.521 ms	30.905 ms
FR2 desk	23.127 ms	1.629 ms	39.451 ms
FR1 plant	26.767 ms	6.334 ms	131.797 ms
FR1 teddy	37.097 ms	22.962 ms	171.980 ms
Total avg	27.346 ms		

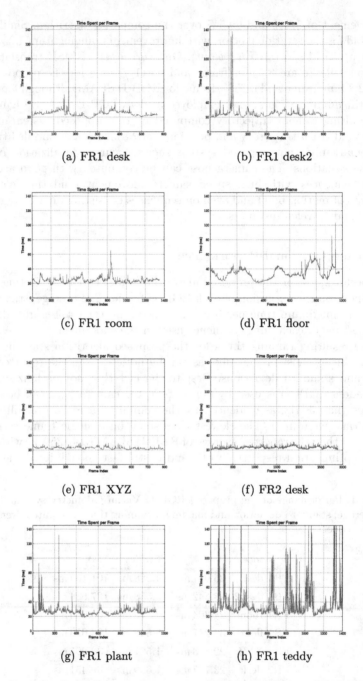

(a) FR1 desk

(b) FR1 desk2

(c) FR1 room

(d) FR1 floor

(e) FR1 XYZ

(f) FR2 desk

(g) FR1 plant

(h) FR1 teddy

Fig. 5. Running times for each image sequence used in the evaluation of the proposed system. The varying quantity of extracted and tracked features and oscillations in the RANSAC runtime explain the peaks in the estimated timings collected among different sequences.

vision based applications ($\sim$7 Hz). The varying quantity of extracted and tracked features and oscillations in the RANSAC runtime explain the peaks in the estimated timings collected among different sequences. Specifically on the sequence *FR1 floor*, a large number of keypoints is tracked in each frame due to the large amount of texture in the scene, which results in an almost uniform sampling of points for tracking and thus in a higher execution time.

4.4 Qualitative Results

We also show qualitative results of the proposed Visual Odometry method. Two resulting 3D maps are shown in Figs. 1 and 6, along with image samples of the respective sequences. A third reconstruction is illustrated on Fig. 7 depicting the result of our system after processing our own datasets. For this, 217 RGB-D frames captured at the Natalnet Laboratory (situated at the Department of Computer Engineering and Automation from the Federal University of Rio Grande do Norte) were supplied to the algorithm. These maps are built in a straightforward manner by simply transforming and concatenating the RGB-D data corresponding to each frame in a globally registered point cloud.

The maps show local consistency and very few noticeable registration errors, even though no global optimization is performed. The resulting point cloud can be post processed and then employed in a number of applications such as an

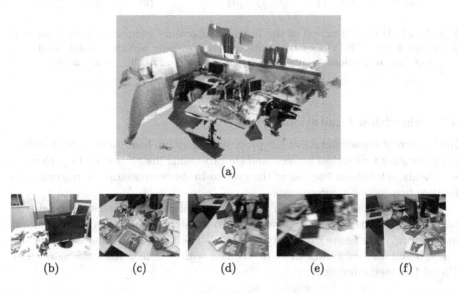

Fig. 6. (a) 3D map of the sequence *FR1 desk2*, obtained by concatenating the RGB-D data of each frame in a single point cloud with 1 cm resolution. The algorithm runs in real-time and is robust against fast camera movements. Note the quality of the map, despite the fact that no SLAM techniques were used in the reconstruction process. (b–f) Some sample images used to build the map (some of them showing noticeable motion blur).

in-hand scanner for object and environment digitalization and also for robot navigation and obstacle avoidance. Additionally, we supply videos of our algorithm processing selected sequences on the YouTube page of the author[2].

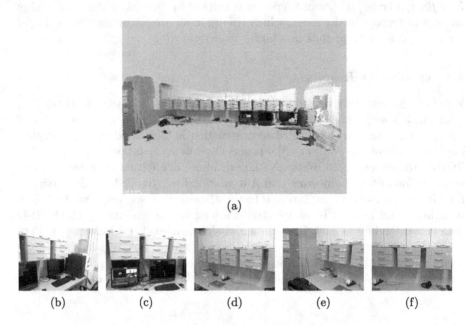

(a)

(b)   (c)   (d)   (e)   (f)

Fig. 7. (a) 3D reconstruction of the Natalnet laboratory computed by the proposed algorithm. Each RGB-D frame is concatenated in a globally registered point cloud with voxels of 1 cm resolution. (b–f) Some sample images used in the reconstruction.

4.5 Algorithm Limitations

In the current implementation, the proposed algorithm has two main limitations: (*a*) processing textureless images; and (*b*) processing images without depth measurements. Therefore, the use of the system in its current state is restricted to texture rich indoor environments.

The former limitation can be tackled by employing strategies to detect textureless environments and then switching to registration methods on range data, as performed by the work of Henry et al. [12]. The latter limitation is inherent to range based methods and can be overcomed with solutions from the monocular Visual Odometry literature.

5 Conclusion

In this work, we propose a Visual Odometry system based on RGB-D sensors that estimates camera poses using appearance/depth measurements. At each

---

[2] https://www.youtube.com/user/brunomfs/videos.

RGB-D frame, visual features are detected and tracked through sparse optical flow with new features being added if they do not fall within regions related to already tracked features. Camera poses computed as the transformation between adjacent frames using RANSAC can then be estimated in a fast and accurate manner.

The accuracy and computational performance of the proposed system is demonstrated by experiments carried out on public available RGB-D datasets and benchmark [32] and a comparison with the state-of-the-art RGB-D SLAM algorithm [7] is presented to clarify how competitive is our proposal. The average RMSE translational and rotational RPE are 8.5 mm/frame and 0.411°/frame for the proposed system and 12.8 mm/frame and 0.758°/frame for RGB-D SLAM, at the same time that the running times for the proposed algorithm are almost one order of magnitude faster on average. This results are achieved without the use of expensive and specialized hardware such as modern GPUs.

The proposed Visual Odometry and mapping algorithm can be employed in a number of important applications related to real-time 3D reconstruction and Robotics, such as object digitalization, indoor mapping and robot navigation.

Future works will focus on detcting loop closures and trajectory optimization algorithms using the Visual Odomety module as a front-end in a full SLAM solution.

Acknowledgments. This work is supported by the Coordination for the Improvement of Higher Education Personnel (CAPES) and the Funding Agency for Studies and Projects (FINEP).

References

1. Aldoma, A., Marton, Z., Tombari, F., Wohlkinger, W., Potthast, C., Zeisl, B., Rusu, R., Gedikli, S., Vincze, M.: Tutorial: point cloud library: three-dimensional object recognition and 6 DOF pose estimation. Robot. Autom. Mag. **19**(3), 80–91 (2012)
2. Besl, P., McKay, N.D.: A method for registration of 3-D shapes. IEEE Trans. Pattern Anal. Mach. Intel. **14**(2), 239–256 (1992)
3. Bouguet, J.Y.: Pyramidal implementation of the lucas kanade feature tracker. Intel Corporation, Microprocessor Research Labs (2000)
4. Calonder, M., Lepetit, V., Fua, P.: Keypoint signatures for fast learning and recognition. In: Forsyth, D., Torr, P., Zisserman, A. (eds.) ECCV 2008, Part I. LNCS, vol. 5302, pp. 58–71. Springer, Heidelberg (2008)
5. Davison, A.: Real-time simultaneous localisation and mapping with a single camera. In: Proceedings of IEEE International Conference on Computer Vision (ICCV) (2003)
6. Du, H., Henry, P., Ren, X., Cheng, M., Goldman, D., Seitz, S., Fox, D.: Interactive 3D modeling of indoor environments with a consumer depth camera. In: Proceedings of the International Conference on Ubiquitous Computing (UbiComp). ACM, New York (2011)
7. Endres, F., Hess, J., Engelhard, N., Sturm, J., Cremers, D., Burgard, W.: An evaluation of the RGB-D SLAM system. In: Proceedings of IEEE International Conference on Robotics and Automation (ICRA), St. Paul, MA, USA, May 2012

8. Fischler, M., Bolles, R.: Random sample consensus: a paradigm for model fitting with applications to image analysis and automated cartography. Commun. ACM **24**(6), 381–395 (1981)
9. Fraundorfer, F., Scaramuzza, D.: Visual odometry: part ii: matching, robustness, optimization, and applications. IEEE Robot. Autom. Mag. **19**(2), 78–90 (2012)
10. Grisetti, G., Stachniss, C., Burgard, W.: Nonlinear constraint network optimization for efficient map learning. IEEE Trans. Intel. Transp. Syst. **10**(3), 428–439 (2009)
11. Hartley, R.I., Zisserman, A.: Multiple View Geometry in Computer Vision, 2nd edn. Cambridge University Press, Cambridge (2004)
12. Henry, P., Krainin, M., Herbst, E., Ren, X., Fox, D.: RGB-D mapping: using kinect-style depth cameras for dense 3D modeling of indoor environments. Int. J. Robot. Res. **31**(5), 647–663 (2012)
13. Howard, A.: Real-time stereo visual odometry for autonomous ground vehicles. In: Proceedings of IEEE/RSJ International Conference on Intelligent Robots and Systems (IROS) (2008)
14. Hu, G., Huang, S., Zhao, L., Alempijevic, A., Dissanayake, G.: A robust RGB-D SLAM algorithm. In: Proceedings of IEEE/RSJ International Conference on Intelligent Robots and Systems (IROS), pp. 1714–1719 (2012)
15. Intel: Threading Building Blocks (TBB) (2014). https://www.threadingbuilding blocks.org/home. Accessed 1 October 2014
16. Kerl, C., Sturm, J., Cremers, D.: Robust odometry estimation for RGB-D cameras. In: Proceedings of IEEE International Conference on Robotics and Automation (ICRA), May 2013
17. Kummerle, R., Grisetti, G., Strasdat, H., Konolige, K., Burgard, W.: G2O: a general framework for graph optimization. In: Proceedings of IEEE International Conference on Robotics and Automation (ICRA), pp. 3607–3613 (2011)
18. Lowe, D.: Distinctive image features from scale-invariant keypoints. Int. J. Comput. Vis. **60**(2), 91–110 (2004)
19. May, S., Droeschel, D., Holz, D., Fuchs, S., Malis, E., Nüchter, A., Hertzberg, J.: Three-dimensional mapping with time-of-flight cameras. J. Field Robot. **26**(11–12), 934–965 (2009)
20. Microsoft: Microsoft Kinect (2014). http://www.xbox.com/en-US/kinect. Accessed 1 October 2014
21. Newman, P., Cole, D., Ho, K.: Outdoor SLAM using visual appearance and laser ranging. In: Proceedings of IEEE International Conference on Robotics and Automation (ICRA), pp. 1180–1187 (2006)
22. Nistér, D., Naroditsky, O., Bergen, J.: Visual odometry. In: Proceedings of IEEE Computer Society Conference on Computer Vision and Pattern Recognition (CVPR), pp. 652–659 (2004)
23. Open Perception: Point Cloud Library (PCL) (2014). http://pointclouds.org. Accessed 1 October 2014
24. OpenCV Foundation: OpenCV Library (2014). http://opencv.org. Accessed 1 October 2014
25. Osteen, P., Owens, J., Kessens, C.: Online egomotion estimation of RGB-D sensors using spherical harmonics. In: Proceedings of IEEE International Conference on Robotics and Automation (ICRA), pp. 1679–1684 (2012)
26. Paton, M., Kosecka, J.: Adaptive RGB-D localization. In: Conference on Computer and Robot Vision (CRV), pp. 24–31 (2012)
27. Rosten, E., Drummond, T.W.: Machine learning for high-speed corner detection. In: Leonardis, A., Bischof, H., Pinz, A. (eds.) ECCV 2006, Part I. LNCS, vol. 3951, pp. 430–443. Springer, Heidelberg (2006)

28. Scaramuzza, D., Fraundorfer, F.: Visual odometry [tutorial]. IEEE Robot. Autom. Mag. **18**(4), 80–92 (2011)

29. Shi, J., Tomasi, C.: Good features to track. In: Proceedings of IEEE Conference on Computer Vision and Pattern Recognition (CVPR), pp. 593–600 (1994)

30. Steinbruecker, F., Sturm, J., Cremers, D.: Real-time visual odometry from dense RGB-D images. In: Workshop on Live Dense Reconstruction with Moving Cameras at the International Conference on Computer Vision (ICCV) (2011)

31. Stückler, J., Behnke, S.: Integrating depth and color cues for dense multi-resolution scene mapping using RGB-D cameras. In: Proceedings of IEEE International Conference on Multisensor Fusion and Information Integration (MFI), September 2012

32. Sturm, J., Engelhard, N., Endres, F., Burgard, W., Cremers, D.: A benchmark for the evaluation of RGB-D SLAM systems. In: Proceedings of IEEE/RSJ International Conference on Intelligent Robot Systems (IROS), October 2012

33. Triggs, B., McLauchlan, P.F., Hartley, R.I., Fitzgibbon, A.W.: Bundle adjustment – a modern synthesis. In: Triggs, B., Zisserman, A., Szeliski, R. (eds.) ICCV-WS 1999. LNCS, vol. 1883, pp. 298–372. Springer, Heidelberg (2000)

34. Umeyama, S.: Least-squares estimation of transformation parameters between two point patterns. IEEE Trans. Pattern Anal. Mach. Intel. **13**(4), 376–380 (1991)

35. Whelan, T., Johannsson, H., Kaess, M., Leonard, J., McDonald, J.: Robust real-time visual odometry for dense RGB-D mapping. In: Proceedings of IEEE International Conference on Robotics and Automation (ICRA), Karlsruhe, Germany, May 2013

From Tele-Operated Robots to Social Robots with Autonomous Behaviors

Rafael Berri, Denis Wolf, and Fernando Osório(✉)

Mobile Robotics Lab (LRM) and Center for Robotics (CRob/USP-SC),
University of São Paulo-ICMC, Trabalhador São-carlense. 400,
São Carlos, São Paulo 13566-590, Brazil
rafaelberri@usp.br, {denis,fosorio}@icmc.usp.br

Abstract. This paper presents a perception/interface device for Telepresence Mobile Robots using a Kinect sensor. Firstly, using the Kinect RGB camera (Webcam) and image processing techniques, it is possible to detect a human face, allowing the robot to track the face, getting closer of a person, moving forward and rotating to get a better pose (position and orientation) to interact with him/her. Then it is possible to recognize hand gestures using the Kinect 3D sensor (Depth camera). The proposed gesture recognition method tracks the hands positions and movements, when moving it forward towards the robot, and then recognizing a set of predefined gestures/commands. Finally, the 3D perception provided by the Kinect also allows us to detect obstacles, avoiding collisions and safely moving the mobile robot base, also allowing to search for someone in the environment. Practical experiments are presented demonstrating the obtained results: (i) in the searching and tracking of human faces; (ii) in the robot positioning related to the user we want to interact with; and also (iii) in the human gesture recognition.

Keywords: Face tracking · Human gesture · Kinect sensor · Perception · Robotics · Telepresence

1 Introduction

The development and application of telepresence mobile robots has significantly increased in the last few years. Telepresence mobile robots allows not only to be virtually present at meetings and into remote places, as we usually do through video-conferencing calls, but also has the mobility and the ability to better interact with other people, as if the remote person were really present in the remote environment. Telepresence robots allow the remote person to control a remote robot avatar, exploring the environment and interacting with people in a more natural way.

There are nowadays several companies that provide robotic telepresence solutions, as for example: Double Robotics [7], Suitable Technologies with Beam Robot [25] (company product initially developed at Willow Garage), iRobot

© Springer-Verlag Berlin Heidelberg 2015
F.S. Osório et al. (Eds.): LARS/SBR/Robocontrol 2014, CCIS 507, pp. 32–52, 2015.
DOI: 10.1007/978-3-662-48134-9_3

with AVA Robot [12], and many others as VGO, Anybots, and even some star-tups like Telemba (Kickstarter crowd funding project which uses the Roomba as mobile base platform).

The large availability and lower costs of these platforms have created new possibilities of applications: (i) virtual visiting of museums and touristic places with the possibility of interact with local people; (ii) remotely take classes or participate into conferences (e.g. some people could participate remotely from the ICAPS 2014 Conference using Beam telepresence robots); (iii) present talks remotely when we are not able to be locally present, as occurred in the presenta-tion of Edward Snowden at TED talk in the United States [23]; (iv) interact with family, friends or co-workers remotely; just to cite a few examples of applications.

Although the mobile robots for telepresence are being largely adopted, the majority of these systems are quite simple mobile robot platforms that are tele-operated, with few or even without any perception capabilities and/or autonomy. When the robot is used in public places (e.g. museums, supermarkets, and shop-ping centers), we can have the following problems:

- *Control:* the person who is controlling the tele-operated robot can have prob-lems to operate it specially in a tight place, e.g., the robot can hit and cause damages in the things located in its way;
- *Movement:* the human controller must know very well the place where the robot is moving for path planning and control of the robot navigation. It also requires a constant attention from the operator in order to send the orders (low abstraction level commands) to the robot, due to its limited autonomy;
- *Interaction:* it is not easy for the robot's controller keeps the robot in a good position/orientation aiming to interact with a person. The human operator should adjust manually the robot pose to keep it well positioned.

In this work, we propose to integrate the Kinect sensors (RGB and depth camera) in a mobile robot platform allowing the robot to: autonomously navi-gate; being tele-operated avoiding collisions with obstacles (semi-autonomous); locate persons into the environment; get closer to a person; and recognize ges-tures from this person, interacting with him/her. The proposed system allows a tele-operated mobile robot base to have: (i) *proxemic behavior*, moving the robot to a good position for interacting with humans and allowing the humans to understand the robot's intention [18]; (ii) *social capacity* of interaction with humans (it is transformed in a social robot) [2]; (iii) it can be used as an autonomous or semi-autonomous system, in other words, a human can control the robot without worrying about obstacles and interact with another human through it (tele-operation, human-human interaction and telepresence).

A typical example of application for this robot is a robotic tour guide for museums and touristic attractions. The robot can act as an autonomous tour guide, moving along the environment and detecting when someone approach the robot and shows the intention to interact with it. The robot should be able to identify the human face and to move itself in order to get closer and better posi-tioned related to the human. Then, the robot should use a audio/video interface (display) to start the interaction with the human, presenting some options of contents presentations, and the human can answer the robot questions selecting the desired options through gestures (hand gesture recognition). An external (remote) operator can also assume the robot operation (telepresence mode) and start to interact with the human, or also to control the robot displacement around the environment. Finally, If the person turns his back to the robot, the robot will detect that the human face has gone away and come back to the initial state, moving along the environment searching for other people, or being tele-operated by a remote operator.

The remainder of this paper is organized as follows: in Sect. 2, we present some related works found in the literature; in Sect. 3 we relate the motivations about the proposed solution; in Sect. 4 we describe some concepts related to the implementation of the proposed solution; in Sect. 5 the robotic system is detailed; the results of our preliminary experiments and tests are shown in Sect. 6; and finally in the Sect. 7 the conclusions and future works are presented.

2   Related Works

Telepresence robots are being developed for a long time, with this term coined by Marvin Minky [11,17] in the 80s. Recently, we have observed a great development expansion of telepresence and tele-operated robots, once the mobile robots and communication technologies have advanced and become cheaper and more sophisticated [15]. Several commercial solutions are available nowadays in the market (e.g. Double Robotics [7], Texai/Suitable Beam Robot [25], iRobot AVA [12], Anybots QB, VGO, and many others [15]), and even a telepresence robot for space activities, the Robonaut, is being developed by NASA [19]).

Despite of this large number of telepresence robots in the market, the majority of the commercial solutions is composed by simple tele-operated robots (with no sensors or autonomous behavior) and providing only teleconference facilities (only video/audio based interaction). In this work, we are interested in providing a local intelligence to the mobile robot (e.g. search for people, automatic positioning, avoid collisions) and natural interface based on gestures (e.g. gestures recognition) [3].

Considering the mobile robot base, there are several solutions for indoor robot navigation [26] and gesture recognition [28], but we are interested in simple, not expensive, mixed solutions (teleoperation with semi-autonomous/autonomous navigation).

An example of autonomous robot for public places is the Grace [22], which uses touch screen, infrared, sonar sensors, stereo camera, and a SICK scanning laser range finder. Grace can speak using a speech synthesizer, and recognize answers using a microphone headset and commercial speech recognition software (IBM's ViaVoice). Michalowski et al. [16] added to the Grace's behaviors the task of finding a person.

The RoboX [13] is a tour-guide robot that uses a camera, two laser range finders (Sick LMS 200), an LED display, two loudspeakers, microphone, and interactive buttons. For interacting with people this robot can have speech recognition (for simple answers as YES/NO). The RGB image is used to track people.

Another tour-guide robot is the Rackham [5], which uses a SICK laser and SLAM for localization and the same laser sensor to avoiding obstacles. For interacting with people, it uses the vocal synthesis and a 3D animated head displayed on the screen. The user answers using the touch screen display.

The Robovie [10, 14] is a robot, which is used in a supermarket. It offers behaviors in a way to help people to carry goods, follow people along the supermarket, suggest and locate products, among other tasks. It uses a face and gesture recognition to identify humans. The Robovie detects the behavior of the users (e.g. walking styles) for better help them.

These related works usually depend on and require expensive sensors, as for example, laser sensors [5, 13, 22], or have a limited predefined set of behaviors and interaction modes with humans [10]. The present work aims to adopt less expensive sensors and also to provide different operation modes: tele-operation, telepresence, autonomous robot moving and positioning and gesture recognition.

Recently the adoption of the Kinect sensor provided by Microsoft/Prime Sense has allowed the development of 3D environment perception with low cost [30]. The Kinect provides RGB images (video stream) and also depth images, allowing to autonomously navigating using this sensor to avoid obstacles [20]. In previous works of our research group we have developed some applications of autonomous navigation [6, 20, 21] and gesture recognition [1] using the Kinect. In this work we adopt the Kinect to provide RGB images for face localization and tracking, and also, to provide depth information allowing obstacle avoidance, positioning and navigation.

3 Motivation

When we use an autonomous mobile robot, we can have a "helper buddy" that is always available for doing some tasks for us. However, we have some difficulty to prepare an autonomous robot for interacting with us, in each possible situation, and also safely moving inside of a specific place. The robotic system can be prepared for some specific situations (local behaviors) that contribute for solving much of the problem. Then, if a telepresence robot is able to autonomously move the robot base, without collisions, we can enjoy the best of both worlds: tele-operate the robot indicating the actions we want to be executed, and, move the robot base autonomously without having to take care of every single step on its moves or constantly paying attention to avoid to hit obstacles. In other words, we can use the robot in semi or completely autonomous mode and a remote human guide can invoke the telepresence mode for interacting with a local user, solving a specific doubt of him/her.

In order to transforming a telepresence robot into an (semi or complete) autonomous robot, we need to develop and made available some behaviors and robot tasks: wander, get closer, and gesture recognition.

In the wander task, the robot needs to move autonomously in the environment. Then, this task does the robot goes ahead with a constant speed and it should detect obstacles to avoid collisions. The objective of the wander task is to be more easily perceived by a possible local user which needs or looks for some help. Then, the user needs to stay in front of the robot declaring his/her intent of interacting with the robot in a "face-to-face interaction". The forward robot speed is slow allowing the human detection and the interaction that can be easily started.

The robot needs to keep autonomously a comfortable proximity to interact with the user, getting closer to the user (but not too close), and demonstrating its "intention" to interact and help the local user. The distance between the robot and the user cannot be too far, causing doubts of which person is now interacting with the robot, but it cannot be too close hampering the data capture (3D perception) from the Kinect, also posing problems to the user gesture recognition.

Interaction is done, between the robot and the user, using a non-verbal communication. The robot shows messages to the user and the user can answer with gestures. Then, the gesture recognition task uses the Kinect data to identify the user's answers and allowing the autonomous interaction of the robot with the local user.

These behaviors/tasks above described allows the robot to be used as a tour guide, acting as a visitor assistant (local user "helper buddy"), but also, allowing a remote user to assume the robot control in order to interact with the user (telepresence mode). On the other hand, the remote user does not need to control every single movement of the robot, since the mobile robot base can move autonomously and also avoid obstacles.

4 Basic Concepts and Techniques

In this section, the basic concepts, techniques and support tools for classifying the face regions in the images, tracking the face, and execute some additional image processing task, as the mathematical morphology processing, are presented.

4.1 Face Detection Using Viola-Jones

Viola-Jones [27] is a detection algorithm applicable for finding human faces regions on grayscale images. A large number of features (Haar-like features) are chosen on Viola-Jones' training. Each feature is a simple threshold function of the image. Figure 1 shows samples of features. The threshold is applied over the gray level difference between the white and black rectangles. A big image dataset is used for choosing the threshold of features. These features are called weak classifiers and when they are combined they contribute to decide whether a region of the image is a face or a non-face.

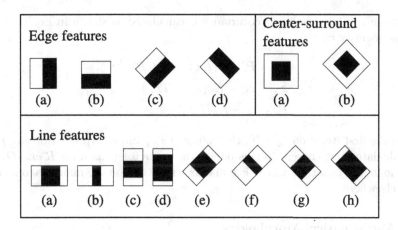

Fig. 1. A set of Haar-like features [4].

4.2   Kalman Filter

The Kalman Filter [29] is a set of mathematical tools which can be used for tracking elements in interactive image processing and computer vision applications. The Discrete Kalman Filter Algorithm uses a series of measurements detected over time, involving noise (random variables), and makes estimates of unknown variables.

The position (image's row and column coordinates in pixels units) of tracking is the input to the Kalman Filter in this paper. The filter estimates the output or the tracked position in the next frame. The iteration on each frame can be divided in a prediction and a correction step.

The prediction step is responsible for projecting the current state ahead and the error covariance estimation for the next time step. The state ahead (x_k^-) is calculated by the Eq. 1, where, A is the state transition matrix, x_{k-1} is the previous state, B is the control-input matrix, and u_{k-1} is the previous control-input vector (parameter). u_{k-1} and B are optional and we do not use in this paper. The Eq. 2 calculates the error covariance estimation (P_k^-), where, P_{k-1} is the previous error covariance estimation, and Q is the estimated process error covariance.

$$x_k^- = Ax_{k-1} + Bu_{k-1} \tag{1}$$

$$P_k^- = AP_{k-1}A^T + Q \tag{2}$$

The correction step is accountable for incorporating a new measurement to get an improved a posteriori estimate. Before the new measurement is obtained, the Kalman Gain (K_k) must be calculated by the Eq. 3, where, H is the observation matrix, and R is the estimated measurement error covariance. Therefore, the new measurement can be calculated by the Eq. 4, where, z_k is the measurement vector (parameter), in other words, this contains the real-world measurement in this frame k. Then, the error covariance is calculated as shown in Eq. 5, where, I is the identity matrix.

$$K_k = P_k^- H^T (H P_k^- H^T + R)^{-1} \tag{3}$$

$$x_k = x_k^- + K_k(z_k - H x_k^-) \tag{4}$$

$$P_k = (I - K_k H) P_k^- \tag{5}$$

On the first iteration ($k = 0$), the values of x_0^-, and P_0^- (prediction step) are not calculated but chosen. In this paper, the value 0.1 is used for R and Q, the A is the identity matrix, and H is a matrix with 0.005 on the main diagonal and zeros elsewhere.

4.3   Mathematical Morphology

Mathematical morphology (MM) comprises the analysis and processing of geometrical structures in the image. Haralick et al. [9] define MM as the way for purging of image data, which essential shape is kept and unnecessary information is removed. It uses a Structuring Element (SE) for defining the neighborhood structure for each image's pixel [24]. The SE is an image (or mask).

There are some morphological operations that can be performed on the images. However, the basic operations are the Dilation and Erosion. Through the basic operations, the Opening and Closing operations are derived [9]. We apply the MM on binary images in this work, but it can be used in other types of images as grayscale.

Erosion: The erosion is a morphological operation that tends to reduce the object's area on the image. The Eq. 6 defines the erosion, where, A is the input image, B is the SE, $\ominus$ is the symbol of erosion, and z is the pixel analyzed (which translates the SE) [24]. Therefore, a pixel of A remains after the erosion whether the SE fit (all pixels of SE must not be over the background) on its neighborhood. Effects and usefulness of erosion on an image are the following: the objects area is reduced, it eliminates object with dimensions smallest of the SE, expanding holes, and it is used for separating object [8].

$$A \ominus B = \{z | (B)_z \subseteq A\}. \tag{6}$$

Dilation: The morphological operation of the dilation tends to increase the object's area. The Eq. 7 describes the dilation, where, A is the input image, B is the SE, $\oplus$ is the dilation's symbol [24]. Then, if any pixel of SE is over the A, the origin of SE (the pixel analyzed) is added into A (assign the value 1). So the dilation increases objects, fills small holes, and connects close objects [8].

$$A \oplus B = \bigcup_{a \in A} (B)_a. \tag{7}$$

Opening: In the morphological opening operation is used the Eq. 8, in other words, the opening (the symbol is ∘) of A by B (SE) is the erosion of A by B, and the result is then processed using a dilation by B. A geometric interpretation can be used which B is translated inside of all objects of A and the regions where B cannot reach are removed. The opening may be used for eliminating protrusions, separating object, and smooth contours [8].

$$A \circ B = (A \ominus B) \oplus B. \tag{8}$$

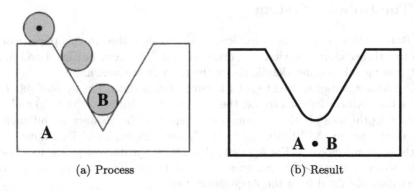

(a) Process   (b) Result

Fig. 2. The closing example for binary image ($A \bullet B$). Based on [8].

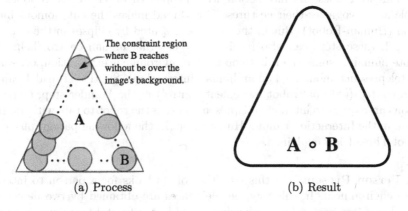

(a) Process   (b) Result

Fig. 3. The opening example for binary image ($A \circ B$). Based on [8].

Closing: The morphological closing operation of A by B (SE) is the dilation of A by B, and then the result is processed using an erosion by B. The Eq. 9 describes the closing (the symbol is •). Geometric interpretation of the binary closing is the displacement of B inside of the image's background, and the positions where B cannot be just over it are added to A. The closing process is shown in Fig. 2, and the Fig. 3 shows the opening process. The closing might be used for filling small holes, connecting close objects, and smooth contours [8].

$$A \bullet B = (A \oplus B) \ominus B. \tag{9}$$

5   The Robotic System

The Robotic System proposed, implemented and described in this paper works with two threads. An overview of Threads 1 and 2 are seen in Figs. 4 and 5. In the following subsections, details about the threads are shown.

The Kinect sensor is used to get the environment data. The system gets two images from Kinect for each frame, the first one is RGBimage (webcam) and the second (DepthImage) is the environmental depth or the distance in millimeters from each pixel in the RGBimage to the Kinect. Examples of RGBimage and DepthImage are shown at Fig. 6(a) and (b), where, the darkest pixels are closest to the Kinect while the lightest ones are the farthest. The two threads get the Kinect data obtained from the Acquisition step.

In the following subsections, details about the threads are discussed.

5.1   Thread 1

The Thread 1 does the interaction with people, in other words, it looks for people and recognizes their gestures. This thread makes the autonomous interaction (Human-Robot). But in the steps represented by ellipses in the diagram of Fig. 4, these steps can also receive some external human control/help (e.g. remote human assume the robot control for environment exploration, or, enters in a telepresence mode for human-human interaction). So, the Thread 1 can be tele-operated (external robot movement control) in the Wander step, and/or a person can request to interact (telepresence) using the robot to talk with another person in the Interaction Human-Human step. In the following paragraphs, each step of Thread 1 is explained.

Is a Person Present? In this step the robots looks for a person to interact in the environment. In this way, people's faces are obtained by two detectors[1] Viola-Jones (see Sect. 4.1), previously trained in the frontal face detection task. People who seek for the robot's attention will be looking for the robot, so the classifiers of frontal faces are used. The small faces are discarded, in other words, people far from the robot are not considered.

---

[1] Viola-Jones detectors from OpenCV (http://opencv.org) with three training files: haar-cascade_frontalface_alt2.xml and haarcascade_frontalface_default.xml.

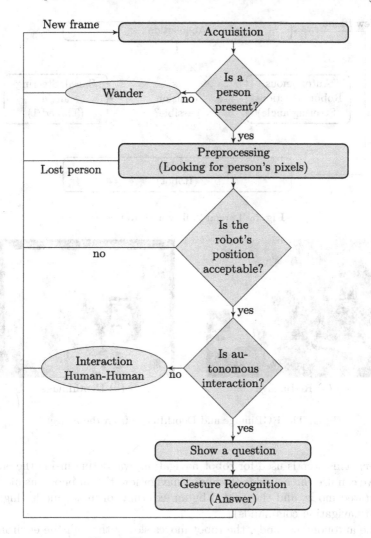

Fig. 4. Thread 1: flow and overview.

Of all detected faces only the largest face found in every frame is selected. A person is considered present or not after a continuous image sequence analysis and face recognition for 1 s. The intersection between the faces of two successive frames is checked, if intersection exists in at least 80 % of the cases examined, the person is declared as being present.

A person is considered to be present until all questions are answered or the preprocessing step (see Sect. 5.1) lose the person.

The robot's Wander behavior is used while no person is detected by the face detector.

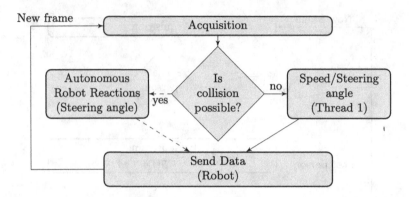

Fig. 5. Thread 2: flow and overview

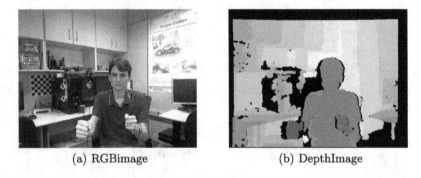

(a) RGBimage   (b) DepthImage

Fig. 6. The RGBimage and DepthImage from the Kinect l.

Wander: This step is used for robot navigation, wandering inside the environment. We can use three modes of wander/navigation: the autonomous mode, the tele-operated mode, and the guided by an external controller mode (high level task and navigation commands).

In the autonomous mode, the robot moves slowly through the environment. It waits for the pro-activity of one person interested in the robot's attention. In this mode, the robot moves without knowing the local map, and no navigation and path planning is predefined.

The tele-operated mode can be activated by an external user (remote control). In this mode, a person can control the robot movement (speed and steering angle). So, the remote person drives the robot until to find a person and execute the next interaction with this person.

In the guided by an external controller mode (get instructions from the master system), the robot receives instructions of speed and steering angle comming from another system. This other system can control the robot remotely into a master-slave operation mode, where the mobile robot is the slave. In this mode, the movements can be better planned, using maps and path planning algorithms, being "smarter" than the other modes. It can do an intelligent path planning and navigation, e.g. moving the robot along of a corridor together with more people moving around in this moment. When a person asks for help (stopping just in front of the robot and facing to it), the planned path execution is stopped until the interaction ends. This mode can work with or without a remote human assistance.

Preprocessing: The face region is received from the "Is a person present?" step in the first time the Preprocessing module is called, which occurs when a local person is detected.

The first task of preprocessing is to avoid disturbances in DepthImage. The Kinect has limitations in measuring very small distances. For this reason, on the pixels with depth less than 100 mm to 250 mm from the Kinect the returned values are the highest level possible (too close).

On the face region, considering the RGBimage and the result obtained from the Viola-Jones detector, we look for the face in the correspondent pixels obtained from the DepthImage, selecting the nearest pixel ($NearestPixelFace$) of the Kinect. An example of the $NearestPixelFace$ position inside of the face region is presented in Fig. 7. All pixels with depth less than $NearestPixelFace+250$ (mm) are selected on a binary image, as shown in Fig. 8.

Fig. 7. The position in RGBimage of the $NearestPixelFace$ inside of the face region (Color figure online).

The morphological closing (see Sect. 4.3) is used for joining the connected-components, which are close to the same component. The Cross Structuring Element is then used, applied to 3 % of the image width for all width and height. An example showing the result (binary image) of this morphological operations is shown in Fig. 9.

Fig. 8. The binary image with the pixels ahead of $NearestPixelFace + 250$ (mm).

The connected-component, obtained from the DepthImage, which has the biggest intersection with the face region detected in the RGBimage, has the target person pixels. The person's pixels are shown in the Fig. 10.

The Preprocessing step adjusts the face region for next frame (face tracking). The search region considered in the new face region search has 102 % to 120 % (adjustable) of the previous region dimensions, and the same center of the actual region face. All pixels of person's binary image inside of the search region are selected. The face region will be repositioned with top set on the highest pixel and in the center set based on the leftmost and rightmost pixels selected.

Fig. 9. The binary image after the morphological Closing.

Fig. 10. The binary image with the person's pixels selected.

A new face detection[2] with Viola-Jones is done each second. Two frontal face detectors and one profile face detector are used. The biggest face regions of each detector are selected. The face region selected with dimensions closest to the actual face region is chosen as the new face region. The maximum allowed variation of face region is 20 %. When the new face from Viola-Jones is rejected, the region face from the tracking is adopted for the next frame. A Viola-Jones detection is done by one second until a compatible face region is found, or, if it can not detect the face region during this time interval (occurs when the person is lost), a new person face is sought in the next frame.

Is the Robot's Position Acceptable? This step verifies whether the robot position is acceptable for interacting with the detected person (face detected and tracked). The main goals here are keeping the face region centered on the image width and inside an acceptable region for image height, as are shown in Fig. 11. When the robot's repositioning is required, the linear and angular speeds are calculated.

The *Angle* value is calculated by the Eq. 10, where, (Pc_x, Pc_y) are the coordinates x and y of the central point of the face region of the person and (Pb_x, Pb_y) are coordinates of the middle and bottom pixel $(\frac{width}{2}, height)$ of image. When the absolute value of Angle is higher than $\frac{\pi}{18}$ (10 degrees) the robot repositioning (reorientation/moving) is required.

$$Angle = arctan(\frac{Pc_y - Pb_y}{Pc_x - Pb_x}) + \frac{\pi}{2} \qquad (10)$$

---

[2] Viola-Jones detectors from OpenCV (http://opencv.org) with three training files: haarcascade_frontalface_alt2.xml, haarcascade_frontalface_default.xml, and haarcascade_profileface.xml.

Fig. 11. An example of acceptable position for the detected face region. The vertical green line is the center of the image width (objective). Between the two horizontal yellow lines are the acceptable height face positions (Color figure online).

The forward speed has a constant value (e.g. 0.2 m/s) and is used for keeping the face region inside of the height acceptable positions. When part of the face is outside of the allowed area, the speed of −0.2 m/s (backward) is adopted. When the face height is smaller than 20 % of the height acceptable positions, then it is adopted the speed of 0.2 m/s. If the speed is non-zero, the robot's repositioning is required.

When the robot repositioning is required, the following steps are not perfomed.

Is Autonomous Interaction Required? This step receives requests from an external person (tutor/guide) to interact with the local user through the robotic system, helping him/her in a specific situation. When this request is made, the steps of the autonomous interaction ("Show a question" and "Gesture Recognition") are not performed, and the system is used for a typical telepresence interaction, operating as the avatar of the remote operator.

Interaction Human-Human: When this step is used, a tutor/guide (remote user) communicates directly through audio and video with the local user, while the robot tries to keep the user face inside of the acceptable region. If the user "is lost" (go away), the interaction is then interrupted.

Show a Question and Gesture Recognition: The "Show a question" and "Gesture Recognition" steps do the autonomous interaction with the person. The first one shows information (questions). The second one gets the answer.

The lower hands, the right hand forward, the left hand forward, and the left and right hands forward are possible interactions and gestures that can be automatically recognized by the system. Therefore, the users can answer in three different ways (e.g. Yes, No, Cancel) to each posed question or give three different commands (e.g. previous, next, select). To lower the hands is reserved as a neutral gesture that indicates the user is waiting for the next question or have not yet provided his/her answer.

The closest pixel from the Kinect in left side of the image, related to the center point of the face region, is adopted as the right hand marker for the right hand forward gesture; and the closest pixel in right side of the image is adopted as the left hand marker for the left hand forward gesture. The hand's marker points must be between 50 and 2000 mm closer than $NearestPixelFace$ (see Sect. 5.1) to be considered, and depending on the distance from $NearestPixelFace$ the hand marker is considered as hand forward (upward towards the sensor) or hand down (downward aligned with the body). The Kalman Filter (see Sect. 4.2) is used to smooth the hands' movements, improving the hands gesture tracking. An example of hands localization is shown in the Fig. 12.

Fig. 12. The hands localization example. The blue dot in the left shows the right hand position and the red dot in the right shows the left hand position. The green dot in the head shows the $NearestPixelFace$. The blue line divides the image frame in two regions used to search the position of the right hand (left side) and left hand (right side) (Color figure online).

Reliable answers are obtained by the system when using periods of one second for gesture recognition. If the same answer is detected at least 80 % of all the time during the answer detection, it is adopted as the final recognized answer. Then, a new recognition period is started, and the system restart to count the detected hand postures. Some interactions require that after each new answer the user should return his hands to the neutral position.

5.2   Thread 2

The Thread 2 finds an obstacle around of the robot. The central row of DepthImage is used to get clearance from obstacles. Any pixel with depth smaller than 60 cm is considered an obstacle in this implementation. When an obstacle is found, the external commands sent to the robot with speed and angle rotation are ignored by the robot. At the same time, the robot start to turn (right or left) in order to avoid collisions. It turns left if the left side of the central image row has the smallest amount of pixels which can be considered as obstacles. Otherwise, the right side is considered the best direction to turn in order to avoid obstacles, then the robot turns right.

6   Experiments

The Human Gesture Interface module (see Sect. 5.1) and Obstacle Detection module (see Sect. 5.2), both based on the use of the Kinect Sensor, were tested. The autonomous robot interaction (Human-Robot) and associated behaviors were used in the experiments described in this section.

In the first set of experiments, the Human Gesture Interface module was tested. Two groups of question were used for Human Gesture Interface test. The first group has the objective to teach the user how to use the system. The questions and messages presente to the user were: "For answering my questions you should use your hands, ok?!!!", "Lower your hands!", "YES Test: move your right hand forward!", "NO Test: move your left hand forward!", and "Both hands: move your left and right hands forward!".

The second group does the interaction itself. The questions were: "Can I help you?", "Did you like this painting?", and "Will you return here in the future?". These questions simulate the interaction into a museum with a robotic tour guide. When the user answer NO on the first question the interaction is stopped. In this case, the other questions will not be presented and the interaction process stops.

Three videos[3] were performed representing the interaction tests. The Videos 1 and 2 show the interaction with the user without any specific problems (see Fig. 13(a)). In the Video 3 an interruption happens (robot's repositioning) as shown in Fig. 13(b), and also a person passed behind the user as shown in Fig. 13(c).

In the second set of experiments, the Obstacle Detection module was tested. In the first experiment the Obstacle Detection tests performed found an obstruction around of the robot. The minimal distance of the central row of DepthImage was obtained for each frame. When this distance was less than 0.6 m, the avoiding collisions step was processed and the robot movements were calculated. In the experiments, the robot turned left whenever the minimal distance is the right side. On the other hand, it turned right whenever the minimal distance

---

[3] See the videos at the link: https://www.youtube.com/channel/UC13inNWCkmGwo AtpbqpJucw.

(a) Normal interaction (Videos 1 and 2)

(b) Reposition (Video 3)

(c) Two people (Video 3)

Fig. 13. Image frames from the video demonstrating the interaction tests that were performed.

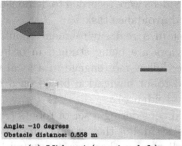

(a) Video 4 (turning left)

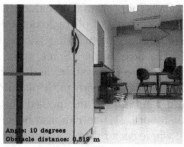

(b) Video 5 (turning right)

Fig. 14. Image frames from the video demonstrating the obstacle detection tests that were performed. The blue pixels in the center row of images represents the minimal distance from Kinect Sensor to obstacles.

occured in the left side. Two videos[3] (Videos 4 and 5) were recorded showing the performance of the obstacle detection tests (see Fig. 14). Both videos show the obstacle avoidance module using the Kinect Sensor to avoid obstacles and collisions.

In another set of experiments, we adopted a Pioneer P3AT robot as the mobile robot platform, and the experiments have been done using the player-stage simulation and robot control tool, in order to test the robot movements. We used the real data obtained from the Kinect sensor, and the robot motor controls were sent to a simulated robot. At present, we are working in the integration of the sensor, real P3AT robot control and Kinect software, in order to make experiments using a real robotic platform.

7   Conclusions

This paper presented a mobile robotic system proposed for Tele-Operarion, Telepresence and Autonomous Navigation tasks, including a human-robot inter-action module which implements gesture recognition. The proposed system uses a Kinect sensor as the main perception/interface device. Several experiments testing the Gesture Interface module and the Obstacle Detection module were performed, demonstrating the reliability and functionality of the system. Three videos were recorded presenting the performed tests with the autonomous inter-action system (face tracking, gesture recognition, and obstacle avoidance). These task demonstrate the system main tasks of interaction between the user and the robot, where it was designed to be used in the next future as a museum robot tour guide.

The Kinect sensor was used for avoiding collisions with obstacles in another set of practical experiments, thus, demonstrating that the same sensor can be used for interaction with the user (face and gesture recognition) and also as a navigation helper (obstacle avoidance). Two videos were recorded to demonstrate the tests performed of obstacle detection and avoidance task.

Tests of the system using the real robot in a real environment should be done in the near future. Some other behaviors are being studied in order to be included into the system, as for example: follow-me (engage in a local user following behavior), and, path planning and robot navigation based on a map (including unmapped/unexpected obstacles avoidance).

This robotic system can also be enhanced considering a set of robots (robot squad), where each robot is an independent system, but they could communicate among themselves. Then, a robot might call out another free robot (without ongoing interaction with a person), when it perceives a new person which is asking for help. There are many other possibilities of multi-robot applications in this context.

Acknowledgment. The authors acknowledge the support granted by the Mobile Robotics Laboratory (LRM Lab.) and the Center for Robotics (CRob/SC) of University of São Paulo at São Carlos.

Rafael Alceste Berri thanks CAPES/DS by the financial support for the graduate program in computer science.

References

1. Alvarenga, M.L.T., Correa, D.S.O., Osório, F.S.: Redes neurais artificiais aplicadas no reconhecimento de gestos usando o kinect. In: Computer on the Beach, p. 10 (2012)
2. Bartneck, C., Forlizzi, J.: A design-centred framework for social human-robot interaction. In: 13th IEEE International Workshop on Robot and Human Interactive Communication, ROMAN 2004, pp. 591–594, Sept 2004
3. Billinghurst, M.: Gesture based interaction (chapt. 14). In: Human Input to Computer Systems: Theories, Techniques and Technology (2011)
4. Chen, Q., Georganas, N.D., Petriu, E.M.: Real-time vision-based hand gesture recognition using haar-like features. In: Instrumentation and Measurement Technology Conference Proceedings, IMTC 2007, pp. 1–6. IEEE, May 2007
5. Clodic, A., Fleury, S., Alami, R., Herrb, M., Chatila, R.: Supervision and interaction. In: Proceedings of the 12th International Conference on Advanced Robotics, ICAR 2005, pp. 725–732, July 2005
6. Correa, D.S.O., Sciotti, D.F., Prado, M.G., Sales, D.O., Wolf, D.F., Osorio, F.S.: Mobile robots navigation in indoor environments using kinect sensor. In: 2012 Second Brazilian Conference on Critical Embedded Systems (CBSEC), pp. 36–41, May 2012
7. DoubleRobotics: Work from anywhere (telepresence). http://www.doublerobotics. com. Accessed: 23 April 2014
8. Gonzalez, R.C., Woods, R.E.: Digital Image Processing. Pearson/Prentice Hall, Upper Saddle River, N. J. (2008)
9. Haralick, R.M., Sternberg, S.R., Zhuang, X.: Image analysis using mathematical morphology. IEEE Trans. Pattern Anal. Mach. Intell. 9(4), 532–550 (1987)
10. Hasanuzzaman, M., Zhang, T., Ampornaramveth, V., Gotoda, H., Shirai, Y., Ueno, H.: Adaptive visual gesture recognition for human-robot interaction using a knowledge-based software platform. Robot. Auton. Syst. 55(8), 643–657 (2007). http://www.sciencedirect.com/science/article/pii/S0921889007000383
11. IJsselsteijn, W.A.: History of telepresence. In: Schreer, O., Kauff, P., Sikora, T. (eds.) 3D Communication: Algorithms, Concepts and Real-time Systems in Human Centred Communication, pp. 7–22. Wiley, Chichester (2005)
12. iRobot: irobot ava® 500 - video collaboration robot.http://www.irobot.com/en/ us/learn/commercial. Accessed: 23 April 2014
13. Jensen, B., Tomatis, N., Mayor, L., Drygajlo, A., Siegwart, R.: Robots meet humans-interaction in public spaces. IEEE Trans. Industr. Electron. 52(6), 1530–1546 (2005)
14. Kanda, T., Glas, D.F., Shiomi, M., Hagita, N.: Abstracting people's trajectories for social robots to proactively approach customers. IEEE Trans. Robot. 25(6), 1382–1396 (2009)
15. Markoff, J.: The boss is robotic, and rolling up behind you. The New York Times - Science, 4 Sep 2010
16. Michalowski, M.P., Šabanović, S., DiSalvo, C., Busquets, D., Hiatt, L.M., Melchior, N.A., Simmons, R.: Socially distributed perception: Grace plays social tag at aaai 2005. Auton. Robots 22(4), 385–397 (2007). http://dx.doi.org/10.1007/ s10514-006-9015-6
17. Minsky, M.: Telepresence. OMNI Magazine, June 1980
18. Mumm, J., Mutlu, B.: Human-robot proxemics: physical and psychological distancing in human-robot interaction. In: Proceedings of the 6th International Conference on Human-Robot Interaction, pp. 331–338. ACM (2011)

19. NASA: Robonaut telepresence. http://robonaut.jsc.nasa.gov/R1/sub/telepresence. asp. Accessed 23 April 2014

20. Sales, D., Correa, D., Osório, F.S., Wolf, D.F.: 3D vision-based autonomous navigation system using ANN and kinect sensor. In: Jayne, C., Yue, S., Iliadis, L. (eds.) EANN 2012. CCIS, vol. 311, pp. 305–314. Springer, Heidelberg (2012)

21. Sales, D.O., Correa, D.O., Fernandes, L.C., Wolf, D.F., Osório, F.S.: Adaptive finite state machine based visual autonomous navigation system. Eng. Appl. Artif. Intell. **29**, 152–162 (2014). http://www.sciencedirect.com/science/article/pii/S0952197613002406

22. Simmons, R., Goldberg, D., Goode, A., Montemerlo, M., Roy, N., Schultz, A.C., Abramson, M., Horswill, I., Kortenkamp, D., Maxwell, B.: Grace: An autonomous robot for the aaai robot challenge. Technical report, DTIC Document (2003)

23. Snowden, E.: Ted talk edward snowden (telepresence - live from ted2014). https://www.ted.com/speakers/edward_snowden. Accessed: 23 April 2014

24. Soille, P.: Morphological Image Analysis: Principles and Applications, 2nd edn. Springer-Verlag New York Inc., Secaucus (2003)

25. Technologies, S.: Beam+ and beam pro (telepresence). https://www.suitabletech.com. Accessed: 23 April 2014

26. Thrun, S., Beetz, M., Bennewitz, M., Burgard, W., Cremers, A.B., Dellaert, F., Fox, D., Hahnel, D., Rosenberg, C., Roy, N., Schulte, J., Schulz, D.: Probabilistic algorithms and the interactive museum tour-guide robot minerva. Int. J. Robot. Res. **19**(11), 972–999 (2000)

27. Viola, P., Jones, M.: Robust real-time object detection. Int. J. Comput. Vis. **57**(2), 137–154 (2001)

28. Waldherr, S., Romero, R., Thrun, S.: A gesture based interface for human-robot interaction. Auton. Robots **9**(2), 151–173 (2000)

29. Welch, G., Bishop, G.: An introduction to the kalman filter. Technical report, Chapel Hill, NC, USA (1995)

30. Wortham, J.: With kinect controller, hackers take liberties. The New York Times 21 (November 2010)

Newton: A High Level Control Humanoid Robot for the RoboCup Soccer KidSize League

Danilo H. Perico[1]([✉]), Isaac J. Silva[1], Claudio O. Vilão Junior[1],
Thiago P.D. Homem[1,3], Ricardo C. Destro[1], Flavio Tonidandel[2],
and Reinaldo A.C. Bianchi[1]

[1] Electrical Engineering Department, Centro Universitário da FEI,
São Bernardo do Campo, SãoPaulo, Brazil
{dperico,isaacjesus,cvilao,thiagohomem,destro,rbianchi}@fei.edu.br
http://www.fei.edu.br
[2] Computer Science Department, Centro Universitário da FEI,
São Bernardo do Campo, SãoPaulo, Brazil
flaviot@fei.edu.br
[3] Computer Science Department, Instituto Federal de São Paulo,
Boituva, SãoPaulo, Brazil
http://www.ifsp.edu.br

Abstract. One of the goals of humanoid robot researchers is to develop a complete – in terms of hardware and software – artificial autonomous agent able to interact with humans and to act in the contemporary world, that is built for human beings. There has been an increasing number of humanoid robots in the last years, including Aldebaran's NAO and Romeo, Intel's Jimmy and Robotis' DARwIn-OP. This research article describes the project and development of a new humanoid robot named Newton, made for research purposes and also to be used in the RoboCup Soccer KidSize League Competition. Newton robot's contributions include that it has been developed to work without a dedicated microcontroller board, using an four-by-four-inch Intel NUC board, that is a fully functioning PC. To work with this high level hardware, a new software architecture comprised of completely independent processes was proposed. This architecture, called Cross Architecture, is comprised of completely independent processes, one for each intelligent system required by a soccer player: Vision, Localization, Decision, Communication, Planning, Sense and Acting, besides having a process used for managing the others. The experiments showed that the robot could walk, find the ball in an unknown position, recover from a fall and kicking the ball autonomously with a good performance.

Keywords: Humanoid robot · Hardware architecture · Software architecture

1 Introduction

Since ancient times mankind dreams with robots capable to perform tasks autonomously to serve and replace human beings in dangerous or repetitive

© Springer-Verlag Berlin Heidelberg 2015
F.S. Osório et al. (Eds.): LARS/SBR/Robocontrol 2014, CCIS 507, pp. 53–73, 2015.
DOI: 10.1007/978-3-662-48134-9_4

tasks. Recently, many humanoids have been developed by universities around the world, like the Robo Erectus Jr-AX [1] and DARwIn-OP [2]. Furthermore, the interest by humanoid robots is not only academic, since some companies have also designed and produced humanoids like the ASIMO [3], produced by Honda, NAO and Romeo [4], produced by Aldebaran, and Jimmy [5], developed by Intel.

However, despite of the large number of researches that have been developed with humanoid robots, they cannot yet perform some tasks that are considered quite simple for the human beings, like playing soccer, for example. Thus, robotic competitions have been held in order to encourage the improvement of the robotics in different domains.

Among the main competitions, it is possible to highlight the RoboCup Soccer. The soccer environment is interesting because it is dynamic and the robots must work cooperatively in order to achieve a common target. Humanoid robots that compete at RoboCup Soccer are complex due to the several number of joints and because of the large number of modules that need to be executed simultaneously, like control for biped locomotion, self-localization, computer vision and learning algorithms to drive the strategy of the team.

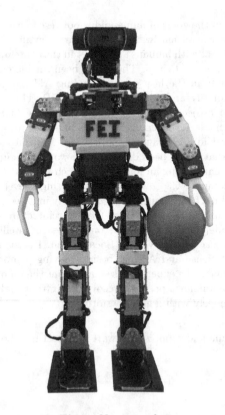

Fig. 1. Newton robot.

This work presents a new humanoid robot, called Newton (Fig. 1), that has been designed to compete at RoboCup Humanoid KidSize League World Competition.

One of the main contributions of Newton is the fact that it has been developed to work without a sub-controller board, commonly used to control the motors. So, the use of electronic parts were reduced and all the controlling and processing needed by the robot is made in its main controller, that is a computer that will be detailed in Sect. 3.1. Another contribution is a new software architecture proposed to make Newton able to deal with all the tasks required in the soccer domain.

This paper is organized as follows: Sect. 2 presents a brief review about the hardware of other humanoid robots used in the KidSize League of RoboCup and also a review about the software paradigms for robotics. Section 3 shows the hardware and software architecture for Newton robot. In Sect. 4 the experiments are presented and Sect. 5 provides the conclusions and indicates avenues for extend and improve Newton capabilities.

2 Research Background

2.1 RoboCup

The RoboCup – Robotic Soccer World Cup – challenge was proposed in 1997 by Kitano et al. [6] with the aim of providing a new challenge that would promote research in Robotics and Artificial Intelligence. The ultimate goal of the RoboCup Initiative can be states as: "By the middle of the 21st century, a team of fully autonomous humanoid robot soccer players shall win a soccer game, complying with the official rules of FIFA, against the winner of the most recent World Cup" [7]. Another important goal of the initiative is to promote engineering and science education among the primary and secondary school children, a goal that is achieved by the RoboCup Junior initiative. Finally the RoboCup initiative also aims to provide "a standard problem so that various theories, algorithms, and architectures can be evaluated" [6].

To develop soccer teams capable of playing, more than the simple integration of AI techniques is needed, according to Kraetzchmar [8], "Mechatronic devices, specialized hardware for controlling sensors and actuators, control theory, sensor interpretation and fusion, neural networks, evolutionary computation, vision, multi-agent cooperation are examples for fields strongly involved with the RoboCup challenge". According to the same author, "engineering a team of robotic soccer players that is able to successfully compete in championship games requires truly interdisciplinary research and the effective cooperation of many disciplines".

RoboCup today is more than soccer competitions: several leagues have been proposed since the competitions started in the 90's. Today the scope of problems involved in the competitions ranges from disaster rescue tasks, involving multi-agent team work coordination, to assistive robot technology for personal domestic applications.

The RoboCup Humanoid League, which started in 2002, is the one that is closest to the RoboCup ultimate goal. In it, humanoid robots – robots with human like dimensions and perception – have to play against each other in a soccer field. The problems involved in this task includes the construction of the robots, dynamic control (the robot must walk and kick without falling), computer vision (as the robot must perceive the ball, the field and other players), self localization and cooperative localization, multi-agent cooperation, among many other research issues that are explored in the League.

Our research is on the humanoid league, with the development of the hardware and software for a new humanoid robot, for the KidSize league.

2.2 Hardware

The hardware is an essential part of humanoid robots, since all the actions that a biped walking robot can perform are physically limited by the set of mechanics, motors, sensors and electronic parts that comprise the robot.

Humanoid robots have been developed since the 1970's with the Wabot-1 [9] created by the Waseda University at Japan. Focusing on the KidSize League of RoboCup, it is possible to quote some examples like the Robo-Erectus Jr-AX (REJr-AX) [1] from the Singapore Polytechnic and one of the most known and used humanoid robot, the DARwIn-OP [2].

REJr-AX [1] was composed for 24 degrees of freedom (DOF), being all of them made with the servomotor Dynamixel DX-117. The robot height was 480 mm and it had four sensors: an USB camera, a tilt sensor to recognize whether it is standing-up, a compass for orientation and a couple of ultrasonic sensors.

Besides the mechanics, REJr-AX electronics has 3 processors, as follows:

- The Main Processor (1 Intel ARM XScale with 400 MHz): responsible for coordinating and synchronizing vision and control processors.
- The Vision Processor (1 Intel ARM XScale with 400 MHz): responsible for processing the images obtained from the USB camera.
- The Control Processor (1 Dual PIC18F8720 with 25 MHz): this microcontroller is in charge of receiving the commands from the main processor and sending the commands to the motors, i.e., it is responsible for the low level control.

REJr have been updated since the REJr-AX and the latest series of Robo-Erectus KidSize humanoids is the REJr-Bv, which is more similar to DARwIn-OP [2]. DARwIn-OP has 20 DOF, its actuators are the Dynamixel MX-28 and it has several sensors, like a 3-axis gyroscope, a 3-axis accelerometer, an USB-based camera and 3 microphones allocated on the head.

DARwIn-OP electronics consists of 2 processors. The main processor is an Intel Atom Z530 1.6 GHz, that is a mini computer, and the sub-controller is an ARM 32-bit Cortex-M3, that is a microcontroller in charge of low level control.

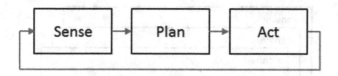

Fig. 2. Hierarchical paradigm for robots [11, p. 43]

There are others humanoid robots in the KidSize League at RoboCup, but most of them are similar to DARwIn-OP when the mechanics, actuators, sensors and electronics are compared. For example, most humanoids have a main processor and a secondary board used for low level control. Besides that, the majority of humanoids that participate at the RoboCup Humanoid League have 20 degrees of freedom.

2.3 Software

The hierarchical paradigm in Artificial Intelligence Framework is historically the first architecture of organized intelligence in robotics. It was proposed in the 1960's along with Shakey robot [10] and it was very common until the late 1980's.

Hierarchical paradigm is based in the sequential and orderly relation between the three primitives of robotics: Sense – Plan – Act. Thus, the robot first senses the world, then it stops its sensors and plans the next action and, finally, the robot acts. After the Sense – Plan – Act sequence finishes, the cycle starts again and the robot senses the consequence of its last action, re-plan and act again (Fig. 2) [11].

Hierarchical paradigm does not provide rapid response time to a dynamic world, once the robot needs to update the whole world model every time the cycle starts. Moreover, sensing and acting are always disconnected.

In the late 1980's the reactive paradigm was created and grew up from the dissatisfaction with hierarchical paradigm. It is possible to see the dissatisfaction with the hierarchical paradigm in some works by Rodney Brooks [12,13], for example. Brooks' works showed that hierarchical paradigms have a horizontal decomposition while ethological literature suggests that intelligence is more like a vertical decomposition. Thus, reactive paradigm is normally based on some aspects of biology.

Using vertical decomposition, the robot has a Sense – Act type of organization. So, the robot can starts with some primitive behaviors and evolves new layers of behaviors. These new layers can reuse the older one, inhibit it or can create parallel tracks of behaviors. Each layer can access the sensors and actuators independently of others layers. Thereby, functions can continue to work independently of others functions.

As in an ethological system, reactive paradigm works using behaviors. These behaviors are transfer functions, that transform sensory inputs into actuator

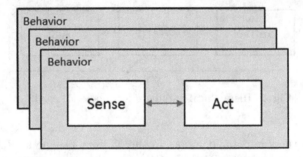

Fig. 3. Reactive paradigm into multiple, concurrent behaviors [11, p. 109]

commands. So, in the reactive paradigm the primitives Sense and Act are clustered into behaviors that can operate either in sequence or concurrently (Fig. 3) [11]. Therefore, reactive paradigm eliminated the Plan component of the primitive robotic paradigm, which means that a Sense – Act organization does not control or coordinate the behaviors. Essentially, reactive paradigm is the opposite of the hierarchical paradigm, since sensing is immediately available to the actuators, and there is no update of the whole world model. Then, the action is almost instantaneous when related to what the robot is sensing.

Programming by behaviors has some advantages linked to the software engineering principles. For example, behaviors are modular and, thus, it is easy to create and test them separately from the system. On top of that, behaviors support incremental expansion and allow execution in real-time. Another advantage of the reactive paradigm is that it normally has low computational cost and the behaviors, working as modules, can function independently of each other, which allows easy reuse [11].

One of the most known architectures that used the reactive paradigm is the subsumption architecture [12]. In the subsumption architecture the behaviors are purely reflexive and memory is not used. The layers are composed by behaviors considering their competence, and lower levels are responsible for more general abilities. Higher level layers coordinate lower level layers.

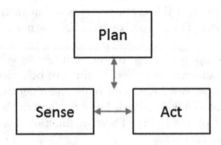

Fig. 4. Hybrid paradigm [11, p. 260]

Table 1. Newton robot key features

Robot name	Newton
Height	500 mm
Weight	3.0 Kg
Walking speed	70 cm/min
Degrees of freedom	22: 6 per leg, 3 per arm,
	2 on the head and 2 on the hip
Motors	Dynamixel RX-28
Sensors	IMU UM6 Ultra-Miniature Orientation Sensor
	Camera Logitech Full HD Pro C920
Computing unit	Intel NUC Core I3-3217 1.8 GHz:
	4 Gb of RAM
	HD Graphics 4000
	5 USB ports

Reactive paradigm has some advantages, however the cost of reactivity is the elimination of the planning, which means no reasoning about the world model. This is a disadvantage because the robot cannot plan about optimal trajectories, cannot track its own performance or even select the best actions to do a task.

In order to have a paradigm that was able to be rapid and behavioral, keeping up the main advantages of the reactive paradigm, without losing the planning abilities, that was the main advantage of the hierarchical paradigm, some hybrids paradigms were proposed: the Autonomous Robot Architecture (AuRA), that was the first hybrid paradigm developed in the mid-1980's [14], followed by the Sensor Fusion Effects (SFX) [15], the Saphira [16] and others.

The hybrid paradigm can be described as: Plan, then Sense – Act (Fig. 4), where the Plan component includes deliberation, world modeling, task and path planning. In hybrid paradigm robots first plan how to do something, then use a behavior, comprised of Sense – Act organization to execute the plan. In a hybrid paradigm the robotic primitives is divided into 2 portions: the reactive one and the deliberative one.

Thereby, planning is not part of the real-time execution. This is good because normally planning algorithms are computationally expensive.

Hybrid architectures are attractive because they can present an organization similar to the organization found in object-oriented programming. This kind of architecture also often try to ensure robustness.

3   Newton Robot

The main premise in Newton's design was the requirement to work with only one processor to simplify electronic embedded in the robot and optimize its energy demand.

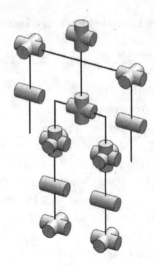

Fig. 5. Newton robot: degrees of freedom

To achieve this premise, in addition to the new hardware design, a completely new software architecture was developed to perform all tasks expected for a robot soccer player with only one processor.

3.1 Hardware Architecture

Hardware design is presented in four groups: Mechanics, Actuators, Sensors and Electronics. All of them are detailed below and Table 1 shows the overall hardware characteristics of Newton robot.

Mechanics. Newton has 22 DOF, being 6 per leg, 3 per arm, 2 on the head, 2 on the hip, distributed according to Fig. 5. The number of degrees of freedom was achieved after an analysis to establish how many DOF the robot needs to walk in a gait similar to the humans. Furthermore, a benchmarking considering the degrees of freedom of others humanoids robots was also performed.

Two equilibrium criteria were used to guarantee the stability of the robot: the Zero Moment Point (ZMP) and the Center of Pressure (CoP) [17]. To ensure the mobility necessary for each joint, avoiding collisions and interferences from simultaneous movements, the positions of the motors were established considering the relative movement between them, keeping the anatomy and the functioning of the robot.

All the aluminum and plastic parts of the robot were designed and made by the group. The mechanical design began as an undergraduate project and has constantly evolved, being, currently, the subject of study of several postgraduate students at the institution.

Fig. 6. Dynamixel RX-28

Actuators. The actuators used to develop Newton Robot were the servo-motor Dynamixel RX-28 [18]. The motors are important components of the robot because they directly influence the velocity and accuracy of the moves. Dynamixel RX-28 (Fig. 6) was chosen because it can generate the needed torque and accuracy, furthermore its geometry favors the fastening in the robot structure. Each motor weights 72 g, so the whole set of motors, considering that the robot has 22 DOF, weights 1.58 Kg.

Dynamixel RX-28 is controlled by packet communication and its protocol type is RS485 Asynchronous Serial Communication. This motor can be supplied with a voltage range from 12 to 18.5 V and its standby current is 50 mA. This motor also have its own sensors, from where it is possible to track data like load, voltage, shaft position, speed and temperature.

Sensors. Newton is basically comprised of 2 sensors: the camera and the inertial measurement unit (IMU).

The camera used is a Logitech Full HD Pro C920 that is an USB-based camera placed on the head of the robot. The robot's head is composed of 2 servomotors, one responsible for the pan movement (rotation in a horizontal plane) and the other for the tilt movement (rotation in a vertical plane). Newton was designed to be a single camera robot.

Logitech C920 is a full high-definition camera and the interface with the robot is made via USB standard. One advantage of using full high-definition camera is that it allows detailed information about the environment. Another advantage of this camera is that it is powered directly by the USB port, so it is not necessary to have a power source exclusive for the camera.

Newton also has an IMU comprised of 3-axis gyroscope, 3-axis accelerometer and 3 axis-magnetometer. For posture estimation and balancing the robot uses only the gyroscope and the accelerometer. The magnetic sensor was tested for localization, however it does not work well due to the noises caused by the motors. The IMU used in the project is the UM6 ultra-miniature produced by CH Robotics. UM6 has an onboard 32-bit ARM Cortex processor for estimating sensor orientation 500 times per second.

Electronics and Electrical Design. One goal of Newton project was to minimize the use of electronic boards in the robot. Therefore, Newton was designed

Fig. 7. Intel Next Unit of Computing (NUC)

to work without a sub-controller board, that is normally a microcontroller board used to control the motors.

Newton has only one processing unit. It is a Intel Next Unit of Computing (NUC) with Core I3-3217. Intel Core I3-3217 is composed of 2 physical cores, but due to the Hyper-Threading Technology, two processing threads are delivered per physical core, which means 4 cores in total. The number of cores is important to the development of the software architecture (Subsect. 3.2). On top of that, NUC is also comprised by 4 Gb of RAM, HD Graphics 4000 and 5 USB ports (Fig. 7). So, instead of controlling the motors with a microcontroller board, all the robot's motors are controlled using NUC's USB port.

Before eliminating the microcontroller board, several tests were conducted to validate the hardware architecture.

Some tests were also performed with NUC in order to analyze its real energy consumption, and, with 4 cores working in 100 %, NUC's power consumption was around 16 W. All USB ports were used during the test.

As the interface of motors is RS485 and a serial port was not available in NUC, a RS485-to-USB adapter was developed, thus the computer can communicate with the motors using its USB port. The IMU UM6 has also a serial interface, but it is TTL. So, the robot uses a serial-to-USB adapter that allows the main computer to receive data, also, via USB port.

3.2 Software Architecture

Due to the advantages presented by the hybrid paradigm, Newton robot works with a hybrid architecture. Thereby, a new software was developed to rule Newton robot. This architecture is named Cross Architecture (solid line boxes in Fig. 8). Each solid line box in the Cross Architecture is a completely independent process, that are briefly detailed hereafter.

Vision. Vision is responsible for obtain images and process them. By using the vision system, the robot must be able to find the ball, the goals, the field lines and the other robots. Besides finding things, Vision must calculate the distances among the robot and the other objects, like the ball, the goal and so on.

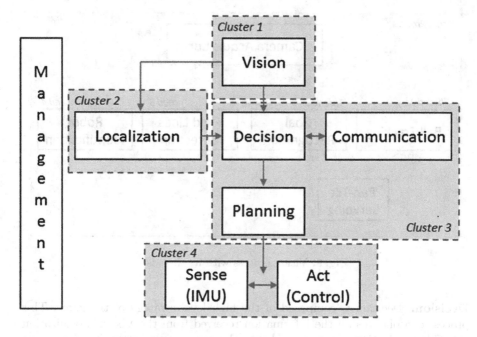

Fig. 8. Cross architecture and its clusters

The Vision process works by using the concepts of active vision [19], so the camera will search for the objects, not just react. Active vision main purpose is to have an active observer that explores and searches things, adjusting camera position to obtain better views.

This process makes a purposive use of a single camera in order to satisfy a set of visual tasks and an Image-Based Visual Servo system [20] is used, considering that the camera pose information is given by the motors position feedback.

Finding the ball, identifying the goal posts, detecting field lines and recognizing robots sequentially consumes a precious time, so vision was designed as a process with four parallel threads, being each one of this tasks a different thread.

After the camera acquisition, one frame is used as an input for all the four threads. Even though all threads works in parallel, the pan-tilt control, that is made by the active vision, needs a sequential structure. This means that only one of these threads can control the pan-tilt at a time. Figure 9 shows the diagram of the four parallel threads and the pan-tilt control. As the more important object during a soccer game is the ball, the ball tracking is, at most times, in control of the pan-tilt system.

The allocation of the vision process in separated threads shows a good gain in real-time application, no matter where the camera is heading to, all threads will continue to grab information from the environment at the same time.

More details about the techniques used in the Vision process can be found at Vilão et al. [21].

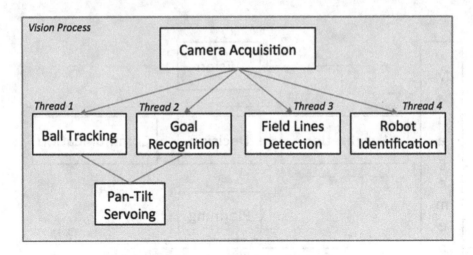

Fig. 9. Vision process with its threads.

Decision. Decision is composed of the high level strategy of the game. This process consolidates all the information received from the Vision, Localization and Communication processes and uses these data to take the decision about what the robot must do. The taken decision is sent to the Planning process.

Decision process has been developed to work using concepts of the Collaborative Spatial Reasoning, which is a derivation of the research on Qualitative Spatial Reasoning [22,23]. With the Collaborative Spatial Reasoning, each agent represents one of the multiple points of view of the environment and all these points of view are integrated using some criteria of spatial constraints.

The Collaborative Spatial Reasoning can contribute substantially in the construction of a model that approximates the real configuration of the objects in the space, making the high level communication among the robots more efficient.

Decision process is still under development, and the ideas of the Collaborative Spatial Reasoning has not yet been completely applied.

Localization. Localization plays an important role in mobile robots, and gives an outstanding advantage in soccer games. In order to know its position in the soccer field, as well as its direction, the robot uses the information received from the vision process.

The particle filter [24] has been tested as a way of deal with multi-modal probabilistic models, using less computational resources than other techniques, with less samples.

By using the particle filter, the robot predicts its position when it moves (prediction phase) and the robot updates its position belief when measurements are made (update phase). During the prediction phase, the robot motion is inserted in all particles' coordinates using inverse kinematics, that is calculated by the Control process.

The update phase normally uses several measurements, provided by the sensors, from some landmarks as input. In this work, all measurements come from the vision sensor, the camera itself. The particles act as virtual robots that have Cartesian coordinates and orientations. In order to compute the Cartesian coordinates of the particles, the distances from all landmarks have to be measured.

Three landmarks were selected: the central circle, the goals, and the penalties marks. As the field is ambiguous, the orientation of the robot is hard to find. So, in order to infer some orientation estimates to the robot, the inclination of the goal posts are used.

Although the above algorithm has the potential to be very robust for this application, it has not yet been entirely integrated with the robot system.

Communication. The Communication is in charge of the wireless communication that is made among the robots and also to control the messages received from the referee. Following the RoboCup Humanoid KidSize rule [25], robots are allowed to communicate by WLAN via UDP. Referee also uses UDP to broadcast any kind of information to the robots.

The robot uses the Communication process to share data, such as its own position in the field, with its teammates, as well as to receive the same kind of data from the other robots. Besides that, Communication is also used to receive instructions from the referee. The referee tells to the robots when the match starts, when it ends and he can punish the robots if they commit any foul or misconduct.

Robots must respect the referee, since the referee has full authority to enforce the Humanoid League rules. So, Communication is extremely important for the robots, once this process allow them to listen to the referee and to communicate with their teammates.

Planning. The Planning process is responsible to send to the Control process the optimal command that makes the robot complete some task. It receives a command from the Decision and an algorithm defines, for example, which path is better for the robot, to go to the ball, diverging from the opponent.

For this, we are investigating some methods like Path Planning, Artificial Potential Fields (APF) and Reinforcement Learning (RL), to propose a new hybrid method, using RL and APF methods to resolve this class of problems.

Reinforcement Learning is a Machine Learning method, in which the agent can learn through interactions with its environment, without any previous knowledge [26]. Basically, the RL method is like a reward system to the agent to each decision: it can be a positive reward, like a prize or a negative reward, like a punishment.

The Artificial Potential Fields, proposed by Khatib [27] in 1986, consists to construct an artificial potential filed around the goal object and a repulsive field around the obstacles. With this, the robot should be attracted to the goal object, dodging the obstacles because of the repulsive field. This method has been widely investigated like Chen et al. [28] and Luo et al. [29]. However, the APF method has some problems like the local minimum problem. This also has been widely investigated because the "local minimums can trap a robot before reaching its goal", for example [30].

The RL method enters in this research and a hybrid method is named when we try to eliminate these problems, punishing the robot when it goes to a local minimum, for example, and prizing the robot when it goes to the goal.

Control. The Control system is in charge of controlling all the servomotors of the body, except the ones of the head, that are controlled by the Vision system. All the movements made by the robot are controlled by the Control process. Control is responsible for making the robot to walk fast, to walk slow, to turn around, to stand up, to kick the ball and so on.

Control process checks all the time whether the robot is standing or fallen. If the robot has fallen down, which can be detected by the accelerometer, the Control stops receiving orders from the Planning process and check whether the robot has fallen with its back or its front facing down.

The robot state (standing or fallen) is given by the rule:

$$\text{Robot state} = \begin{cases} \text{Fallen robot} & \text{if axis } z > -0.7, \\ \text{Robot standing} & \text{otherwise.} \end{cases} \tag{1}$$

Where:

- z is a data received from the accelerometer: z is equal to -1 when the robot is standing in the upright position and 1 when the robot is in the upside down position $(-1 \leqslant z \leqslant 1)$.

If the robot is fallen, the following rule is adopted to identify its position on the floor:

$$\text{Robot position} = \begin{cases} \text{Fallen with its back facing down.} & \text{if axis } x > 0, \\ \text{Fallen with its front facing down.} & \text{otherwise.} \end{cases} \tag{2}$$

Where:

- x is also a data received from the accelerometer: $-1 \leqslant x \leqslant 1$.

Then the Control makes the robot stand up. Once the robot is standing, it starts to receive instructions from the Planning again.

The control system also monitors the battery voltage. When the battery voltage is below the safe operating range, the robot sits down and turn off the servomotors.

Table 2. Processes per core

Core 0	Cluster 1	Vision
Core 1	Cluster 2	Localization
Core 2	Cluster 3	Decision, Communication and Planning
Core 3	Cluster 4	Sense and Act (IMU and Control)

Management. The Cross Architecture has also a Management process that is used to launch, synchronize and monitor all the processes. If any problem is detected with some process, the management can interrupt this specific process and restart it. The Management is the only process that is not linked to any cluster, because this process can run at any core of the computer.

Returning to the overall functioning of the Cross Architecture, as only one processor is used, the processes were divided into 4 clusters due to their computational cost (dashed line polygons in Fig. 8), and each cluster was allocated in one core of the processor (Table 2).

Cross architecture is hybrid because there are some aspects of the reactive paradigm as well as of the hierarchical paradigm in the architecture. Cluster 4 is an example of reactivity, since the relation between Control and IMU is a type of Sense – Act organization. There is no planning at all if the robot falls. It is just a matter of sensing and acting.

The relation between the Decision and the Communication processes is also reactive. Even considering that there is no direct actuators in this relation, the Decision process can be considered the Act component of the organization, since this process uses the information received from the Communication, that can be considered the Sense component, to act immediately and change the decisions of the robot.

In the other hand, Vision, Localization, Decision, Planning and Control have a traditional hierarchical relationship.

As quoted before, Cross Architecture is a set of completely independent process and it requires an interprocess communication structure. Newton's software is based upon a blackboard architecture [31] to address this communication requirement. By using the blackboard, independent processes can access a common memory area to share their information.

In the proposed architecture, this common area is a shared memory, which contributed to increase the speed of the data exchange among processes.

So, through the blackboard, processes can publish their shared variables in this common area and any other process can read this value. In order to guarantee the functionality of the architecture, all shared variables are mapped before the begin of the software development.

Basically, the Cross Architecture allows the elimination of the sub-controller board to the motors, once they can be directly controlled by an exclusive core

Fig. 10. Newton robot walking towards the ball and kicking it.

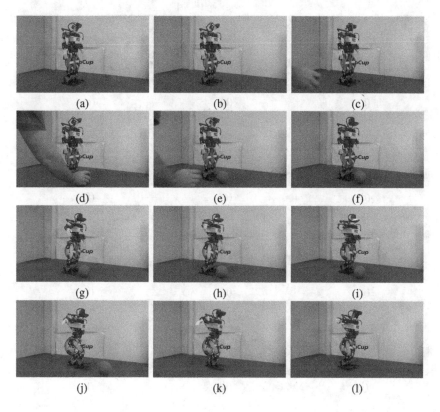

Fig. 11. Newton robot finding an unknown position ball and kicking it.

on the multicore processor computer (Table 2), using the reactive paradigm concept to keep the lower level activity, which is the control of the robot, working independently of any other deliberation.

4   Experiments

Newton was tested with some tasks, like walking towards the ball, finding the ball in an unknown position, kicking the ball and recovering itself from a fall. For those experiments, a similar RoboCup KidSize League orange ball was used.

The operating system used in the computer during the experiments was the Ubuntu 12.04 and the proposed architecture was implemented using C++. As the Operating System is preemptive, the maximum priority was given to the Sense – Act process, responsible for the low level control. The movements were implemented via finite-state machine, where some motion scripts were previously programmed.

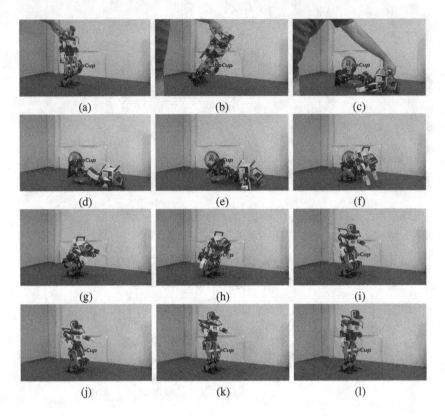

Fig. 12. Newton robot recovering itself from a fall (fallen with its front facing down).

The experiment for walking towards the ball is shown in Fig. 10. First the robot detects the ball through its color and shape. Then, using the diameter of the detected ball, the Vision process send to the blackboard the information about the distance between the ball and robot. The Decision process collects, from the blackboard, data related to the Localization and to the Communication processes and takes a decision about what to do. In the experiment, the initial decisions were to go towards the ball (from Fig. 10a to j), then, when the robot was near to the ball, the decision was to kick the ball (from Fig. 10k to u). During the experiment, the robot never lost the ball from its field of view.

In order to perform the experience of finding a ball in an unknown position, the ball was hidden from Newton. During this period, Newton searched the ball (from Fig. 11a to e). As soon as the ball was placed on the field, Newton robot could quickly find it and could, also, take the decision of kicking the ball, since the ball was near to the robot (from Fig. 11f to l).

Newton robot can recovery itself from a fall, regardless the way it falls. If it falls with its front facing down, it can get up as shown in Fig. 12. If it falls with its back facing down, it can get up as shown in Fig. 13.

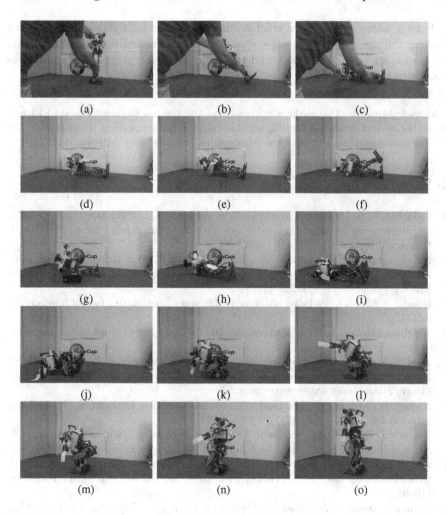

Fig. 13. Newton robot recovering itself from a fall (fallen with its back facing down).

5   Conclusions

This paper presented the hardware and software description of a new humanoid robot, named Newton.

Newton robot contributions are: the elimination of a secondary processor, that reduced the number of electronic parts in the robot, and the new software architecture, that is based on the hybrid paradigm and uses a blackboard concept to allow interprocess communication.

Experimental results proved the efficiency of the multitasking approach for a humanoid robot, since the robot could execute different tasks that are necessary during a soccer game, keeping a good performance.

Future works will involve reinforcement learning for optimizing the robot walking, the use of a collaborative spatial reasoning to improve communication and decision among the robots and the analysis of the proposed architectures along with the ROS.

Acknowledgment. The authors acknowledge the Centro Universitário da FEI and the Robotics and Artificial Intelligence Laboratory for supporting this project. The authors would also like to thank the scholarships provided by CAPES and CNPq.

References

1. Calderon, C.A.A., Mohan, R.E., Zhou, C., Hu, L., Yue, P.K., Hu, H.: A modular architecture for humanoid soccer robots with distributed behavior control. Int. J. Humanoid Rob. **5**(3), 397–416 (2008)
2. Ha, I., Tamura, Y., Asama, H., Han, J., Hong, D.W.: Development of open humanoid platform DARwIn-OP. In: Proceedings of SICE Annual Conference (SICE), pp. 2178–2181. IEEE (2011)
3. Honda - ASIMO, Website. Accessed: 22 May 2014. http://world.honda.com/ASIMO/
4. Aldebaran Robotics, Website. Accessed: 20 May 2014. http://www.aldebaran.com/en/
5. Intel Research - 21st century robot - Jimmy, Website. Accessed: 19 March 2015. http://www.intel.com/content/www/us/en/corporate-responsibility/better-future/21st-century-robot-program.html
6. Kitano, H., Minoro, A., Kuniyoshi, Y., Noda, I., Osawa, E.: Robocup: a challenge problem for AI. AI Mag. **18**(1), 73–85 (1997)
7. RoboCup.org, Website. Accessed: 10 October 2014. http://www.robocup.org/
8. Kraetzschmar, G.K., et al.: The Ulm sparrows: research into sensorimotor integration, agency, learning, and multiagent cooperation. In: Asada, M., Kitano, H. (eds.) RoboCup 1998. LNCS (LNAI), vol. 1604, pp. 452–457. Springer, Heidelberg (1999)
9. Wabot-1, Website. Accessed: 22 May 2014. http://www.humanoid.waseda.ac.jp/booklet/kato_2.html
10. Shakey, Website. Accessed: 20 May 2014. http://www.ai.sri.com/shakey/
11. Murphy, R.: Introduction to AI Robotics. MIT Press, Cambridge (2000)
12. Brooks, R.A.: A robust layered control system for a mobile robot. IEEE J. Rob. Autom. **2**(10), 14–23 (1986)
13. Brooks, R.: Intelligence without representation. Artif. Intell. **47**, 139–159 (1991)
14. Arkin, R.C., Balch, T.: Aura: principles and practice in review. J. Exp. Theor. Artif. Intell. **9**, 175–189 (1997)
15. Murphy, R.R., Arkin, R.C.: Sfx: an architecture for action-oriented sensor fusion. In: IEEE/RSJ International Conference on Intelligent Robots and Systems (1992)
16. Konolige, K., Myers, K., Ruspini, E., Saffiotti, A.: The saphira architecture: a design for autonomy. J. Exp. Theor. Artif. Intell. **9**, 215–235 (1997)
17. Sardain, P., Bessonnet, G.: Forces acting on a biped robot. center of pressure-zero moment point. Trans. Sys. Man Cyber. Part A **34**, 630–637 (2004)
18. Robotis - Dynamixel, RX-28's Manual. Accessed: 16 January 2014. http://support.robotis.com/en/product/dynamixel/rx_series/rx-28.htm

19. Aloimonos, J., Weiss, I., Bandyopadhyay, A.: Active vision. Int. J. Comput. Vis. **1**, 333–356 (1988)
20. Chaumette, F., Hutchinson, S.: Visual servo control, part i: basic approaches. IEEE Rob. Autom. Mag. **13**(4), 82–90 (2006)
21. Vilão, C., et al.: A single camera vision system for a humanoid robot. In: IEEE SBR-LARS-Robocontrol (2014)
22. Randell, D.A., Cui, Z., Cohn, A.: A spatial logic based on regions and connection, pp. 165–176 (1992)
23. Moratz, R., Renz, J., Wolter, D.: Qualitative spatial reasoning about line segments, pp. 234–238 (2000)
24. Thrun, S., Fox, D., Burgard, W., Dellaert, F.: Robust monte carlo localization for mobile robots. Artif. Intell. **128**, 99–141 (2001)
25. RoboCup. RoboCup Soccer Humanoid League Rules and Setup. RoboCup Soccer, Hefei, China (2015)
26. Sutton, R.S., Barto, A.G.: Reinforcement Learning: An Introduction. MIT, Cambridge (1998)
27. Khatib, O.: Real-time obstacle avoidance for manipulators and mobile robots. Int. J. Robot. Res. **5**(1), 90–98 (1986)
28. Chen, L., Liu, C., Shi, H., Gao, B.: New robot planning algorithm based on improved artificial potential field. In: Third International Conference on Instrumentation, Measurement, Computer, Communication and Control, pp. 228–232 (2013)
29. Luo, N., Liu, L., Gong, D., Wang, L.: Study on robot path planning based on an improved artificial potential field method. J. Commun. Comput. **10**, 1360–1363 (2013)
30. Lee, S.H., Park, J.: Artificial potential field based path planning for mobile robots using a virtual obstacle concept. In: Proceedings of International Conference on Advanced Intelligent Mechatronics, vol. 2, pp. 735–740 (2003)
31. Hayes-Roth, B.: A blackboard architecture for control. Artif. Intell. **26**, 251–321 (1985)

Trajectory Control of Wheeled Mobile Robots Not Satisfying Ideal Velocity Constraints by Using Slipping and Skidding Variations: A Singular Perturbation Approach

C.A. Peña Fernández[1]([⊠]), J.J.F. Cerqueira[1], and A.M.N. Lima[2]

[1] Robotics Laboratory - Department of Electrical Engineering,
Federal University of Bahia, Rua Aristides Novis, 02,
Federação, Bahia, Salvador 40210-630, Brazil
{cesar.pena,jes}@ufba.br
[2] Center of Electrical and Computer Engineering - Department of Electrical
Engineering, Federal University of Campina Grande, Rua Agripio Veloso, 882,
Universitário, Paraíba, Campina Grande 58429-970, Brazil
amnlima@dee.ufcg.br

Abstract. Control of wheeled mobile robots (WMRs) on trajectory tracking problems has given rise to an abundant proposals at recent years. Normally, WMRs are subject to phenomena like sliding, deformability or flexibility, which are strongly associated with violation of velocity constraints. Here, we propose a method to reduce the effects of slipping and skidding in WMRs by using an auxiliary control law whose robustness is based on slipping and skidding variations. It is considered the control law based on state-feedback linearization whose robustness with respect to the deformability of wheel will be based on singular perturbation methods. The tracking problem is studied by using the auxiliary control law proposed in a feedforward loop. The results show that the law proposed is robust to slipping and skidding and that tracking error converges toward zero.

Keywords: Skidding · Slipping · Rolling dynamics · Singular perturbations · Wheeled mobile robots

1 Introduction

Usually in wheeled mobile robots (WMRs) the kinematic constraints are conditions of pure rolling and nonslipping, both associated with the velocity of contact point between each wheel and the surface motion (see [1, 2, 7]). The analysis of WMRs is often based on assumption that full set of constraints are satisfied at each time instant along the motion of WMR [19]. However, these kinematic constraints are violated due to phenomena, as sliding, deformability and flexibility, which affect the WMR's motion on a trajectory, either accelerating or decelerating, or cornering at a high speed. For this reason, the control of WMRs on

© Springer-Verlag Berlin Heidelberg 2015
F.S. Osório et al. (Eds.): LARS/SBR/Robocontrol 2014, CCIS 507, pp. 74–95, 2015.
DOI: 10.1007/978-3-662-48134-9_5

trajectory tracking problems with those phenomena has given rise to an abundant literature in recent years, e.g., [3–6,13].

In work reported here, it is considered the classical control by using static state-feedback linearization whose robustness with respect to the deformability of wheel will be based on singular perturbation methods and an auxiliary control law that includes estimated behaviors, at time domain, of slipping and skidding variations. Basically, the slipping and skidding variations are included to define a neighborhood where occurs loss of traction force. Thus, compensation schemes have been designed by using parametric estimators whose robustness is based on such loss. Generally, these compensation schemes can be found in hybrid control laws, e.g., fuzzy logic and sliding modes or singular perturbation methods and sliding modes [5,6]. However, the chattering phenomena associated with the sliding control law makes of those methodologies rather impracticable [3,4]. Here, we will study the tracking problem related to WMRs when auxiliary control law proposed is used in the outer closed loop (associated with kinematic behavior of the WMR) in order to that the tracking error converges to zero.

This paper is organized as follows: In Sect. 2, key aspects regarding WMRs are discussed. Complementarily, WMR's dynamic model and its trajectory control, by using singular perturbation methods, will be presented in Sect. 3. In order to make a robust trajectory control, in Sect. 4 will be made an analysis on the slipping and skidding variations into the rolling dynamics. Next, in Sect. 5, the result of this analysis is used to design an auxiliary control law whose robustness of closed loop is studied through simulation results. Finally, conclusions and closing remarks will be shown in Sect. 6.

2   Theoretical Preliminaries on Constrained WMRs

A WMR can be specified in its workspace by using the vector ξ:

$$\xi = [x, y, \theta]^T$$

with three DOF or $\xi = [x, y, \theta, \sigma_1 \dots, \sigma_{N_{ind}}]^T$ with $3 + N_{ind}$ DOF where N_{ind} is associated with the angular position of the wheels that can be oriented independently. The variables $x, y \in \mathbb{R}$ represent the pose of the local frame $\{L\}$ with respect to a global frame $\{W\}$. The variable $\theta \in \mathbb{R}$ represents the orientation (guidance).

There are two types of constraints depending on movements in relation to the wheel plane and the velocity of the contact point with the ground: the *pure rolling* constraint, where the longitudinal component of this velocity is null, and the *nonslipping* constraint, where the transversal component is null [7].

Let consider a WMR whose total motion is executed by the action of N wheels such that $N = N_f + N_c + N_o + N_s$, where N_f, N_c, N_o, N_s represent the number of *fixed* wheels, *centered orientable* wheels, *off-centered orientable* wheels and *swedish* wheels, respectively [7]. Thus, the configuration of WMRs can be fully described by the vector of the generalized coordinates $q \in \mathbb{R}^{3+N+N_c+N_o}$:

$$q = [z \ \beta_o \ \varphi]^T \tag{1}$$

where $z = [\xi \ \beta_c]^T \in \mathbb{R}^{3+\delta_d}$, $\beta_c = [\beta_{1_c} \ \cdots \ \beta_{N_c}] \in \mathbb{R}^{N_c}$, $\beta_o = [\beta_{1_o} \ \cdots \ \beta_{N_o}] \in \mathbb{R}^{N_o}$ and $\varphi = [\varphi_{1_f} \ \cdots \ \varphi_{N_f} \ \varphi_{1_c} \ \cdots \ \varphi_{N_c} \ \varphi_{1_o} \ \cdots \ \varphi_{N_o} \ \varphi_{1_s} \ \cdots \ \varphi_{N_s}] \in \mathbb{R}^N$. Each pair $(\beta_{i_c}, \varphi_{i_c})$ is associated with guidance and angular pose of the i-th *centered orientable* wheel, for $i = 1_c, \ldots, N_c$, and each pair $(\beta_{i_o}, \varphi_{i_o})$ is associated with with guidance and angular pose of the i-th *off-centered orientable* wheel, for $i = 1_o, \ldots, N_o$. The constant δ_d is known as *steerability degree*.

Subsequently, let also consider that the WMR is subjected to K_r independent velocity constraints at Pfaffian form:

$$A^T(q)\dot{q} = 0 \quad \left(\text{i.e.,} \quad \begin{bmatrix} A_1(q) \\ A_2(q) \end{bmatrix}^T \begin{bmatrix} \dot{z} \\ \dot{\beta}_o \\ \dot{\varphi} \end{bmatrix} = 0 \right) \tag{2}$$

where $A^T(q) \in \mathbb{R}^{K_r \times (3+N+N_c+N_o)}$, for $K_r < 3+N+N_c+N_o$, and whose generic *kinematic configuration* is defined by

$$\dot{q} = S(q)\eta \quad \left(\text{i.e.,} \quad \begin{bmatrix} \dot{z} \\ \dot{\beta}_o \\ \dot{\varphi} \end{bmatrix} = \begin{bmatrix} S_1(q) \\ S_2(q) \end{bmatrix}\eta \right) \tag{3}$$

where $S(q) \in \mathbb{R}^{(3+N_o+\delta_d+N) \times \delta_u}$ is known as Jacobian, $\eta \in \mathbb{R}^{\delta_u}$ represents linear and angular velocities of the WMR and δ_u represents its *degree of maneuverability*.

From (2) and (3) we have

$$A^T(q)S(q) = 0, \tag{4}$$

i.e., at each instant $\dot{q}$ belongs to the space generated by the columns[1] of $S(q)$ [8].

By using the lagrange equations, the generic *dynamic model* for WMRs has the following standard form:

$$M(q)\ddot{q} = C(q, \dot{q}) + B(q)\tau + F(q) \tag{5}$$

where $M(q) \in \mathbb{R}^{(3+\delta_d+N_o+N) \times (3+\delta_d+N_o+N)}$ is the inertia matrix of the WMR, $C(q, \dot{q}) \in \mathbb{R}^{(3+\delta_d+N_o+N)}$ is the vector with torques of centrifuge/coriolis forces, $B(q) \in \mathbb{R}^{(3+\delta_d+N_o+N) \times \delta_u}$ is assumed to be full rank, $F(q) \in \mathbb{R}^{3+\delta_d+N_o+N}$ is the vector with generalized coordinates associated with interaction forces and $\tau \in \mathbb{R}^N$ is the vector with torques of motors. Usually torques are uniformly bounded in order to represent the saturation nonlinearity, i.e.,

$$\tau_{\min} \leq \tau \leq \tau_{\max} \quad \text{for } \tau_{\min}, \tau_{\max} \in \mathbb{R}. \tag{6}$$

Whenever the degree of maneuverability δ_u is full, the range of $S^T(q)B(q)$ is also full and the matrix $S^T(q)M(q)S(q)$ is nonsingular, the generic *static state-feedback* linearization of (5) is defined by the global feedback control:

$$\tau = [S^T(q)B(q)]^{-1} \left\{ S^T(q) \left[M(q)S(q)\upsilon + M(q) \left[\frac{\partial S}{\partial q} S(q)\eta \right] \eta - C(q, S(q)\eta) \right] \right\}, \tag{7}$$

---

[1] Usually, $S(q)$ is considered a matrix whose elements are harmonic functions of the angular variables, e.g., $\sin \theta$, $\cos \beta_{1_o}$, etc.

where v represents an *auxiliary control* law described by

$$v = \Delta_v^{-1}(z)\left(\ddot{h}_{\text{ref}} - K_1\tilde{h}(t) - K_2\dot{\tilde{h}} - \dot{\Delta}_v(z)\eta(t)\right) \in \mathbb{R}^{\delta_u} \tag{8}$$

being $\tilde{h} = h - h_{\text{ref}}$ the tracking error, $K_1 \in \mathbb{R}^{2\times 2}$ and $K_2 \in \mathbb{R}^{2\times 2}$ are arbitrary matrices positive definite and, by using (3), $\Delta_v(z)$ is a singular matrix defined by

$$\Delta_v(z) = \frac{\partial h_z(z)}{\partial z} S_1(q) \in \mathbb{R}^{2\times \delta_u}.$$

The case nonsingular is valid for $\delta_u = 2$.

By substituting (7) into the model (5) yields the following *output linearization condition*:

$$\dot{\eta} = v. \tag{9}$$

3 Singularly Perturbed Model for WMRs and Tracking Problem

We will consider the real case where the velocity constraints (2) are not satisfied but the interaction forces are nevertheless applied to the system. For this purpose, it will be introduced an assumption ensuring the *dissipative* nature of these forces, like in [8], i.e., the generalized force $F(q,\dot{q})$ associated with interaction forces will be defined by

$$F(q,\dot{q}) = -\frac{1}{\varepsilon}A(q)K(q,\dot{q})A^T(q)\dot{q}. \tag{10}$$

where $K(q,\dot{q}) \in \mathbb{R}^{(2N-N_s)\times(2N-N_s)}$ is a definite positive matrix and $\varepsilon \in \mathbb{R}_+$ is a scale factor that is used to represent the *flexibility* in WMRs.

Since the constraints (2) are not satisfied, $\dot{q}$ does not belong to the space generated by the columns of $S(q)$ and can therefore be expressed as

$$\dot{q} = S(q)\eta + A(q)\varepsilon\mu = \begin{bmatrix} S(q) & A(q) \end{bmatrix}\begin{bmatrix} \eta \\ \varepsilon\mu \end{bmatrix} \tag{11}$$

where $\mu \in \mathbb{R}^{K_r}$ is a vector associated with the violation of the velocity constraints and $\begin{bmatrix} S(q) & A(q) \end{bmatrix}$ a square nonsingular matrix. Premultiplying (11) by $A^T(q)$ and by using (4), (2) becomes

$$A^T(q)\dot{q} = A^T(q)A(q)\varepsilon\mu$$

and consequently, (10) can be rewritten as:

$$F(q,\dot{q}) = -A(q)K(q,\dot{q})A^T(q)A(q)\mu$$

being $K(q,\dot{q}) = K(q,\eta,\varepsilon\mu) = K(q, S(q)\eta + A(q)\varepsilon\mu)$.

Differentiating (11) and substituting it in (5) and premultiplying it by the matrix $\begin{bmatrix} S^T(q) \\ A^T(q) \end{bmatrix}$ a *singular perturbation model* for a WMR can be defined by the following space-state [9,10,13]:

$$\begin{cases} \dot{x} = Z_0(q)\eta + [\varepsilon Z_1(q) + Z_2(q)]\,\mu + Z_3(q)\tau \triangleq Z(x,\mu,\varepsilon,t),\ x(0) = x_0 & (12) \\ \varepsilon\dot{\mu} = G_0(q)\eta + [\varepsilon\,G_1(q) + G_2(q)]\,\mu + G_3(q)\tau \triangleq G(x,\mu,\varepsilon,t),\ \mu(0) = \mu_0 & (13) \end{cases}$$

where $x = [q\ \eta]^T \in \mathbb{R}^{3+\delta_d+N_o+N+\delta_u}$ is the state vector with the slow variables, $\mu \in \mathbb{R}^{K_r}$ is the vector with the fast variables [8], $Z_0 \in \mathbb{R}^{(3+\delta_d+N_o+N+\delta_u)\times\delta_u}$; $Z_1, Z_2 \in \mathbb{R}^{(3+\delta_d+N_o+N+\delta_u)\times K_r}$; $Z_3 \in \mathbb{R}^{(3+\delta_d+N_o+N+\delta_u)\times N}$; $G_0 \in \mathbb{R}^{K_r\times\delta_u}$, $G_1, G_2 \in \mathbb{R}^{K_r\times K_r}$; $G_3 \in \mathbb{R}^{K_r\times N}$. $Z(x,\mu,\varepsilon,t) \in \mathbb{R}^{3+\delta_d+N_o+N+\delta_u}$ and $G(x,\mu,\varepsilon,t) \in \mathbb{R}^{K_r}$ are vectorial fields continuously differentiable on parameters $(x,\mu,\varepsilon,t) \in D_x \times D_\mu \times [0,\varepsilon_0] \times [0,t]$, being $D_x \in \mathbb{R}^{3+\delta_d+N_o+N+\delta_u}$ and $D_\mu \in \mathbb{R}^{K_r}$ open and convex sets. In this state-space formulation the input τ depends on x and μ, i.e., it is a function defined by $\tau \triangleq \tau(q,\eta,\mu)$. When $\varepsilon = 0$ the dimension of system (12)–(13) is reduced to $3 + \delta_d + N_o + N$ while (13) becomes algebraic equation[2], i.e.:

$$0 = G_0(q)\eta + G_2(q)\mu + G_3(q)\tau. \tag{14}$$

Definition 1 (Standard Singular Form [14]**).** *The system* (12)–(13) *is a standard singular form if and only if* (14) *has* $k \geq 1$ *different and isolated roots, denoted by:*

$$\bar{\mu}_i = H_i(\bar{x},t), \qquad i = 1,\dots,k. \tag{15}$$

For each i-th function, $\bar{\mu}_i$, it is defined the following *reduced system*:

$$\dot{\bar{x}} = Z_0(q)\eta + Z_2(q)H(\bar{x},t) + Z_3(q)\tau, \qquad \bar{x}(0) = x_0 \tag{16}$$

corresponding to the case $\varepsilon = 0$.

Definition 2 (Flexible Manifold [14]**).** *For system* (12)–(13) *a flexible manifold is defined by*

$$\mu = H(x,t). \tag{17}$$

Definition 3 (Boundary Layer System [8,14]**).** *Let be the boundary layer system defined on the coordinates* $\hat{\mu}$ *and expressed as:*

$$\frac{d\hat{\mu}}{dt^*} = G(x_0,\hat{\mu} + H(x_0,t_0),0,t_0), \qquad \hat{\mu}(0) = \mu_0 - H(x_0,t_0)$$
$$= G_0(q_0)\eta_0 + G_2(q_0)[\hat{\mu} + H(q_0,\eta_0,t_0)] + G_3(q_0)\tau_0, \tag{18}$$

where $x_0 = [q_0\ \eta_0]^T$, t_0 *are interpreted as fixed parameters,* $\tau_0 \triangleq \tau(q_0,\eta_0,\mu_0)$ *is the initial condition and* $t^* = t/\varepsilon$.

---

[2] By substituting $\varepsilon = 0$ in $G(x,\mu,\varepsilon,t)$ give $G(x,\mu,0,t)$.

Now, let consider an open ball centered at origin with radius $\bar{r}$ into D_x $(\subset \mathbb{R}^{3+\delta_d+N_o+N+\delta_u})$, $B_{\bar{r}}(0 : \bar{r})$, and an open ball and centered at origin with radius $\bar{\rho}$ into D_y $(\subset \mathbb{R}^{K_r})$, $B_{\bar{\rho}}(0 : \bar{\rho})$. Next, it can be imposed the following conditions:

Condition 1 ([14]). *There exist T, $\bar{r}$, $\bar{\rho}$, $\varepsilon_0 \in \mathbb{R}_+$ such that: (i) $Z(x, \mu, \varepsilon, t)$, $G(x, \mu, \varepsilon, t)$ and its partial derivatives with respect to x, μ and ε are continuous in $B_{\bar{r}} \times B_{\bar{\rho}} \times [0, \varepsilon_0] \times [0, T]$; (ii) $H(x, t)$ and jacobian $\partial G(x, \mu, 0, t)/\partial \mu$ have partial derivatives continuous, and, (iii) the reduced model (16) has unique solution $\bar{x}$ defined on $[0, T]$ which belongs to $B_{\bar{r}}$.*

Condition 2 ([14]). *There exists $t^* \geq 0$ such that: (i) $\hat{\mu} = 0$ is an exponentially stable equilibrium point of the boundary layer system (18), uniformly in the parameters x_0 and t_0, and, (ii) $\mu_0 - \bar{\mu}(0)$ belongs to its domain of attraction, i.e., $\lim_{t^* \to \infty} \hat{\mu}(t^*) = 0$.*

Theorem 1 (Tikhonov's Theorem [8,14]**).** *For a system in a standard form (12)–(13), if Conditions 1 and 2 are satisfied, then there exist positive constants $\nu_1 \in \mathbb{R}_+$, $\nu_2 \in \mathbb{R}_+$ and $\varepsilon^* \in \mathbb{R}_+$ such that if $\|x_0\| < \nu_1$, $\|\mu_0 - H(x_0, 0)\| < \nu_2$ and $\varepsilon < \varepsilon^*$ then the following approximations are valid for $\forall t \in [0, T]$, $T \in \mathbb{R}_+$: $x(t) = \bar{x}(t) + \mathcal{O}(\varepsilon)$ and $\mu(t) = \bar{\mu}(t) + \hat{\mu}(t^*) + \mathcal{O}(\varepsilon)$ where $\mathcal{O}(\varepsilon)$ represents a quantity in terms of ε.*

Condition 3 ([8]). *The origin of reduced system (16) is exponentially stable.*

Theorem 2 (Uniformity with Respect to T [8]**).** *For a system in a standard form (12)–(13), if Conditions 1, 2 and 3 are satisfied then the approximations in Theorem 1 are satisfied uniformly with respect to T.*

One way to ensure Condition 3 is to suppose that the outputs controlled are a subset of the vector of the generalized coordinates q. Thus, let assume that there exists a partition of the system defined by (12)–(13) in three parts:

$$\begin{cases} \dot{z} = Z_0^a(q)\eta + [\varepsilon Z_1^a(q) + Z_2^a(q)]\mu + Z_3^a(q)\tau, & z(0) = z_0 & (19) \\ \dot{w} = Z_0^b(q)\eta + [\varepsilon Z_1^b(q) + Z_2^b(q)]\mu + Z_3^b(q)\tau, & w(0) = w_0 & (20) \\ \varepsilon\dot{\mu} = G_0(q)\eta + [\varepsilon G_1(q) + C_2(q)]\mu + G_3(q)\tau, & \mu(0) = \mu_0 & (21) \end{cases}$$

where $z = [\xi \;\; \beta_c]^T \in \mathbb{R}^{3+\delta_d}$, $w = [\beta_o \;\; \varphi \;\; \eta]^T \in \mathbb{R}^{N_o+N+\delta_u}$, $Z_0^a(q)\eta + [\varepsilon Z_1^a(q) + Z_2^a(q)]\mu + Z_3^a(q)\tau = Z_a(z, w, \mu, \varepsilon, t) \in \mathbb{R}^{3+\delta_d}$ and $Z_0^b(q)\eta + [\varepsilon Z_1^b(q) + Z_2^b(q)]\mu + Z_3^*(q)\tau = Z_b(z, w, \mu, \varepsilon, t) \in \mathbb{R}^{N_o+N+\delta_u}$. For WMRs, the controlled outputs in tracking problems are defined by z, i.e., the WMR's pose in $\{W\}$. Now, let consider the following assumption about the system (19)–(21):

Assumption 1. *There exist constants T, $\bar{r}$, $\bar{\rho}$, $\varepsilon_0 \in \mathbb{R}_+$ such that: $z \in B_{\bar{r}}$, $\mu(t) - H(z, w, t) \in B_{\bar{\rho}}$, and, $Z_a(z, w, \mu, \varepsilon, t)$, $G(z, w, \mu, \varepsilon, t)$ and its partial derivatives are uniformly limited with respect to w, t and $\varepsilon < \varepsilon_0$; Conditions 1 and 2 are satisfied for the system (19)–(21); and for system $\dot{\bar{z}} = Z_a(z, w, H(z, w, t), 0, t)$ the origin is exponentially stable uniformly with respect to any smooth time function w.*

Under Assumption 1 there exist three positive constants $\nu_1 \in \mathbb{R}_+$, $\nu_2 \in \mathbb{R}_+$ and $\varepsilon^* \in \mathbb{R}_+$ such that if $\|z_0\| < \nu_1$, $\|\mu_0 - H(z_0, w_0, 0)\| < \nu_2$ and $\varepsilon < \varepsilon^*$ then the approximations $z(t) = \bar{z}(t) + \mathcal{O}(\varepsilon)$ and $\mu(t) = \bar{\mu}(t) + \hat{\mu}(t^*) + \mathcal{O}(\varepsilon)$ are valid in $t \in [0, T]$.

3.1   Tracking Problem and Weighting Factor Δ_σ

The tracking problem is to find a state-feedback controller that allows that any point P, into the frame $\{L\}$, can achieve the tracking, with stability, of a given moving reference position P_{ref}. Let $h_{\text{ref}} = \begin{bmatrix} x_{\text{ref}} & y_{\text{ref}} \end{bmatrix}^T$ be the position of point P_{ref} assumed a 2-diffeomorphism (i.e., $h_{\text{ref}} \in \mathcal{C}^2$) and defined by $\begin{bmatrix} x_{\text{ref}} \\ y_{\text{ref}} \end{bmatrix} : \mathbb{R}_+ \rightarrow \mathbb{R}^2$. In addition, let also define the coordinates of point P by

$$h = h_z(z) = \begin{bmatrix} x' \\ y' \end{bmatrix} = \begin{bmatrix} x - L\sin\theta \\ y + L\cos\theta \end{bmatrix} \in \mathbb{R}^2 \tag{22}$$

where L is the distance between the WMR's center to P.

By assuming the vector h as the set of linearizing outputs we will apply an auxiliary control law whose robustness is based on a specific function, which we will call *weighting factor*. The weighting factor will make a strategic reduction of the WMR's acceleration with respect to frame $\{L\}$.

Differentiating two times (22) we have

$$\ddot{h} = \frac{d}{dt}\left(\frac{\partial h_z}{\partial z}\right)\dot{z} + \frac{\partial h_z}{\partial z}\ddot{z}.$$

From (3), we have that $\dot{z} = S_1(q)\eta$ and $\ddot{z} = \dot{S}_1(q)\eta + S_1(q)\dot{\eta}$. Then, by replacing these expressions in the above expression gives

$$\ddot{h} = \frac{d}{dt}\left(\frac{\partial h_z}{\partial z}\right)S_1(q)\eta + \frac{\partial h_z}{\partial z}\dot{S}_1(q)\eta + \frac{\partial h_z}{\partial z}S_1(q)\dot{\eta}.$$

It can be verified that $\frac{d}{dt}\left(\frac{\partial h_z}{\partial z}\right)S_1(q)\eta + \frac{\partial h_z}{\partial z}\dot{S}_1(q)\eta = \frac{d}{dt}\left(\frac{\partial h_z}{\partial z}S_1(q)\right)\eta$, thus $\ddot{h} = \frac{d}{dt}\left(\frac{\partial h_z}{\partial z}S_1(q)\right)\eta + \frac{\partial h_z}{\partial z}S_1(q)\dot{\eta}$. On the other hand, due to $\Delta_v(z) = \frac{\partial h_z}{\partial z}S_1(q)$ then

$$\ddot{h} = \dot{\Delta}_v(z)\eta + \Delta_v(z)\dot{\eta}. \tag{23}$$

In order to reduce the WMR's acceleration (refered to $\{L\}$) a weighting factor $\Delta_\sigma \in \mathbb{R}_+$ is introduced into above equation such that:

$$\ddot{h} = \dot{\Delta}_v(z)\eta + \Delta_v(z)\Delta_\sigma\dot{\eta} \tag{24}$$

where $0 \leq \|\Delta_\sigma\| \leq 1$. By imposing the target dynamic of tracking error as $\ddot{\tilde{h}} + K_2\dot{\tilde{h}} + K_1\tilde{h}$ (with $\tilde{h} = h - h_{\text{ref}}$) then

$$\ddot{h} = \ddot{h}_{\text{ref}} - K_1\tilde{h} - K_2\dot{\tilde{h}}. \tag{25}$$

Now, by equating (24) with (25) we obtain

$$\dot{\eta} = \Delta_\sigma^{-1}\Delta_v^{-1}(z)\left(\ddot{h}_{\text{ref}} - K_1\tilde{h} - K_2\dot{\tilde{h}} - \dot{\Delta}_v(z)\eta\right),$$

otherwise, by using (8) and (9), we conclude that

$$v^*(t) = \Delta_\sigma^{-1}v, \tag{26}$$

being v^* the *modified auxiliary control law*.

4   Analysis of Slipping and Skidding Variations

We consider the violations of the constraints due to deformability of the wheels and to the fact that the contact zones between wheels and ground can not be reduced to single points [9,13,15]. Let consider the i-th wheel with radius r in motion along a straight line. Let V_i the velocity of centre of the i-th wheel whose angular velocity is denoted by $\dot{\varphi}_i$. $V_{i,x}$ and $V_{i,y}$ denote the transversal and longitudinal components of V_i, respectively. The longitudinal slip for the i-th wheel is define by

$$s_i = \frac{\|V_{i,y} - r\dot{\varphi}_i\|}{\|V_i\|}. \tag{27}$$

where $V_{i,y} - r\dot{\varphi}$ represents the slipping velocity, which is equal to zero in the ideal case. In (27) s_i is related with condition $s = +1$ when $V_{i,y} < 0$, $\dot{\varphi} > 0$ and $s = -1$ when $V_{i,y} > 0$, $\dot{\varphi} < 0$. The slip angle $\delta_{x,i}$ associated with skidding, or transversal slip, at i-th wheel is defined as the angle between the wheel plane and the velocity of its centre. Let $\delta_{x,i}$ characterized by

$$\delta_{x,i} \approx \sin\delta_{x,i} = \frac{\|V_{i,x}\|}{\|V_i\|}. \tag{28}$$

Based on proposal by [17], here it will be guaranteed that the transversal and longitudinal forces of the i-th wheel, $F_{i,x}$ and $F_{i,y}$, respectively, are uniformly bounded [16]. Thus, for *small values* of s_i and $\delta_{x,i}$ (both less than 0.1) the longitudinal and transversal forces applied by the ground will be given by

$$F_{i,x} = D\frac{V_{i,x}}{\|V_i\|} \text{ and } F_{i,y} = G\frac{V_{i,y} - r\dot{\varphi}_i}{\|V_i\|}, \tag{29}$$

where G and D are known as *slip stiffness* and *cornering stiffness* coefficients, respectively, both strongly related with nature of contact between the wheel and the ground.

For motion of a WMR on a trajectory there are N conditions, corresponding to N wheels, [11,12,18], defined by

$$\delta_{x,i} = \dot{\delta}_{x,i} = 0 \quad \text{and} \quad s_i = \dot{s}_i = 0, \qquad \text{for } i = 1,\ldots,N. \tag{30}$$

Particularly, for WMRs that use swedish wheels the N conditions associated with slip angle are rewritten as $\delta_{x,i} \neq \dot{\delta}_{x,i} \neq 0$. This condition means the mechanical torques are not large enough to ensure that wheel-ground contact point is not stationary. It is important to point out that such condition is an inherent and proper feature of those type of WMRs [12]. For applications with WMRs it is common to associate $\dot{\delta}_{x,i}$ and $\dot{s}_i$ with targets in the controller design [20] while $\delta_{x,i}$ and s_i are considered always nonzero [12]. In work reported here, $\dot{\delta}_{x,i}$ and $\dot{s}_i$ will be a powerful tool to construct (26).

Slipping Variation. The slipping variation associated with the i-th wheel can be written by differentiating (27) without norms:, i.e.,

$$\dot{s}_i = \frac{\dot{V}_{i,y} - r\ddot{\varphi}_i}{V_i} - \frac{(V_{i,y} - r\dot{\varphi}_i)\,\dot{V}_i}{V_i^2}.$$

Assume that the slip angle $\delta_{i,x}$ is sufficiently small such that $V_i \approx V_{i,y}$, then

$$\dot{s}_i = \frac{r\dot{\varphi}_i\dot{V}_i - r\ddot{\varphi}_iV_i}{V_i^2}. \tag{31}$$

By using the Euler-Lagrange formulation in [11] for the i-th wheel we have

$$I_w\ddot{\varphi}_i = \tau_i - rF_i \tag{32}$$

where τ_i is the control action applied to the i-th wheel, F_i is the i-th traction force (resulting of the compositions of $F_{i,x}$ and $F_{i,y}$) and I_w the inertia of the i-th wheel. Substituting (32) in (31) and manipulating for N wheels yields

$$\dot{S}_tV_t = (I_{N\times N} - S_t)\,\dot{V}_t - m_\gamma T + rm_\gamma F_t \tag{33}$$

where $m_\gamma = r/I_w$, $T \triangleq T(q,\eta,\mu) = \begin{bmatrix} \tau_1 \dots \tau_N \end{bmatrix}^T \in \mathbb{R}^N$, $F_t = [F_1,\dots,F_N]^T \in \mathbb{R}^N$, $V_t \triangleq V_t(q,\eta,\mu) = \begin{bmatrix} V_1(q,\eta,\mu) \dots V_N(q,\eta,\mu) \end{bmatrix}^T \in \mathbb{R}^N$ (being $V_i \triangleq V_i(q,\eta,\mu)$) and $S_t = \mathrm{diag}\{s_1,\dots,s_N\} \in \mathbb{R}^{N\times N}$.

As consequence of the linear approximations in (29) the force F_t can be expressed as $F_t = GS_t + D\Delta_t$, being $\Delta_t = \mathrm{diag}\{\delta_{x,1},\dots,\delta_{x,N}\} \in \mathbb{R}^{N\times N}$. Substituting (30) in (33) gives

$$m_\gamma T = \dot{V}_t + rm_\gamma F_t, \tag{34}$$

which will be called *dynamic condition of appropriate rolling.*

Due to F_y and F_x are uniformly bounded, then $\|F_t\| \leq Y_T$ being $Y_T > 0$ a known value. Next, by calculating the pseudo-inverse for V_t we can rewrite (33) as

$$\dot{S}_t = \left[(I_{N\times N} - S_t)\,\dot{V}_t - m_\gamma T\right]V_t^+ + rm_\gamma F_tV_t^+,$$

and due to $-1 \leq s_i \leq +1$ (in (27)) then it is immediate that $\|S_t\| \leq S_T$, where $S_T > 0$ is a known value. Similarly, from (6), we have $\tau_{\min} \leq \tau \leq \tau_{\max}$, thus $\|T\| \leq T_T$, being $T_T > 0$ a known value.

Now, by applying an appropriate norm $\|\cdot\|$ in above equation and by using the Minkowski inequality we have:

$$\|\dot{S}_t\| \leq \left\|\left[(I_{N \times N} - S_t)\dot{V}_t - m_\gamma T\right]V_t^+\right\| + \|rm_\gamma F_t V_t^+\|,$$

where it can be obtained the following inequality, by using the Cauchy-Schwarz inequality:

$$\|\dot{S}_t\| \leq \|V_t^+\|\|\dot{V}_t\| + \|V_t^+\|\|\dot{V}_t\|\|S_t\| + \|m_\gamma V_t^+\|\|T\| + \|rm_\gamma V_t^+\|\|F_t\|.$$

From (3) it can be seen that ξ depends on harmonic functions, thus $\dot{V}_t$ and V_t^+ are bounded, i.e., $\|\dot{V}_t\| \leq V_T$ and $\|V_t^+\| \leq V_T^*$, for $V_T, V_T^* \geq 0$ known values. Next, substituting V_T and V_T^* in the above inequality, we obtain

$$\|\dot{S}_t\| \leq V_T^* V_T + V_T^* V_T S_T + m_\gamma V_T^* T_T + rm_\gamma V_T^* Y_T. \tag{35}$$

The Eq. (31) allow us to see that $\dot{s}_i$ is inversely proportional to V_i, thus it is hoped that $f_1(V_t, S_t) \leq \|V_t\|\|\dot{S}_t\|$ being $f_1(\cdot) > 0$ a known function. Indeed, from Cauchy-Schwarz inequality we know that $\|V_t \dot{S}_t\| \leq \|V_t\|\|\dot{S}_t\|$ and by applying an appropriate norma in (33) we have

$$\|V_t\|\|\dot{S}_t\| \geq \|(I_{N \times N} - S_t)\dot{V}_t - m_\gamma T + rm_\gamma F_t\| = f_1(V_t, S_t). \tag{36}$$

On the other hand, it is also valid that

$$V_T + V_T S_T + m_\gamma T_T + rm_\gamma Y_T \geq \|(I_{N \times N} - S_t)\dot{V}_t - m_\gamma T + rm_\gamma F_t\|. \tag{37}$$

Now, by dividing (36) with (37), and by manipulating algebraically, we have

$$\|V_t\| \geq \gamma_{11} \|\dot{S}_t\|^{-1} \tag{38}$$

where $\gamma_{11} = (V_T + V_T S_T + m_\gamma T_T + rm_\gamma Y_T)$. Consequently, by using (35) we have that $\|\dot{S}_t\| \leq V_T^* \gamma_{11}$ and due to ξ depends on harmonic functions then $\|V_t\| \leq V_R$. With last this, it is valid to state that

$$\|V_t\| \leq V_R V_T^* \gamma_{11} \|\dot{S}_t\|^{-1}. \tag{39}$$

Next, from inequalities (38) and (39) we can conclude that

$$V_{\inf}(\|\dot{S}_t\|) \leq \|V_t\| \leq V_{\sup}(\|\dot{S}_t\|) \tag{40}$$

where $V_{\inf}(\|\dot{S}_t\|) = \gamma_{11} \|\dot{S}_t\|^{-1}$ and $V_{\sup}(\|\dot{S}_t\|) = V_R V_T^* \gamma_{11} \|\dot{S}_t\|^{-1}$.

Skidding Variation. The skidding variation $\dot{\delta}_{x,i}$ associated with the i-th wheel can be calculated by differentiating (28) without the norms, i.e.,

$$\dot{\delta}_{x,i} = \frac{\dot{V}_{i,x} V_i - \dot{V}_i V_{i,x}}{V_i^2}. \tag{41}$$

The above expression for N wheels can be rewritten, through algebraic manipulation, as the following compact form

$$\dot{\Delta}_t V_t = \dot{V}_x - \Delta_t \dot{V}_t \tag{42}$$

where $V_x = \begin{bmatrix} V_{1,x} \cdots V_{N,x} \end{bmatrix}^T \in \mathbb{R}^N$ and $\Delta_t = \text{diag}\{\delta_{x,1}, \ldots, \delta_{x,N}\} \in \mathbb{R}^{N \times N}$. It can be noted that (42) do not include F_t and it do not depend on the control law τ. In this case, the dynamic condition associated to the skidding is represented by the *dynamic condition of the appropriate skidding* and defined by $\dot{V}_x = 0$ (obtained just replacing (30) in (42)).

From (28) it is possible to state that Δ_t is uniformly bounded, i.e., $\|\Delta_t\| \leq D_T$ where $D_T > 0$ is a known value. Next, by calculating of pseudo-inverse for V_t, we can rewrite (42) as

$$\dot{\Delta}_t = \dot{V}_x V_t^+ - \Delta_t \dot{V}_t V_t^+. \tag{43}$$

Due to $\|\dot{V}_t\| \leq V_T$, $V_{x,i} = \sin \delta_{x,i} V_i$ and $\|V_t^+\| \leq V_T^*$, for $V_T, V_T^* > 0$ known values, then $\dot{V}_{x,i} = \dot{\delta}_{x,i} \cos \delta_{x,i} V_i + \sin \delta_{x,i} \dot{V}_i$, or in compact form as

$$\dot{V}_x = \dot{\Delta}_t \begin{bmatrix} \cos \delta_{x,1} & \cdots & 0 \\ \vdots & \ddots & \vdots \\ 0 & \cdots & \cos \delta_{x,N} \end{bmatrix} V_t + \begin{bmatrix} \sin \delta_{x,1} & \cdots & 0 \\ \vdots & \ddots & \vdots \\ 0 & \cdots & \sin \delta_{x,N} \end{bmatrix} \dot{V}_t.$$

We known that $|\cos \delta_{x,i}| \leq 1$ and $|\sin \delta_{x,i}| \leq 1$. Thus, by applying Minkowski and Cauchy-Schwarz inequality in above equation yields

$$\|\dot{V}_x\| \leq \|\dot{\Delta}_t\| V_R + V_T. \tag{44}$$

Proceeding similarly with (43) and by using (44) we have

$$\|\dot{\Delta}_t\| \leq \|V_t^+\| \|\dot{V}_x\| + \|V_t^+\| \|\dot{V}_t\| \|\Delta_t\| \leq V_T^* \left(\|\dot{\Delta}_t\| V_R + V_T \right) + V_T^* V_T D_T$$

or, by manipulating algebraically, as

$$\|\dot{\Delta}_t\| \leq \frac{V_T^* V_T + V_T^* V_T D_T}{1 - V_T^* V_R}. \tag{45}$$

The Eq. (41) allows us to note that $\dot{\delta}_{i,x}$ is inversely proportional to V_i, thus it is hoped that $f_2(V_t, S_t) \leq \|V_t\| \|\dot{S}_t\|$ being $f_2(\cdot) > 0$ a known function. Indeed, from Cauchy-Schwarz inequality, we know that $\|\dot{\Delta}_t V_t\| \leq \|V_t\| \|\dot{\Delta}_t\|$, thus, by applying of the appropriate norm in (42) we have

$$\|V_t\| \|\dot{\Delta}_t\| \geq \|\dot{V}_x - \Delta_t \dot{V}_t\|. \tag{46}$$

On the other hand, it is also valid that

$$\left(\frac{V_T^* V_T + V_T^* V_T D_T}{1 - V_T^* V_R} \right) V_R + V_T + V_T D_T \geq \|\dot{V}_x - \Delta_t \dot{V}_t\|. \tag{47}$$

Now, dividing (46) by (47), and by manipulating algebraically, we have

$$\|V_t\| \geq \gamma_{12} \|\dot{\Delta}_t\|^{-1} \tag{48}$$

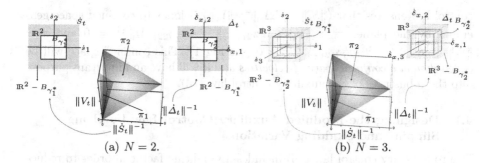

Fig. 1. Representation of the dynamic confined space of velocities for (a) $N = 2$ and (b) $N = 3$.

where $\gamma_{12} = \left(\frac{V_T + V_T D_T}{1 - V_T^* V_R}\right)$. It is known that $\|V_t\| \leq V_R$ and, by using (45), $\|\dot{\Delta}_t\| \leq V_T^* \gamma_{12}$. Thus, it is valid to state that

$$\|V_t\| \leq V_R V_T^* \gamma_{12} \|\dot{\Delta}_t\|^{-1}. \tag{49}$$

From inequalities (48) and (49) we can conclude that

$$V_{\inf}^*(\|\dot{\Delta}_t\|) \leq \|V_t\| \leq V_{\sup}^*(\|\dot{\Delta}_t\|) \tag{50}$$

where $V_{\inf}^*(\|\dot{\Delta}_t\|) = \gamma_{12}\|\dot{\Delta}_t\|^{-1}$ and $V_{\sup}^*(\|\dot{\Delta}_t\|) = V_R V_T^* \gamma_{12}\|\dot{\Delta}_t\|^{-1}$.

Now, the *total effect of slipping and skidding variations* can be compacted by adding (40) and (50), i.e.,

$$\frac{1}{2}\left[V_{\inf}^*(\|\dot{\Delta}_t\|) + V_{\inf}(\|\dot{S}_t\|)\right] \leq \|V_t\| \leq \frac{1}{2}\left[V_{\sup}^*(\|\dot{\Delta}_t\|) + V_{\sup}(\|\dot{S}_t\|)\right]$$

By substituting (38), (39), (48) and (49) in above expression yields

$$V_{t,\inf}(\|\dot{S}_t\|, \|\dot{\Delta}_t\|) \leq \|V_t\| \leq V_{t,\sup}(\|\dot{S}_t\|, \|\dot{\Delta}_t\|). \tag{51}$$

being $V_{t,\inf}(\|\dot{S}_t\|, \|\dot{\Delta}_t\|) = \frac{1}{2}\gamma_{11}\|\dot{S}_t\|^{-1} + \frac{1}{2}\gamma_{12}\|\dot{\Delta}_t\|^{-1}$ and $V_{t,\sup}(\|\dot{S}_t\|, \|\dot{\Delta}_t\|) = \frac{1}{2}\gamma_{21}\|\dot{S}_t\|^{-1} + \frac{1}{2}\gamma_{22}\|\dot{\Delta}_t\|^{-1}$, where $\gamma_{21} = V_R V_T^* \gamma_{11}$ and $\gamma_{22} = V_R V_T^* \gamma_{12}$. In other words, whenever (51) is satisfied the behavior of V_t can be manipulated by slipping and skidding variations.

By defining $\gamma_1^* = V_T^* \gamma_{11}$ and $\gamma_2^* = V_T^* \gamma_{12}$ in (35) and (45) then $\|\dot{S}_t\|^{-1} \geq 1/\gamma_1^*$ and $\|\dot{\Delta}_t\|^{-1} \geq 1/\gamma_2^*$. Thus, there exist two closed balls $B_{\gamma_1^*}$ and $B_{\gamma_2^*}$ such that

$$\dot{S}_t \in \mathbb{R}^{N \times N} - B_{\gamma_1^*} \quad \text{and} \quad \dot{\Delta}_t \in \mathbb{R}^{N \times N} - B_{\gamma_2^*} \tag{52}$$

whit $B_{\gamma_1^*} = \{\dot{S}_t \in \mathbb{R}^{N \times N} | \|\dot{S}_t\|^{-1} \leq 1/\gamma_1^*\}$, $B_{\gamma_2^*} = \{\dot{\Delta}_t \in \mathbb{R}^{N \times N} | \|\dot{\Delta}_t\|^{-1} \leq 1/\gamma_2^*\}$.

Let consider triples at form $\langle \|\dot{S}_t\|^{-1}, \|\dot{\Delta}_t\|^{-1}, \|V_t\| \rangle$. We will assume that slipping and skidding variations remain in sets (52) such that the auxiliary control law ensures that $\langle \|\dot{S}_t\|^{-1}, \|\dot{\Delta}_t\|^{-1}, \|V_t\| \rangle$ belongs to confined space generated by the planes $\pi_1 : \|V_t\| - \frac{1}{2}\gamma_{21}\|\dot{S}_t\|^{-1} - \frac{1}{2}\gamma_{22}\|\dot{\Delta}_t\|^{-1} = 0$ and $\pi_2 :$ $\|V_t\| - \frac{1}{2}\gamma_{11}\|\dot{S}_t\|^{-1} - \frac{1}{2}\gamma_{12}\|\dot{\Delta}_t\|^{-1} = 0$ (see Fig. 1). This confined space will be called *dynamic confined space of velocities* and it will have an important purpose into the robustness of the auxiliary control law (26).

4.1 Designing the Modified Auxiliary Control Law by Using Slipping and Skidding Variations

Due to auxiliary control law (26) includes a weighting factor in order to reduce the WMR's acceleration then it is necessary to understand how the influence of slipping and the skidding can be used in order to improve the robustness of the auxiliary control law. Firstly, let rewrite (11) as

$$\dot{q} = S(q)\int_0^t v^*(\lambda)\,d\lambda + A(q)\varepsilon\mu = S(q)\int_0^t \Delta_\sigma^{-1}v(\lambda)\,d\lambda + A(q)\varepsilon\mu, \qquad (53)$$

due to $\dot{\eta} = v^*$ (see (26)), i.e., $\eta = \int_0^t v^*(\lambda)\,d\lambda$.

Now, let consider the following assumption:

Assumption 2. *The velocity at center of the wheels of the WMR are considered equal, more precisely, equal to its average:*

$$\|V_i\| = \|V(q,\eta,\mu)\| = (\dot{x}^2 + \dot{y}^2)^{1/2} = \left[\mathrm{Tr}\left(\dot{\xi}\,\dot{\xi}^T\right)\right]^{1/2}, \quad for\ i = 1,2,\ldots,N.$$

By using (53) and its parcel associated with the modified auxiliary control law then

$$\dot{\xi} = \bar{S}_1(q)\int_0^t \Delta_\sigma^{-1}v(\lambda)\,d\lambda,$$

being $\bar{S}_1(q) \in \mathbb{R}^{3\times\delta_u}$ a submatrix of $S_1(q)$ (due to $\xi \in z$, see (3)). With the above expression and Assumption 2 we can verify that

$$\left[\mathrm{Tr}\left(\bar{S}_1(q)\int_0^t \Delta_\sigma^{-1}v(\lambda)\,d\lambda\left(\int_0^t \Delta_\sigma^{-1}v(\lambda)\,d\lambda\right)^T \bar{S}_1^T(q)\right)\right]^{1/2} = \left[\mathrm{Tr}\left(\dot{\xi}\,\dot{\xi}^T\right)\right]^{1/2}. \quad (54)$$

In order to obtain an expression for Δ_σ we will assume that the slipping and skidding variations belong to the space confined by the planes π_1 and π_2. For this purpose, let choose the induced norm for matrices, defined by

$$\|A\|_2 = \left[\sigma_{\max}\left(AA^T\right)\right]^{1/2},$$

where A represents any matrix and $\sigma_{\max}(A)$ represents its maximum eigenvalue. Thus, we can state that

$$\|V_t\|_2 = \begin{cases} \frac{1}{2}\gamma_{11}\|\dot{S}_t\|_2^{-1} + \frac{1}{2}\gamma_{12}\|\dot{\Delta}_t\|_2^{-1}, & V_t \in V_{t,\inf} \\ \frac{1}{2}\gamma_{21}\|\dot{S}_t\|_2^{-1} + \frac{1}{2}\gamma_{22}\|\dot{\Delta}_t\|_2^{-1}, & V_t \in V_{t,\sup} \end{cases}. \quad (55)$$

Now, let consider the following assumption on individual effect of the slipping and skidding variations at each wheel.

Assumption 3. *The velocity at center of the* i-*th wheel of WMR for the intervals* $V_{t,\inf}$ *and* $V_{t,\sup}$ *can be expressed as*

$$\left[\text{Tr}\left(\dot{\xi}\,\dot{\xi}^T\right)\right]^{1/2} = \|V_i\| = \begin{cases} \frac{1}{2}\gamma_{11}\|\dot{s}_i\|_2^{-1} + \frac{1}{2}\gamma_{12}\|\dot{\delta}_{x,i}\|_2^{-1}, & V_i \in V_{t,\inf} \\ \frac{1}{2}\gamma_{21}\|\dot{s}_i\|_2^{-1} + \frac{1}{2}\gamma_{22}\|\dot{\delta}_{x,i}\|_2^{-1}, & V_i \in V_{t,\sup} \end{cases} \quad (56)$$

Noting Assumption 3 it can be stated that $\|\dot{s}_i\|_2$ and $\|\dot{\delta}_{x,i}\|_2$ are inversely proportional to V_i. Therefore, it is hoped that for a suitable increment of the norm $\|\dot{s}_i\|$ (or $\|\dot{\delta}_{x,i}\|$) corresponds, when necessary, with a decrement of V_i.

Let see the case $V_i \in V_{t,\inf}$ (the case $V_i \in V_{t,\sup}$ is similar). By multiplying both sides of (56) by $\|\dot{s}_i\|_2$ and manipulating algebraically we obtain

$$\left[\text{Tr}\left(\|\dot{s}_i\|_2\dot{\xi}\,\|\dot{s}_i\|_2\dot{\xi}^T\right)\right]^{1/2} = \frac{1}{2}\gamma_{11} + \frac{1}{2}\gamma_{12}\|\dot{s}_i\|_2\|\dot{\delta}_{x,i}\|_2^{-1}. \quad (57)$$

Due to $\|\dot{s}_1\|_2 = |\dot{s}_1|, \ldots, \|\dot{s}_N\|_2 = |\dot{s}_N|$, $\|\dot{\delta}_{x,1}\|_2 = |\dot{\delta}_{x,1}|, \ldots, \|\dot{\delta}_{x,N}\|_2 = |\dot{\delta}_{x,N}|$, $\gamma_{11} + \gamma_{12}\|\dot{S}_t\,\dot{\Delta}_t^{-1}\|_2 = \|\text{diag}\{\frac{1}{2}\gamma_{11} + \frac{1}{2}\gamma_{12}\|\dot{s}_1\|_2\|\dot{\delta}_{x,1}\|_2^{-1}, \ldots, \frac{1}{2}\gamma_{11} + \frac{1}{2}\gamma_{12}\|\dot{s}_N\|_2\|\dot{\delta}_{x,N}\|_2^{-1}\}\|$, $\|\dot{S}_t\|_2 = \|\text{diag}\{\|\dot{s}_1\|_2, \ldots, \|\dot{s}_N\|_2\}\|$ the Eq. (57) can be rewritten for N wheels as

$$\left[\text{Tr}\left(\|\dot{S}_t\|_2\dot{\xi}\,\|\dot{S}_t\|_2\dot{\xi}^T\right)\right]^{1/2} = \frac{1}{2}\gamma_{11} + \frac{1}{2}\gamma_{12}\|\dot{S}_t\,\dot{\Delta}_t^{-1}\|_2, \quad (58)$$

or, by using $\dot{\xi} = \bar{S}_1(q)\int_0^t v(\lambda)\,d\lambda$, as

$$\frac{1}{2}\gamma_{11} + \frac{1}{2}\gamma_{12}\|\dot{S}_t\,\dot{\Delta}_t^{-1}\|_2 = \left[\text{Tr}\left(\bar{S}_1(q)\|\dot{S}_t\|_2\int_0^t v(\lambda)d\lambda\left(\|\dot{S}_t\|_2\int_0^t v(\lambda)d\lambda\right)^T \bar{S}_1^T(q)\right)\right]^{1/2}. \quad (59)$$

Likewise, the above expression can be expressed by using the norm $\|\dot{\Delta}_t\|_2$ as

$$\frac{1}{2}\gamma_{11}\|\dot{\Delta}_t\dot{S}_t^{-1}\|_2 + \frac{1}{2}\gamma_{12} = \left[\text{Tr}\left(\bar{S}_1(q)\|\dot{\Delta}_t\|_2\int_0^t v(\lambda)d\lambda\left(\|\dot{\Delta}_t\|_2\int_0^t v(\lambda)d\lambda\right)^T \bar{S}_1^T(q)\right)\right]^{1/2}. \quad (60)$$

Similarly, when $V_i \in V_{t,\sup}$ yields

$$\frac{1}{2}\gamma_{21} + \frac{1}{2}\gamma_{22}\|\dot{S}_t\,\dot{\Delta}_t^{-1}\|_2 = \left[\text{Tr}\left(\bar{S}_1(q)\|\dot{S}_t\|_2\int_0^t v(\lambda)d\lambda\left(\|\dot{S}_t\|_2\int_0^t v(\lambda)d\lambda\right)^T \bar{S}_1^T(q)\right)\right]^{1/2}, \quad (61)$$

$$\frac{1}{2}\gamma_{21}\|\dot{\Delta}_t\dot{S}_t^{-1}\|_2 + \frac{1}{2}\gamma_{22} = \left[\text{Tr}\left(\bar{S}_1(q)\|\dot{\Delta}_t\|_2\int_0^t v(\lambda)d\lambda\left(\|\dot{\Delta}_t\|_2\int_0^t v(\lambda)d\lambda\right)^T \bar{S}_1^T(q)\right)\right]^{1/2}. \quad (62)$$

By adding (59) with (60) and (61) with (62) is obtained

$$\left[\text{Tr}\left(\bar{S}_1(q)h_\gamma\int_0^t v(\lambda)\,d\lambda\left(h_\gamma\int_0^t v(\lambda)\,d\lambda\right)^T \bar{S}_1^T(q)\right)\right]^{1/2}$$

$$= \begin{cases} \frac{1}{2}\gamma_{11}(\|\dot{\Delta}_t\,\dot{S}_t^{-1}\|_2 + 1) + \frac{1}{2}\gamma_{12}(\|\dot{S}_t\,\dot{\Delta}_t^{-1}\|_2 + 1), & V_t \in V_{t,\inf} \\ \frac{1}{2}\gamma_{21}(\|\dot{\Delta}_t\,\dot{S}_t^{-1}\|_2 + 1) + \frac{1}{2}\gamma_{22}(\|\dot{S}_t\,\dot{\Delta}_t^{-1}\|_2 + 1), & V_t \in V_{t,\sup}, \end{cases} \quad (63)$$

where $h_\gamma = \|\dot{\Delta}_t\|_2 + \|\dot{S}_t\|_2$. Thus, by comparing the right side of (55) with the right side of (63) is immediate that

$$\|\dot{S}_t\|_2^{-1} = \|\dot{\Delta}_t \dot{S}_t^{-1}\|_2 + 1 \quad \text{and} \quad \|\dot{\Delta}_t\|_2^{-1} = \|\dot{S}_t \dot{\Delta}_t^{-1}\|_2 + 1. \tag{64}$$

The left side of (63) is equal to the left side of (54) if and only if

$$h_\gamma \int_0^t \upsilon(\lambda)\, d\lambda = \int_0^t \Delta_\sigma^{-1} \upsilon(\lambda)\, d\lambda. \tag{65}$$

Then, by differentiating both sides of (65) and due to $\dot{\eta} = \upsilon$, the modified auxiliary control law (26) can be expressed in terms of the slipping and skidding variations as:

$$\upsilon^* = \Delta_\sigma^{-1} \upsilon = h_\gamma \upsilon + \dot{h}_\gamma \eta \quad \left(\text{i.e., } \upsilon^* = \frac{d}{dt}\left(h_\gamma \eta\right)\right). \tag{66}$$

In work reported here, (66) will represent the *modified output linearization condition*.

5   Trajectory Tracking Control Based on the Modified Auxiliary Control Law

In this section we will formulate a method to calculate the function h_γ in (66) by using an extension of methods proposed in [12,13]. From (34) and due to $V_i \approx V_{i,y} = r\dot{\varphi}_i$ (for small values of $\delta_{x,i}$ and s_i) then

$$\tilde{F} \triangleq r^{-1}T(\bar{q}, \eta, \varepsilon) - F_t = m_\gamma^{-1}\ddot{\varphi}(\bar{q}, \eta, \mu) \in \mathbb{R}^N, \tag{67}$$

where $\tilde{F}$ will be called *apparent force*. By comparing (3) with (11) it is possible to note that $S(q)\eta = \dot{q} - A(q)\varepsilon\mu \triangleq \dot{\bar{q}}$ where $\dot{\bar{q}}$ will be called *apparent generalized velocities*[3]. Thus, the *apparent kinematic configuration model* is defined by

$$\dot{\bar{q}} = S(\bar{q})\bar{\eta} \quad \left(\text{i.e., } \begin{bmatrix} \dot{\bar{z}} \\ \dot{\bar{\beta}}_o \\ \dot{\bar{\varphi}} \end{bmatrix} = \begin{bmatrix} S_1(\bar{q}) \\ S_2(\bar{q}) \end{bmatrix} \bar{\eta} \right). \tag{68}$$

Now, from (68) we have $\dot{\bar{\varphi}} = \bar{S}_2(\bar{q})\bar{\eta}$ being $\bar{S}_2(\bar{q})$ a submatrix of $S_2(\bar{q})$. However, [7] shows that

$$\bar{S}_2(\bar{q}) = \begin{bmatrix} D_\varphi \Sigma(\bar{\beta}_c) & 0_{N \times \delta_d} \end{bmatrix} \in \mathbb{R}^{N \times \delta_u}.$$

By substituting (68) in $\dot{\bar{\varphi}} = \bar{S}_2(\bar{q})\bar{\eta}$ is obtained

$$\dot{\bar{\varphi}} = \begin{bmatrix} D_\varphi \Sigma(\bar{\beta}_c) & 0_{N \times \delta_d} \end{bmatrix} S^+(q)\dot{\bar{q}} \triangleq \Lambda(\bar{q})\dot{\bar{q}} \tag{69}$$

with $\Lambda(\bar{q}) \in \mathbb{R}^{N \times (3 + \delta_d + N_o + N)}$.

---

[3] From here any element of $\bar{q}$ will be represented by a bar over it, e.g., $\bar{\beta}_c$, $\bar{z}$, $S(\bar{q})$, etc.

The methods proposed in [12,13] are based on the chain rule for differentiation of $\tilde{F}$ maps. Let consider the following differentials taking into account (67):

$$\dot{S}_t 1_N = \Lambda_1 \dot{\tilde{F}} = \Lambda_1 \ddot{\varphi}(\bar{q},\bar{\eta}) \quad \text{and} \quad \dot{\Delta}_t 1_N = \Lambda_2 \dot{\tilde{F}} = \Lambda_2 \ddot{\varphi}(\bar{q},\bar{\eta}) \qquad (70)$$

where $1_N = [1 \ldots 1]^T \in \mathbb{R}^N$, $\Lambda_1 = m_\gamma^{-1}\mathrm{diag}\left\{\frac{ds_i}{dF_i}\right\}$ and $\Lambda_2 = m_\gamma^{-1}\mathrm{diag}\left\{\frac{d\delta_{x,i}}{dF_i}\right\}$ for $i = 1,\ldots,N$.

Now, by differentiating two times (69) and substituting it in (70) yields

$$\dot{S}_t 1_N = \Lambda_1 \ddot{A}(\bar{q})\dot{\bar{q}} + 2\Lambda_1 \dot{A}(\bar{q})\ddot{\bar{q}} \quad \text{and} \quad \dot{\Delta}_t 1_N = \Lambda_2 \ddot{A}(\bar{q})\dot{\bar{q}} + 2\Lambda_2 \dot{A}(\bar{q})\ddot{\bar{q}} \qquad (71)$$

where $\dot{A}(\bar{q}) = \frac{\partial\Lambda}{\partial\theta}\dot{\theta} + \sum_{i=1}^N \frac{\partial\Lambda}{\partial\beta_{i_c}}\dot{\beta}_{i_c} + \sum_{i=1}^N \frac{\partial\Lambda}{\partial\beta_{i_o}}\dot{\beta}_{i_o}$ and $\ddot{A}(\bar{q}) = \frac{\partial^2\Lambda}{\partial t\partial\theta}\dot{\theta} + \frac{\partial\Lambda}{\partial\theta}\ddot{\theta} + \sum_{i=1}^N \frac{\partial^2\Lambda}{\partial t\partial\beta_{i_c}}\dot{\beta}_{i_c} + \sum_{i=1}^N \frac{\partial\Lambda}{\partial\beta_{i_c}}\ddot{\beta}_{i_c} + \sum_{i=1}^N \frac{\partial^2\Lambda}{\partial t\partial\beta_{i_o}}\dot{\beta}_{i_o} + \sum_{i=1}^N \frac{\partial\Lambda}{\partial\beta_{i_o}}\ddot{\beta}_{i_o}$.

From (29) and (67) it is immediate that $\frac{ds_i}{dF_i} = -\frac{1}{G}$ and $\frac{d\delta_{x,i}}{dF_i} = -\frac{1}{D}$. Thus,

$$\Lambda_1 = -\,\mathrm{diag}\left\{(m_\gamma G)^{-1} 1_N\right\} \quad \text{and} \quad \Lambda_2 = -\,\mathrm{diag}\left\{(m_\gamma D)^{-1} 1_N\right\}. \qquad (72)$$

We propose to include nonzero slipping and skidding into the trajectory control problem (i.e., $S_t \neq 0$ and $\Delta_t \neq 0$) and considering them constant values. Nevertheless, slipping and skidding variations (i.e., $\dot{S}_t$ and $\dot{\Delta}_t$) will be specifications in the controller design with aid of a condition on the slipping and skidding variations. Let this condition defined by the following theorem:

Theorem 3 (Condition on Slipping and Skidding Variations). *For a WMR that moves on a trajectory with slipping and skidding a necessary and sufficient condition for $\|\dot{S}_t\| = 0$ and $\|\dot{\Delta}_t\| = 0$ is defined by*

$$\|R_\Lambda(\bar{q},\dot{\bar{q}})\| = \|\ddot{A}(q)\dot{\bar{q}} + 2\dot{A}(q)\ddot{\bar{q}}\| = 0. \qquad (73)$$

Proof. From (72) we have $\|\Lambda_1\|_2 = (m_\gamma G)^{-1}$ and $\|\Lambda_2\|_2 = (m_\gamma D)^{-1}$. Thus, by using the Cauchy-Swarchz inequality in (71) is obtained

$$\|\dot{S}_t 1_N\| \leq \Lambda_1 \ddot{A}(\bar{q})\dot{\bar{q}} + 2\Lambda_1 \dot{A}(\bar{q})\ddot{\bar{q}} \leq (m_\gamma G)^{-1}\|\ddot{A}(q)\dot{\bar{q}} + 2\dot{A}(q)\ddot{\bar{q}}\|$$
$$\|\dot{\Delta}_t 1_N\| \leq \Lambda_2 \ddot{A}(\bar{q})\dot{\bar{q}} + 2\Lambda_2 \dot{A}(\bar{q})\ddot{\bar{q}} \leq (m_\gamma D)^{-1}\|\ddot{A}(q)\dot{\bar{q}} + 2\dot{A}(q)\ddot{\bar{q}}\|,$$

thus $\|\dot{S}_t 1_N\| = \|\dot{\Delta}_t 1_N\| = 0$ if and only if

$$\|\ddot{A}(q)\dot{\bar{q}} + 2\dot{A}(q)\ddot{\bar{q}}\| = 0,$$

what ends the proof.

By applying the Cauchy-Schwarz inequality to (71) we obtain

$$\|\dot{S}_t\|_2 + \|\dot{\Delta}_t\|_2 \leq (\|\Lambda_1\|_2 + \|\Lambda_2\|_2)\|\ddot{A}(\bar{q})\dot{\bar{q}} + 2\dot{A}(\bar{q})\ddot{\bar{q}}\|_2 = \alpha_0^*\|R_\Lambda(\bar{q},\dot{\bar{q}})\|_2,$$

where $\alpha_0^* = \frac{L_w}{r}\left(\frac{1}{D} + \frac{1}{G}\right)$. However, there exists a nonzero value $0 < c^* \leq 1$ such that

$$h_\gamma = \|\dot{S}_t\|_2 + \|\dot{\Delta}_t\|_2 = \alpha^*\|R_\Lambda(\bar{q},\dot{\bar{q}})\|_2. \qquad (74)$$

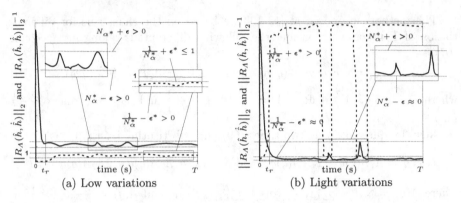

Fig. 2. Representation of the norms $\|R_\Lambda\|_2$ (solid line) and $\|R_\Lambda\|_2^{-1}$ (dot line) for (a) *low variations* (For $\forall t \geq t_r$ the norm $\|R_\Lambda\|_2$ is not zero. i.e., $N_\alpha^* \neq 0$, for $\epsilon > 0$, can be considered a constant value. It is noted that $\|R_\Lambda\|_2^{-1} \leq 1$) and (b) *light variations* (for $\forall t \geq t_r$ any regions $\|R_\Lambda\|_2$ are close to zero. It can be verified that $\|R_\Lambda\|_2^{-1} \to \infty$ when $\|R_\Lambda\|_2 \to 0$).

and $\alpha^* = \alpha_0^* c^*$.

By assuming that $\alpha^* = \alpha_1^* + \alpha_2^*$ (i.e., α^* is partitioned) and by using (64) and (74) then

$$\frac{D}{G+D} = \alpha_1^* \|R_\Lambda(\bar{q}, \dot{\bar{q}})\|_2 \quad \text{and} \quad \frac{G}{G+D} = \alpha_2^* \|R_\Lambda(\bar{q}, \dot{\bar{q}})\|_2. \qquad (75)$$

So that

$$\alpha^* = \alpha_1^* + \alpha_2^* = \|R_\Lambda(\bar{q}, \dot{\bar{q}})\|_2^{-1}. \qquad (76)$$

Here, the method proposed assumes situations whose slipping and skidding have low and light variations. In Fig. 2 is represented the situation of low and light variations through the norm $\|R_\Lambda(\bar{q}, \dot{\bar{q}})\|_2$.

Now, let $t_r \in [0, T]$ be the duration of the initial transient of $\|R_\Lambda(\bar{q}, \dot{\bar{q}})\|_2$ and N_α its average value. We proposes that in a situation of low variations, by using the average value theorem for integrals, N_α is defined by

$$\frac{1}{T - t_r} \int_{t_r}^T \|R_\Lambda(\bar{q}, \dot{\bar{q}})\|_2 d\lambda,$$

however, by Assumption 1 we will choose a parcel of the vector $\bar{q}$ in order to guarantee $z(t) = \bar{z}(t) + \mathcal{O}(\varepsilon)$ and $\mu(t) = \bar{\mu}(t) + \hat{\mu}(t^*) + \mathcal{O}(\varepsilon)$ for $t \in [0, T]$, i.e., the uniformity of the control scheme with respect to T. Thus, there exists a known value N_α^* such that

$$N_\alpha^* = \frac{1}{T - t_r} \int_{t_r}^T \|R_\Lambda(\hat{h}, \dot{\hat{h}})\|_2 d\lambda, \quad \left(\text{i.e.,} \left| \|R_\Lambda(\hat{h}, \dot{\hat{h}})\|_2 - N_\alpha^* \right| \leq \epsilon, \text{ for } t \in [t_r, \infty) \right)$$

where $\hat{h} = \begin{bmatrix} \bar{h} & \bar{\theta} \end{bmatrix}^T$ due to $\bar{h} = h_z(\bar{z})$ (see (22)).

With previous arguments, the parameter α^* will be calculated, taking into account (76), as

$$\alpha^* = \frac{1}{N_\alpha^*}. \tag{77}$$

Feedforward of the Slipping and Skidding Variations. In order to improve the robustness of the auxiliary control law (26), the slipping and skidding variations will be used to synthesize a control scheme based on feedforward loop. The slipping and skidding variations of the reference trajectory will be measured and forwarded to external control loop defined by v^* (defined by (26)). To this end, it is necessary that the slipping and skidding variations can be measured by using the pose information of reference point P_{ref}. Thus, the function h_γ in (74) can be rewritten as

$$h_\gamma = \alpha^* \| R_\Lambda(\hat{h}_{\text{ref}}, \dot{\hat{h}}_{\text{ref}}) \|_2, \tag{78}$$

where $\hat{h}_{\text{ref}} = [h_{\text{ref}} \ \theta_{\text{ref}}]^T$, being $h_{\text{ref}} \in \mathbb{R}^2$ the pose of P_{ref} in Subsect. 3.1 and $\theta_{\text{ref}} \in \mathbb{R}$ the guidance of the WMR. Consequently, (66) can be rewritten as

$$\Delta_\sigma^{-1} v = \alpha^* \| R_\Lambda(\hat{h}_{\text{ref}}, \dot{\hat{h}}_{\text{ref}}) \|_2 v + \frac{d}{dt} \left(\alpha^* \| R_\Lambda(\hat{h}_{\text{ref}}, \dot{\hat{h}}_{\text{ref}}) \|_2 \right) \eta. \tag{79}$$

Let consider that $\hat{h}_{\text{ref}}$ and $\dot{\hat{h}}_{\text{ref}}$ in (79) are calculated by using pseudo-differentiators with command input $\hat{h}_{\text{ref}}^{\text{com}}$, i.e.,

$$\frac{d}{dt} \left(\begin{bmatrix} \hat{h}_{\text{ref}} \\ \dot{\hat{h}}_{\text{ref}} \end{bmatrix} \right) = \begin{bmatrix} 0_{3\times3} & I_{3\times3} \\ -\omega_{n,\text{dif}}^2 I_{3\times3} & -2\zeta^* \omega_{n,\text{dif}} I_{3\times3} \end{bmatrix} \begin{bmatrix} \hat{h}_{\text{ref}} \\ \dot{\hat{h}}_{\text{ref}} \end{bmatrix} + \begin{bmatrix} 0_{3\times3} \\ G_{\text{dif}} \omega_{n,\text{dif}}^2 I_{3\times3} \end{bmatrix} \hat{h}_{\text{ref}}^{\text{com}}$$

where $\hat{h}_{\text{ref}}$ is the filtered signal of $\hat{h}_{\text{ref}}^{\text{com}}$, $\dot{\hat{h}}_{\text{ref}}$ is the approximated derivative of $\hat{h}_{\text{ref}}^{\text{com}}$, ζ^* is the damping ratio, $\omega_{n,\text{dif}}$ the natural frequency proportional to the pass band of a low-pass filter and G_{dif} the gain of that filter [21]. Particularly, any increasing of G_{dif} represents a increasing of $\dot{\hat{h}}_{\text{ref}}$ and $\| R_\Lambda(\hat{h}_{\text{ref}}, \dot{\hat{h}}_{\text{ref}}) \|_2$. Moreover, the term $\frac{d}{dt}(\alpha^* \| R_\Lambda(\hat{h}_{\text{ref}}, \dot{\hat{h}}_{\text{ref}}) \|_2)$ adds very high *on-peaks*. In order to reduce the on-peaks at norm we will consider known values $0 < \lambda^* < 1$ and $\bar{G}_{\text{dif}}$ such that

$$\Delta_\sigma^{-1} v = \alpha^* \bar{G}_{\text{dif}} \| R_\Lambda(\hat{h}_{\text{ref}}, \dot{\hat{h}}_{\text{ref}}) \|_2 v + \alpha^* \bar{G}_{\text{dif}} \lambda^* \frac{d}{dt} \left(\| R_\Lambda(\hat{h}_{\text{ref}}, \dot{\hat{h}}_{\text{ref}}) \|_2 \right) \eta. \tag{80}$$

5.1   Assessing the Controller: Simulation Results

In order to evaluate the controller proposed we consider the WMR shown in Fig. 3(a), which has two identical fixed wheels on the same axle and one free wheel whose mass can be neglected. The vector of configuration coordinates reduces to $q = \begin{bmatrix} x & y & \theta & \varphi_1 & \varphi_2 \end{bmatrix}^T$ and the matrices associated with the kinematic and dynamic model are:

$$Z_0(q) = \begin{bmatrix} S(\theta) \\ \Delta_0 \end{bmatrix}, \ Z_1(q) = \begin{bmatrix} A(\theta) \\ \Delta_1 \end{bmatrix}, \ Z_2(q) = \begin{bmatrix} 0_{5\times3} \\ \Delta_2 \end{bmatrix}, \ Z_3(q) = \begin{bmatrix} 0_{5\times2} \\ \Delta_3 \end{bmatrix},$$

$$G_0(q) = \begin{bmatrix} -\dot\theta\cos2\theta & 0 \\ \frac{1}{3}\dot\theta\sin2\theta & 0 \\ -\frac{1}{3}\dot\theta\sin2\theta & 0 \end{bmatrix}, \ G_1(q) = \begin{bmatrix} 0 & \dot\theta & -\dot\theta \\ \frac{1}{3}\dot\theta & 0 & 0 \\ \frac{1}{3}\dot\theta & 0 & 0 \end{bmatrix}, \ G_2(q) = \begin{bmatrix} a_3D_o & 0 & 0 \\ 0 & a_4G_o & a_4G_o \\ 0 & a_4G_o & a_4G_o \end{bmatrix},$$

$$G_3(q) = \begin{bmatrix} 0 & 0 \\ a_1 & 0 \\ 0 & a_1 \end{bmatrix}, \ \Delta_0 = \begin{bmatrix} \frac{1}{3}\dot\theta\sin2\theta & 0 \\ 0 & 0 \end{bmatrix}, \ \Delta_1 = \begin{bmatrix} -\frac{1}{3}\dot\theta & 0 & 0 \\ 0 & 0 & 0 \end{bmatrix}, \ \Delta_2 = \begin{bmatrix} 0 & 0 & 0 \\ 0 & a_2G_o & a_2G_o \end{bmatrix},$$

$$S_1(q) = \begin{bmatrix} -\sin\theta & 0 \\ \cos\theta & 0 \\ 0 & 1 \end{bmatrix}, \ S_2(q) = \begin{bmatrix} -\frac{1}{r} & -\frac{l}{r} \\ \frac{1}{r} & -\frac{l}{r} \end{bmatrix} \text{ and } \Delta_3 = \begin{bmatrix} -a_1 & a_1 \\ -a_1 & -a_1 \end{bmatrix}$$

where $a_1 = \frac{r^2}{3\,I_w}, a_2 = -\frac{2\,I_w\,l^2 - 2\,I_c\,r^2}{I_c\,I_w\,\|V(q,\eta,\mu)\|}, a_3 = -\frac{4}{M\,\|V(q,\eta,\mu)\|}$ and $a_4 = -\frac{2\,l^2}{I_c\,\|V(q,\eta,\mu)\|}$ $-\frac{r^2}{I_w\,\|V(q,\eta,\mu)\|}$. The parameters chosen are $r = 0.35$ m, $l = 1$ m, $L = 1$ m, $M = 1000$ Kg, $I_c = 500$ Kg-m^2 and $I_w = 1.6$ Kg-m^2 (see [8]). By using the analysis in [9,10], the parameter ε was chosen such that its value was less than 9×10^{-11} (see Fig. 3(b)) and it ensures lower computational cost[4]. Therefore, let use $\varepsilon = 10^{-15}$.

The reference trajectory used was the rhombus with

$$x_{\text{ref}} = 2\sin^{-1}(\cos4\pi t), \ y_{\text{ref}} = 2\sin^{-1}(\sin4\pi t), \ \theta_{\text{ref}} = \tan^{-1}\left(\frac{4\pi t}{4\pi t + \pi/2}\right)$$

and $V_i = 1.18$ m/s. In the rhombus the corners represent a greater deviation at high values of V_i [9,13]. The auxiliary control law (80) was set with $K_1 = 500\,I_{2\times2}$, $K_2 = 120\,I_{2\times2}$. In Fig. 3(c) is observed the evolution of the norm $\|R_\Lambda(\hat h, \dot{\hat h})\|_2$ for $T = 15$ s. The value of N_α^* was calculated as

$$N_\alpha^* \approx \frac{1}{2}\left(\max_{0.261\le t\le15}\left\{\|R_\Lambda(\hat h,\dot{\hat h})\|_2\right\} + \min_{0.261\le t\le15}\left\{\|R_\Lambda(\hat h,\dot{\hat h})\|_2\right\}\right) = 16.75$$

and, consequently, by using (77) $\alpha^* = 0.0597$. The values for $\bar G_{\text{dif}}$ and λ^* were 2000 and 0.02, respectively. The control performance of (80) is measured by using the IAE index and shown in the Table 1. In Fig. 3(d) is shown the trajectory tracking and it can be observed that the WMR has a better tracking when $\alpha^*\bar G_{\text{dif}}$ and $\alpha^*\bar G_{\text{dif}}\lambda^*$ are increased. In Table 1 can be observed that setting $(\alpha^*\bar G_{\text{dif}}, \alpha^*\bar G_{\text{dif}}\lambda^*)$ as $(300.8, 12.35)$ and varying V_i the deviation at corner of the rhombus is smaller as well as occurring with IAE index.

6   Final Remarks

It can be said that static linearizing feedback laws supported by an auxiliary control law whose robustness is based on the slipping and skidding variations are quite robust to deformation and flexibility phenomena when WMRs makes tracking of a reference trajectory at significant velocities. For that purpose, the auxiliary control law was set by using the Theorem 3 and a feedforward outer loop. Similarly as [8,9,13], such robustness has been complemented by using singular perturbations method.

---

[4] In [9], the computational cost of the control law for the trajectory tracking is associated with the nonlinearity dead-zone, which is strongly related to the static friction at wheels.

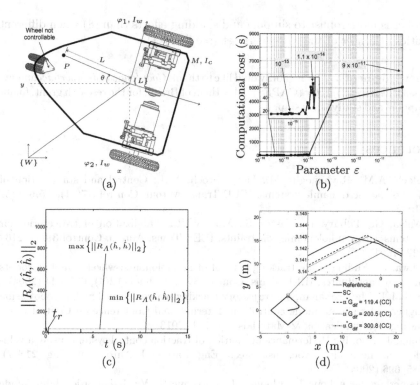

Fig. 3. (a) Kinematic and dynamic variables of WMR with two fixed wheels. The free wheel is not controllable. (b) Computational cost for the trajectory tracking controller. Imminent instability when $\varepsilon \geq 9 \times 10^{-11}$. (c) Norm $\|R_\Lambda\|_2$ with $t_r = 0.261$ s, $T = 15$ s, $\max\{\|R_\Lambda\|_2\} \approx 33.5$, $\min\{\|R_\Lambda\|_2\} \approx 5.6 \times 10^{-5}$. (d) Trajectory tracking control by using slipping and skidding variations.

Table 1. Performance of the modified auxiliary control law (80).

$V_i = 1.18$ m/s				$\alpha^* \bar{G}_{\mathrm{dif}} = 300.8$; $\alpha^* \bar{G}_{\mathrm{dif}} \lambda^* = 12.35$				
$\alpha^* \bar{G}_{\mathrm{dif}}$	$\alpha^* \bar{G}_{\mathrm{dif}} \lambda^*$	IAE CC	IAE[a] SC	V_i (m/s)	IAE CC	IAE SC	CD CC (cm)	CD SC (cm)
119.4	2.35	2.188		1.18	0.220	0.6356	7.33×10^{-2}	1.29
200.5	8.35	1.4371	0.6356	2.36	1.133	27.069	3.22	3.98
300.8	12.35	0.2204		3.55	1.392	28.624	1.523	3.95

[a] The IAE index used to measure the performance of controller was defined by IAE $= \sqrt{\mathrm{Tr}\left[\int_0^T \tilde{h}(\lambda)\,d\lambda \int_0^T \tilde{h}^T(\lambda)\,d\lambda\right]} = \sqrt{\mathrm{IAE}_{x'}^2 + \mathrm{IAE}_{y'}^2}$. The labels CC represent the modified control law (26) and SC represent the convencional control law (8). The label CD represent the corner deviation when the modified control law (26) is used.

Contrarily to [8], where was shown that a linearizing static feedback law based on (8) guarantees the Theorem 1 for ε sufficiently smalls, we used a modified expression for the auxiliary control law (see (26)) and it was noted that this controller is more robust to slipping and skidding effects than (8) when different velocities at center of the wheels are set (see Table 1).

Acknowledgments. The authors would like to thank *Coordenação de Aperfeiçoamento de Pessoal de Nível Superior* (CAPES), all of them of Brazil, for the research grant, financial support and study fellowship.

References

1. Bloch, A.M., Reyhanoglu, M., McClamroch, N.H.: Control and stabilization of nonholonomic dynamic systems. IEEE Trans. Autom. Control **37**(11), 1746–1757 (1992)
2. Walsh, G., Tilbury, D., Sastry, S., Murray, R.: Stabilization of trajectories for systems with nonholonomic constraints. IEEE Trans. Autom. Control **39**(1), 216–222 (1994)
3. Chwa, D.: Sliding-mode tracking control of nonholonomic wheeled mobile robots in polar coordinates. IEEE Trans. Control Syst. Technol. **12**(4), 637–644 (2004)
4. Aithal, H., Janardhanan, S.: Trajectory tracking of two wheeled mobile robot using higher order sliding mode control. In: International Conference on Control Computing Communication & Materials, pp. 1–4 (2013)
5. Song, J., Boo, K.: Performance evaluation of traction control systems using a vehicle dynamic model. Proc. Inst. Mech. Eng. Part D J. Automobile Eng. **218**(7), 685–696 (2004)
6. Hamerlain, F., Achour, K., Floquet, T., Perruquetti, W.: Higher order sliding mode control of wheeled mobile robots in the presence of sliding effects. In: 44th IEEE Conference on Decision and Control, pp. 1959–1963 (2005)
7. Campion, G., Bastin, G., D'Andréa-Novel, B.: Structural properties and classification of kinematic and dynamic models of wheeled mobile robots. IEEE Trans. Robot. Autom. **12**(1), 47–62 (1996)
8. D'Andréa-Novel, B., Campion, G., Bastin, G.: Control of wheeled mobile robots not satisfying ideal velocity constraints: a singular perturbation approach. Int. J. Robust Nonlinear Control **5**(4), 243–267 (1995)
9. Fernández, C.A.P., Cerqueira, J.J.F., Lima, A.M.N.: Trajectory tracking control of an omnidirectional wheeled mobile robot with slip and deformation: a singular perturbation approach. In: 20th Brazilian Congress of Automatic. Belo Horizonte, Brazil (2014)
10. Fernández, C.A.P., Cerqueira, J.J.F., Lima, A.M.N.: Trajectory tracking control of nonholonomic wheeled mobile robots with slipping on curvilinear coordinates: a singular perturbation approach. In: 20th Brazilian Congress of Automatic. Belo Horizonte, Brazil (2014)
11. Fernández, C.A.P., Cerqueira, J.J.F.: Identificação de uma base holonômica para robôs moveis com escorregamento nas rodas usando um modelo narmax polinomial. In: 9th Brazilian Symposium on Intelligent Automation. Brasilia D.F., Brazil (2009)
12. Fernández, C.A.P., Cerqueira, J.J.F., Lima, A.M.N.: Dinâmica não-linear do escorregamento de um robô móvel omnidirecional com restrição de rolamento. In: 19th Brazilian Congress of Automatic. Campina Grande, Brazil (2012)

13. Fernández, C.A.P., Cerqueira, J.J.F., Lima, A.M.N.: Control of nonholonomic mobile bases supported by measuring of the slipping and skidding variations. In: Proceedings of the 2014 Joint Conference on Robotics: SBR-LARS Robotics Symposium and Robocontrol. IEEE Computer Society, São Carlos (2014)
14. Khalil, H.: Nonlinear Systems, 3rd edn. Prentice Hall, New Jersey (2002)
15. Motte, I., Campion, G.: A slow manifold approach for the control of mobile robots not satisfying the kinematic constraints. IEEE Trans. Robot. Autom. 16(6), 875–880 (2000)
16. Thuilot, B., D'Andréa-Novel, B., Micaelli, A.: Modeling and feedback control of mobile robots equipped with several steering wheels. IEEE Trans. Robot. Autom. 12(3), 375–390 (1996)
17. Bakker, E., Nyborg, L., Pacejka, H.: Tire modeling for use in vehicle dynamics studies. Soc. Autom. Eng. 2(870421), 190–204 (1987)
18. Stonier, D., Cho, S.-H., Choi, S.-L., Kuppuswamy, N.S., Kim, J.-H.: Nonlinear slip dynamics for an omniwheel mobile robot platform. In: IEEE International Conference on Robotics and Automation, Roma, Italy, pp. 2367–2372 (2007)
19. Balakrishna, R., Ghosal, A.: Modeling of slip for wheeled mobile robots. IEEE Trans. Robot. Autom. 11(1), 126–132 (1995)
20. Terry, J.D., Minor, M.A.: Traction estimation and control for mobile robots using the wheel slip velocity. In: IEEE International Conference on Intelligent Robots and Systems, Nice, France, pp. 2003–2009 (2008)
21. Liu, Y., Zhu, J.J., Williams II, R.L., Wu, J.: Omni-directional mobile robot controller based on trajectory linearization. Robot. Auton. Syst. 56(5), 461–479 (2008)

Automatic Semantic Waypoint Mapping Applied to Autonomous Vehicles

Matheus Zoccoler, Patrick Y. Shinzato, Alberto Y. Hata$^{(\boxtimes)}$, and Denis F. Wolf

Mobile Robotics Laboratory – LRM/ICMC, University of São Paulo,
São Carlos, São Paulo, Brazil
{matheusz,shinzato,hata,denis}@icmc.usp.br

Abstract. Road network maps have been used for autonomous vehicle path planning. These maps are basically formed by GPS waypoints and can contain semantic information about the environment to help following traffic codes. This paper describes a novel method for automatic construction of a waypoint map containing semantic information about roads. The collected GPS points are stored into flexible waypoint data structures that can represent any relevant information for vehicle navigation. The mapping method also reduces the amount of waypoints by recognizing and converting them into traffic structures. The resulting waypoint map is stored in a text file which is both human and machine-readable. This work makes part of CaRINA II platform, an autonomous vehicle under development by the Mobile Robotics Laboratory (LRM) - ICMC/USP. Tests were conducted in urban environment and the resulting maps were consistent when compared to publicly available satellite maps.

1 Introduction

In order to determine the optimal path for an autonomous vehicle reach a destination, it is important to maintain the road network of the environment. The road network is an environment representation that informs the traversable paths and may contain information about traffic signals and obstacles present in the streets. Basically, the road network map is formed by a set of waypoints that can be expanded to store semantic information as lanes, crosswalks and stop signs. Some authors denominate this structure as topological maps [10,14].

Some road network mapping methods focus only on storing a set of GPS data in a graph structure to represent the connection between locations. In [17] vehicle GPS pose data are plotted in a bitmap and its skeleton computed. Then a graph extraction algorithm is applied to extract the road network graph. The work in [14] combines GPS and LIDAR sensor to detect the road surface and build a metric map. A road skeletonization algorithm is used to convert the metric map

D.F. Wolf—The authors acknowledge the grant provided by FAPESP (process no. 10/01305-1 and 12/02354-1) and CNPq (process no. 158581/2013-0), and thank the Mobile Robotics Laboratory members for their support.

F.S. Osório et al. (Eds.): LARS/SBR/Robocontrol 2014, CCIS 507, pp. 96–113, 2015.
DOI: 10.1007/978-3-662-48134-9_6

into a topometric map (topological map with metric information). Some works add semantic information in the obtained road network map. [9] represented static and dynamic obstacles in a map to retrieve the trajectory of the obstacles. [10] developed a topological map that integrates geographic information system (GIS) data. The topological map node stores the type of horizontal signalization, type of lane, lane width and curb height. The work of [5] extended the Route Network Definition File (RNDF) format specified for DARPA Urban Challenge. The proposed file named RNDFGraph adds graph structure in which the nodes can store any traffic information such as traffic lights and stop restrictions.

Despite the automatic construction of the road network, these works require manual specification of the traffic information associated with each node. Thus, the map building process can be exhaustive and take long time. In this work we propose a road network map that automatically relates waypoints with any traffic information. The mapping method is integrated with the vehicle perception system, therefore, the detected traffic elements are associated on-the-fly with the waypoints that corresponds to the detected pose. In this work, we focused on the detection of roundabouts and lane structures. The roundabouts are represented using its centers and radiuses. Lanes are represented through a list of waypoints. We also store the interconnections between these structures. This representation model allows us to reduce the stored data size. Another advantage of our mapping process is the capability of handling sparse GPS data thanks to the lane points smoothing. The map data is stored in YAML format which is a human-readable markup like language.

We tested the proposed road network mapping using GPS data collected in real urban environments through an autonomous vehicle prototype named CaRINA II [6]. The reconstruction of roundabouts and lanes were compared with publicly available satellite aerial maps and were integrated with navigation system of CaRINA II to experimental tests in the campus of University of São Paulo (USP).

This paper is structured as follows. Section 2 details the automatic semantic waypoint mapping method. Section 3 describes all the software framework used to build and represent the map and the navigation system of CaRINA II. Section 4 presents the obtained results in urban environments and Sect. 5 concludes this work.

2   Route Map Processing

The route map processing is the core of this work as it converts the GPS points into more compact and suitable information for vehicle navigation. These structures allow us to classify each point with different semantic values, for instance, roundabouts points and lane points. In short, we eliminate points without losing world information by applying filters and detecting traffic structures. Also, specific tags can be appended to a waypoint to indicate location or traffic information.

The entire system follows eight steps performed sequentially to obtain the road network map. The first one is the speed bump detection, followed by a

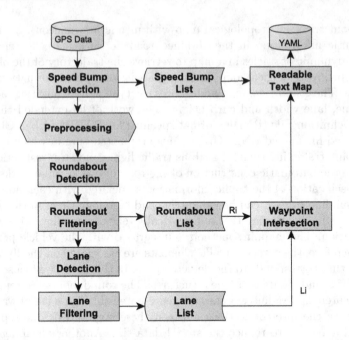

Fig. 1. Route map processing steps.

preprocessing step to eliminate a great amount of points obtained by the GPS. Then, the detection and filtering of roundabouts is performed. The same idea is applied to lanes. The subsequent step is responsible for evaluating and defining waypoint connections. At last, the resulting map is converted into human and machine readable text (YAML file). In Subsect. 2.9 we provide additional explanation on the visualization of the map, giving an overview of the steps performed after the map is generated. Figure 1 synthesizes the mapping method.

2.1 Speed Bump Detection

The information about the position of speed bumps make possible to set up the velocity of the vehicle to smoothly cross these structures. To detect speed bumps, the pitch value provided by an IMU was analyzed.

As speed bumps are formed by a steep ascend and descend, three events are produced in an IMU:

1. **Primary Pitch Variation:** Occured after front tires pass over the speed bump.
2. **Slight Pitch Variation:** Occured after the first event, front and back tires are between the speed bump.
3. **Secondary Pitch Variation:** Occured after back tires pass over the speed bump.

The red line of Fig. 2 shows the pitch signal produced by a car that traversed a speed bump. The pitch graph forms two peaks: the first (0.5 s ~ 1.5 s) is originated by event 1 and the second (2.0 s ~ 2.5 s) is originated by event 3.

In order to classify a sequence of pitch signals as a speed bump, we analyzed the pitch variation relative to the time. Basically, a simplified differential operator defined in Eq. 1 is applied in each pitch measurement.

$$\frac{df(t)}{dx} = \frac{\Delta f(t)}{\Delta t} \approx \frac{f(t+1) - f(t-1)}{(t+1) - (t-1)}$$
$$= \frac{f(t+1) - f(t-1)}{2}$$
$$\approx f(t+1) - f(t-1), \tag{1}$$

where $f(t)$ is the pitch value in time t. The effect of this operator in the pitch signal is illustrated by the blue line of Fig. 2.

Later, each differential value is compared if it is higher than a predefined threshold. Two consecutive positive results for the comparison implies in the detection of a speed bump. For our system, this detection implies in a specific tag for respective waypoint that is explained in the next section.

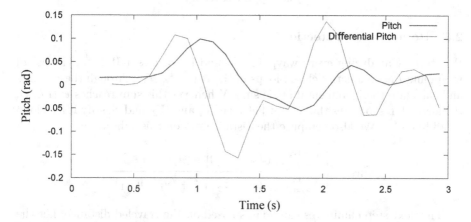

Fig. 2. Red line: pitch signal when crossing a speed bump. Two pikes are formed in the graph, each one representing respectively event 1 and 3. Blue line: differential operator appliend in the pitch values. Again, two peaks representing event 1 and 3 are formed (Color figure online).

2.2   Preprocessing

This stage is responsible for taking the GPS raw points and eliminating those where the distance is smaller than ϵ meters in relation to previous collected points. In other words, we skip points that do not add relevant trajectory information for vehicle navigation. We will denote the resulting list of points as L_{pp}.

Later, we compute the orientation for all points in L_{pp}. For every three points (p_{i-1}, p_i, p_{i+1}), the angle of p_i is calculated from the orientation of its neighbors (Eq. 2). This strategy is derived from the Mean Value Theorem and gives less orientation noise than if we used the angle from pairs of points.

$$\theta_i = tan^{-1}\left(\frac{y_{i+1} - y_{i-1}}{x_{i+1} - x_{i-1}}\right) \tag{2}$$

Eventually, point information are stored in a structure named *Waypoint* (W_i), which is comprised by the following items: *id* field to store an unique number to identify each point; x, y, θ fields to store the point position; *flag* field to classify the point type; and *tag* field for additional semantic information. Equation 3 summarizes the *Waypoint* structure.

$$W_i = \begin{cases} id: & \text{unique identifier} \\ x: & \text{longitudinal coordinate} \\ y: & \text{lateral coordinate} \\ \theta: & \text{orientation} \\ tag: & \text{point properties} \\ flag: & \text{point category.} \end{cases} \tag{3}$$

2.3   Roundabout Detection

We start by analyzing every waypoint W_i and its successor W_{i+1} in the list of waypoints L_W to identify closed-loops in the map. We seek through these points and calculate the incremental angle sum. Whenever this sum reaches ψ (Eq. 4), the algorithm separates this subset between W_1 and W_2, and classify it as a loop candidate C_W. We also compute the distance ran on this subset.

$$C_{W_i} = \begin{cases} \left|\sum_{j=W_1}^{W_2} (\theta_{j+1} - \theta_j)\right| = \psi \\ \sum_{j=W_1}^{W_2} \sqrt{(x_j - x_{j+1})^2 + (y_j - y_{j+1})^2} \end{cases} \tag{4}$$

The next step eliminates candidates based on the traveled distance. Let the greatest roundabout length be $2\pi\rho$ meters. We eliminate C_{W_i} if its distance ran is greater than $2\pi\rho$. This strategy avoids considering enormous closed-loop cycles (e.g. any subset starting and ending on the same point defines a loop).

We divide the remaining subset candidates into different groups G_W. Each G_W includes the subsets containing a possible roundabout (Fig. 3(a)). We notice the roundabout cycles that best define a roundabout are those where the traveled distance is the smallest among its group (Fig. 3(b)). Therefore, we take the subsets with smallest distance in every G_W and classify them as our roundabout candidates RC_W.

In order to find the optimal circle that best fits RC_W, we end up with a least squares problem. Specifically, this is a two-dimensional circle fitting as described in [16]. We define the cost function as the squared distance from each point to the calculated solution:

$$J(x,y,r) = \sum_{i=W_1}^{W_2} \left(\sqrt{(x_i - C_x)^2 + (y_i - C_y)^2} - r \right)^2 \tag{5}$$

where the pair (C_x, C_y) represents the estimated circle center coordinates, r is the estimated radius and (x_i, y_i) are each sample point coordinates belonging to RC_W.

Since this is a non-linear problem for which no closed-form solutions can be derived, we apply iterative methods [3,4]. Here, we choose the Gauss-Newton method with the Levenberg-Marquardt correction [11,12]. Also known as Levenberg-Marquardt method, this solution was adopted for its high rate of convergence and high probability of convergence given a random initial guess [3,8]. We used as the initial guess, the first data set point position and the maximum roundabout radius parameter ρ.

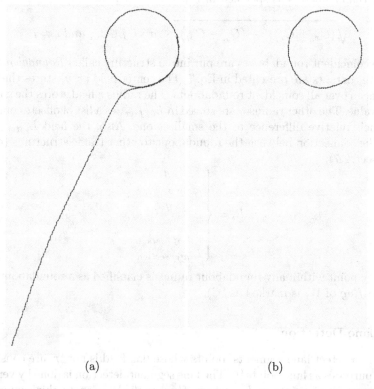

(a)   (b)

Fig. 3. Closed-loop detection. In (a) several subset candidates with distance smaller than $2\pi\rho$ meters are represented. The subset with the smallest traveled distance is selected in (b).

The Levenberg-Marquardt minimization was performed through MINPACK library (details in Subsect. 3.1). The method results a list L_R containing roundabouts centers and radiuses (Fig. 4(a)).

The last step applies a statistical analysis to check the fitting performance and, therefore, evaluate the calculated roundabouts. There are some fitting performance methods described in literature as Anderson-Darling, Kolmogorov-Smirnov and Chi-Square goodness-of-fit tests [18]. We take the latter one, the Chi-Square goodness-of-fit test, as it applies to discrete distributions, while the others can only be applied to continuous distributions.

The Chi-Square method is taken for a significance percentage level α. Any element in L_R with P-value smaller than α is rejected.

2.4   Roundabout Filtering

This filter groups together roundabouts detected in the previous step. We first compare the center of each roundabout with others present in L_R. Two roundabouts are considered coincident if the Euclidean distance between their centers is lower than σ meters as specified in Eq. 6.

$$\sqrt{\left(C_{x_i} - C_{x_j}\right)^2 + \left(C_{y_i} - C_{y_j}\right)^2} < \sigma \; \forall i, j \in L_R \; and \; i \neq j \tag{6}$$

The coincident roundabouts are put into a structure called *Roundabout*. This structure contents are presented in Eq. 7. The center field (x, y) stores the arithmetic mean over all coincident roundabouts. The radius r field stores the smallest radius value. The other radiuses are stored in $L_{offsets}$ as a list of offsets computed from their relative difference to the smallest one. Also, the field $L_{intersections}$ stores the connection between the roundabout to other traffic structures (details in Subsect. 2.7).

$$R_i = \begin{cases} id \\ x \\ y \\ r \\ L_{offsets} \\ L_{intersection} \end{cases} \tag{7}$$

Every point within any roundabout radius is classified as a roundabout point (i.e. the *flag* of W_i is marked as 'r').

2.5   Lane Detection

In order to detect lane segments, points whose flag field is not 'r' are considered for our purposes as lane points 'l'. The lane segment detection is done by verifying every sequence of points in L_W where $flag_i$ is 'l'. We denote this sequence as $L_{lane\,point}$. In this work, without loss of generality, every $L_{lane\,point}$ will end in a roundabout or in the last point of L_W. Hereafter, they may end in other detectable structures implemented. The notation used for lane segments is shown in Eq. 8.

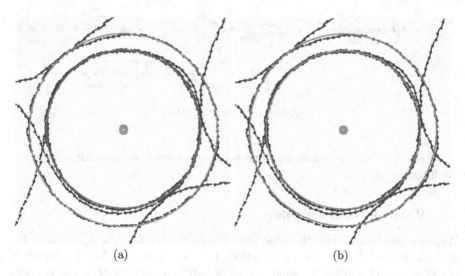

(a)   (b)

Fig. 4. Levenberg-Marquardt fitting results. The orange and the magenta roundabout in (a) were collected at different times and have slightly different centers. In (b) we perform the roudabout filtering to merge them into one *Roundabout* structure (Color figure online).

$$L_i = \begin{cases} id \\ L_{lane\,point} \\ L_{intersection}. \end{cases} \tag{8}$$

2.6 Lane Filtering

The method for eliminating unnecessary lane points is performed on those points located in straight paths where a line can be defined between a waypoint W_A and a waypoint W_B. Any points between W_A and W_B can be eliminated without losing map information.

Considering a lane L_i, let W_c denote the current waypoint being analyzed, which is initially set as the first point of $L_{lane\,point}$. We append W_c to our filtered list FL_W and set $j = c + 1$. The loop starts by taking W_j in $L_{lane\,point}$. We compare the absolute angle difference between W_j and W_c as in Eq. 9. If it is smaller than ϕ degrees, then we proceed to the next loop iteration with $j = j + 1$. Otherwise, we append W_j to FL_W and set it as the new W_c. Figure 5 presents the lane filtering flowchart.

$$|\theta_j - \theta_c| < \phi \tag{9}$$

Eventually, we obtain the FL_W and compute orientation corrections as specified in Eq. 2. Another filtering is performed on FL_W originating an auxiliary structure $FL_{W_{new}}$. We repeat this filtering algorithm until the size of $FL_{W_{new}}$ is equal to FL_W, meaning that the process can no longer filter out points.

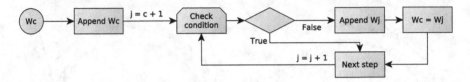

Fig. 5. Lane filter algorithm.

In Fig. 6 we illustrate how the lane points are greatly reduced after applying the filtering process.

2.7 Waypoint Intersections

We have seen previously that the intersection field - $L_{intersection}$ defined for *Roundabout* and *Lane* - stores connections between structures. We developed an algorithm to automatically connect roundabouts and lane points. These connections allow the vehicle to navigate through the map.

The solution involves concepts from analytic geometry applied to a line to circle intersection problem. The two possible cases we might encounter are represented in Fig. 7, where P represents the last point in $L_{lane\,point}$, C is the roundabout center, C_l is the closest point to C and X is the desired connection.

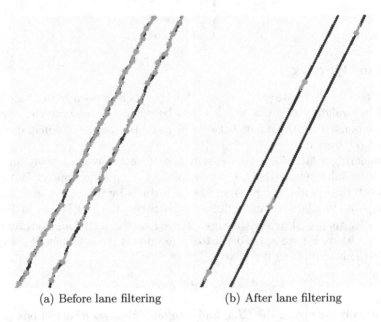

(a) Before lane filtering   (b) After lane filtering

Fig. 6. Lane noise reduction. The lane points are shown in green and the red lines represent the trajectory calculated through splines (explained in Subsect. 2.9) (Color figure online).

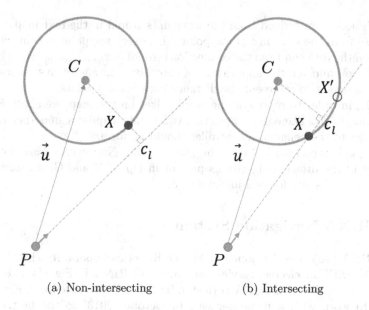

(a) Non-intersecting   (b) Intersecting

Fig. 7. Intersection estimation between lanes and roundabouts.

2.8   Readable Text Map

The production of a readable text map involves writing the main structures created in the previous steps. By main structures we mean those necessary to reconstruct the map if only the text file is provided. In our work we have to write *Roundabout* and *Lane* structures. The organization and readability of the text file is facilitated using YAML format.

YAML is a human-readable data serialization file format. It provides a simple and unified synthax for the main data types found in most programming languages (e.g. scalars, arrays and dictionaries). It was designed to be more human-friendly than existing markup languages. The structures written to YAML file can be easily comprehended and modified by the user - an advantage if one wants to add new waypoints to the map or make changes to the semantic information.

2.9   Map Visualization

We will briefly describe the strategies used to graphically represent waypoints and intersections. Although these strategies do not integrate a step in route map processing, they are important to correctly visualize the map according to the trajectory a controller will follow if it uses our map. The results presented in Sect. 4 use these strategies.

The read map is transported to a directed graph structure. This idea best defines the traversable paths the car can follow given a destination. Moreover, any shortest path algorithm may be used to calculate the best route.

Graph nodes are defined from the waypoints stored in the text map. Graph edges arise from the sequence of waypoints (i.e. every waypoint is connected to the next on the list) and from the connections stored in $L_{intersection}$. For a better representation and for the application of shortest path algorithms, edges may also have a weight to represent the distance between waypoints.

Finally, in order to represent the graph edges on the map, we apply Bézier spline concepts [7]. The edges connecting two points acquire a smoother trajectory, similar to the behavior a controller should perform.

This graph structure is better organized using NetworkX. Also, we take advantage of the drawing algorithms present in OpenCV and Gephi softwares. These frameworks are detailed in Subsect. 3.1.

3   CaRINA Navigation System

The CaRINA project is developed at Mobile Robotics Laboratory (LRM) since April 2010 with an electric service car named CaRINA I (Fig. 8(a)). In July 2011, the acquisition of CaRINA II (a standard Fiat Palio Adventure, Fig. 8(b)) enabled to work with a passenger car. In October 2013, to the best of our knowledge it has been the first commercial vehicle in Latin America capable of performing autonomous navigation in the streets. This section describes some software frameworks used in this work and the navigation system architecture of CaRINA II using our semantic waypoint map.

3.1   Software Framework

This section describes the frameworks that provide connection between the mapping service and the car navigation module. They are responsible for the construction and the graphical representation of the road network.

(a) CaRINA I   (b) CaRINA II

Fig. 8. The platforms of CaRINA project.

- The MINPACK-1 library provides several performance optimized algorithms to solve least squares minimization problems [13].
- NetworkX is a library used for graph manipulation and study. It depicts graph adjacencies and provides standard graph algorithms.
- OpenCV provides an extensive set of functions for computer vision and machine learning [2].
- Gephi is an open source software for graph and network analysis [1]. The software produces good visualizations of graph structures.
- ROS is a service-based architecture for robot software development [15]. In ROS, robot subsystems are separated into nodes and their communication is performed by sending messages or subscribing to topics. This architecture makes the integration with different subsystems easier. ROS also provides a set of visualization and log data managing tools.

3.2   CaRINA II Platform and Architecture

As CaRINA II is developed under ROS [6], then the entire system is divided by modules that each one is responsible for a specific task. The proposed mapping

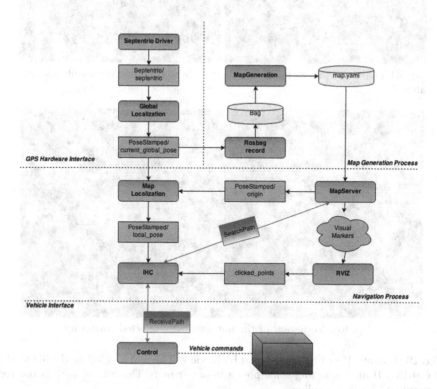

Fig. 9. System architecture: In currently navigation system, the higher level is divided in two major parts: the map generation process, and the navigation process.

system is inserted in the higher level of navigation system (showed in Fig. 9) of CaRINA II using several ROS libraries. The currently navigation system is divided in two major parts: the "Map Generation Process" and the "Navigation Process". The first one is responsible for recording all poses from a path to a posterior offline map-processing that generates our semantic map-file. The latter loads our map file and provides some services to interact with the user, giving it the option to select a goal for the robot vehicle to follow.

As shown in Fig. 9, the part of flowchart named "GPS Hardware Interface" is required for both process (Map-Generation and Navigation) and it is a set of programs used to connect to the GPS device and transform information like latitude, longitude, roll, pitch and yaw to a 3D pose. The part called "Map Generation Process" contains only two steps: first is a recorder of all pose-3D, and the second is an offline program that performs all methods presented in the previous section. This node is responsible to compute all information of an urban environment, compose our semantic map and save this information in a file.

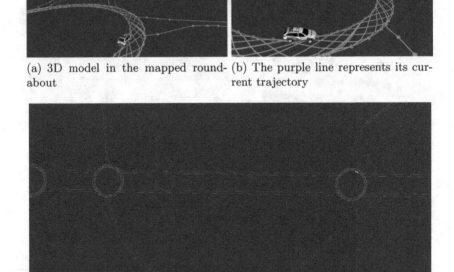

(a) 3D model in the mapped round-about

(b) The purple line represents its current trajectory

(c) A top down view of the automatically selected trajectory

Fig. 10. Campus II of USP São Carlos RVIZ view. The user can follow the 3D model of CaRINA II after selecting some points from our map. The current path is painted in purple (Color figure online).

The second major part of Fig. 9 ("Navigation Process") contains a set of programs that provide all required information to path selection, localization, control and interface with the user. The "MapServer" is a node that loads our map-file and provides a visual structure through RVIZ node (see Fig. 10). Also, our MapServer node provides the global position of the map to "MapLocalization" node in order to compute the position of the vehicle using only GPS information. At last, IHC node is responsible for listening a specific topic from RVIZ program. The topic *clicked_points* is activated whenever the user selects a goal point from our map. The IHC node gets the current position and the goal point, and uses "MapServer" service to calculate the shortest path on the map. This path is sent to the control module (described in [7]) that will generate several command actions to CaRINA II execute.

Although the vehicle interface is composed of several nodes, Fig. 9 shows a single node for simplicity. The control module receives an array of 3D points representing the path to follow. In this module, the longitudinal and lateral control are decoupled and they depend on a reduced number of parameters that can be easily set. The longitudinal control considers inclined roads, then tries to establish the relationship between acceleration and throttle or brake pedal position in order to maintain a constant velocity. The lateral controller uses a cubic Bézier curve to find a short trajectory defined by the path received from IHC node.

4   Experimental Results and Discussions

The proposed road network mapping method defines a set of parameters that can be adjusted according to the scenario.

- ϵ – minimum distance in meters between points for initial preprocessing.
- ψ – loop detection angle in radians (close to 2π).
- ρ – maximum detectable roundabout radius in meters.
- σ – coincident roundabout tolerance in meters.
- ϕ – curvature threshold in degrees.
- α – significance percentage level for Chi-Square goodness-of-fit test.
- δ – distance in meters between reconstructed roundabout points.

These parameters are essential for our detection methods as they help on generating a simplified map. Nevertheless, they do not limit the robustness of the proposed solution as their values are simple to set based on visual characteristics observed in any real world scenario.

We collected the data set for our tests in an urban environment (Campus II of USP São Carlos) using a Xsens MTI-G GPS/INS device. The location is convenient as it has a good number of roundabouts with one or two lanes.

The test track has around 5 km and the corresponding satellite aerial map is illustrated in Fig. 11. Every two-way road was driven on both directions and we did a complete loop in every roundabout lane.

Fig. 11. Campus II of USP São Carlos satellite view and resulting map shown in red (Color figure online).

The resulting map (red lines of Fig. 11) matched the satellite view of the same area without applying any correction (e.g. SLAM). The slight offset could be corrected if a DGPS device was used.

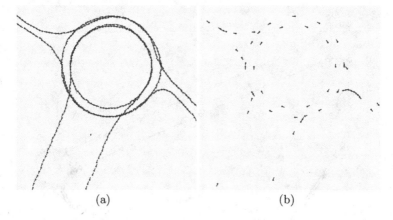

(a)   (b)

Fig. 12. Overall points reduction. (a) Preprocessed GPS points and (b) the resulting points for $\delta = 10$ meters.

The roundabout and lane filters could reduce the amount of waypoints as illustrated in Fig. 12. Dense waypoint dataset (Fig. 12(a)) are simplified to sparse waypoints without losing road shape (Fig. 12(b)). The roundabouts were transformed into artificial points with a distance δ due to the fact CaRINA II control system only works given a list of points.

Using graph structure to represent the road network map (Subsect. 2.9) we obtained the map shown in Fig. 13. Lane waypoints are shown in green and roundabout waypoints in blue. The edge weights, that correspond to the distance between nodes, are represented by a red color gradient (darker red is associated with higher weights).

For the method presented in Subsect. 2.3 an important consideration has to be respected. In order to detect a roundabout, the vehicle must have driven around the roundabout completing a full loop. If the dataset was not recorded respecting this restriction, the roundabouts may not be properly detected. Besides, a poorly set ρ parameter can result in the detection of roundabouts that actually are city blocks with a circular shape.

Although the roundabouts are mostly circular, one may find elliptical roundabouts or similar shaped objects. Our method will most likely reject these structures due to our Chi-Square approach. However, it will fail to reject two-level circular loops (such as in cloverleaf interchanges) because our method does not consider elevation coordinates.

The evaluation of the route map processing method was conducted visually. There are few options to compare the results numerically. The only recommended option involves the utilization of a ground truth. However, we could not apply it to our data as the GPS used to record them did not have a good precision (about 2.5 m).

The navigation experiments were performed in campus 2 of USP - São Carlos and showed a robust and user-friendly navigation system. Also, the navigation

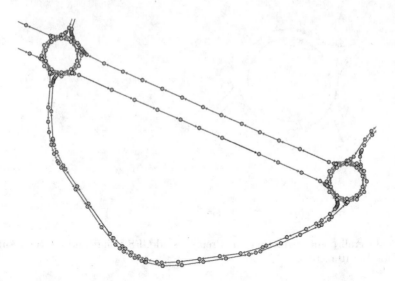

Fig. 13. Graph visualization of the east area of Fig. 11 using Gephi (Color figure online).

system architecture divided in several modules and the possibility to show the path that the vehicle is following allows integration with several other experiments like control and perception systems.

5   Conclusion

In this paper we presented a novel method for automatic construction of a waypoint map containing semantic information about roads. We developed processing steps that implement flexible waypoint structures and help reducing the number of waypoints. In the future, we plan to append more information to the semantic waypoint structures by integrating data collected from other sensors. We will study detection solutions for cross intersections and cloverleaf interchanges. Also, maps from different datasets collected in the same region shall be put together. In addition to this, the upcoming acquisition of a GPS unit with RTK will enable state-of-the-art comparative results.

References

1. Bastian, M., Heymann, S., Jacomy, M.: Gephi: An Open Source Software for Exploring and Manipulating Networks (2009)
2. Bradski, G., Kaehler, A.: Learning OpenCV: Computer Vision with the OpenCV Library. O'Reilly Media, Sebastopol (2008)
3. Chernov, N., Lesort, C.: Least squares fitting of circles. J. Math. Imaging Vis. **23**(3), 239–252 (2005)

4. Chernov, N.: Circular and Linear Regression: Fitting Circles and Lines by Least Squares. CRC Press, Boca Raton (2010)
5. Czerwionka, P., Wang, M., Wiesel, F.: Optimized route network graph as map reference for autonomous cars operating on German autobahn. In: 2011 5th International Conference on Automation, Robotics and Applications (ICARA), pp. 78–83, Dec 2011
6. Fernandes, L.C., Souza, J.R., Pessin, G., Shinzato, P.Y., Sales, D., Mendes, C., Prado, M., Klaser, R., Magalhães, A.C., Hata, A., Pigatto, D., Branco, K.C., Grassi Jr., V., Osorio, F.S., Wolf, D.F.: CaRINA intelligent robotic car: architectural design and applications. J. Syst. Architect. **60**(4), 372–392 (2014)
7. Filho, C.M., Wolf, D.F., Grassi Jr., V., Osório, F.S.: Longitudinal and lateral control for autonomous ground vehicles. In: 2014 IEEE Intelligent Vehicles Symposium (IV) (2014)
8. Gander, W., Golub, G., Strebel, R.: Least-squares fitting of circles and ellipses. BIT Num. Math. **34**(4), 558–578 (1994)
9. Jin, P., Zhang, X.: A new approach to modeling city road network. In: 2010 International Conference on Computer Application and System Modeling (ICCASM), vol. 2, pp. V2–305–V2–309, Oct 2010
10. Lee, Y.C., Christiand, Yu, W., Kim, S.: Satellite image based topological map building method for intelligent mobile robots. In: 2012 IEEE Intelligent Vehicles Symposium (IV), pp. 867–872, June 2012
11. Levenberg, K.: A method for the solution of certain non-linear problems in least squares. Quart. Appl. Math. **2**, 164–168 (1944)
12. Marquardt, D.W.: An algorithm for least-squares estimation of nonlinear parameters. SIAM J. Appl. Math. **11**(2), 431–441 (1963)
13. Moré, J.J., Garbow, B.S., Hillstrom, K.E.: User Guide for MINPACK-1. ANL-80-74, Argonne National Laboratory (1980)
14. Qin, B., Chong, Z., Bandyopadhyay, T., Ang, M.: Metric mapping and topo-metric graph learning of urban road network. In: 2013 6th IEEE Conference on Robotics, Automation and Mechatronics (RAM), pp. 119–123, Nov 2013
15. Quigley, M., Conley, K., Gerkey, B.P., Faust, J., Foote, T., Leibs, J., Wheeler, R., Ng, A.Y.: ROS: an open-source robot operating system. In: ICRA Workshop on Open Source Software (2009)
16. Shakarji, C.M.: Least-squares fitting algorithms of the NIST algorithm testing system. J. Res. Nat. Inst. Stand. Technol. **103**(6), 633–641 (1998)
17. Shi, W., Shen, S., Liu, Y.: Automatic generation of road network map from massive GPS, vehicle trajectories. In: 12th International IEEE Conference on Intelligent Transportation Systems, ITSC 2009, pp. 1–6, Oct 2009
18. Snedecor, G., Cochran, W.: Statistical Methods. Statistical Methods, vol. 276. Iowa State University Press, Ames (1989)

RoboSeT: A Tool to Support Cataloging and Discovery of Services for Service-Oriented Robotic Systems

Lucas Bueno Ruas Oliveira[1,2](✉), Felipe Augusto Amaral[1], Diogo B. Martins[1], Flavio Oquendo[2], and Elisa Yumi Nakagawa[1]

[1] Department of Computer Systems, University of São Paulo - USP, São Carlos, SP, Brazil
{oliveira,elisa}@icmc.usp.br, {felipeaa,dbrdem}@usp.br
[2] IRISA Research Institute, University of South Brittany, Vannes, France
flavio.oquendo@irisa.fr

Abstract. Robotics has played an increasingly important role in several sectors of the society. Nowadays, robots are not only used to support activities in factories, but also to assist house cleaning, border surveillance, and even surgeries. The variety of application domains and the rising complexity are challenging the design of robotic systems that control such robots. In this perspective, Service-Oriented Architecture (SOA) has been adopted as a promising architectural style to design large, complex robotic systems in a flexible and reusable manner. Several Service-Oriented Robotic Systems (SORS) have been developed in the recent years and a large number of services are available for reuse. Nevertheless, none of the environments dedicated to the development of SORS provide an efficient mechanism for publishing and discovering services. As a consequence, services for SORS have to be manually searched, reducing significantly the potential of reuse and productivity provided by SOA. This paper presents RoboSeT, a mechanism that supports cataloging and discovery of services for robotic systems. RoboSeT is based on semantic search and classifies the services using a taxonomy of the robotics domain. Results of our case study indicate that RoboSeT facilitates the development of robotic systems, since it presents the potential to widely promote reusability of services for SORS.

1 Introduction

The rapidly growing advancements in robot technology are enabling its use in a broad range of applications for the society. Robots are no longer exclusively used to perform fast, repetitive tasks in controlled environments of factories. The actual generation of robots is being produced to operate along with humans and to support daily activities inside hospitals [37], houses [22], and on the streets [13,40]. Robotic systems that are used to control such robots are becoming increasingly large, complex, and integrated to other devices of the environment. As a consequence, reusability, productivity, scalability, and flexibility are now

© Springer-Verlag Berlin Heidelberg 2015
F.S. Osório et al. (Eds.): LARS/SBR/Robocontrol 2014, CCIS 507, pp. 114–132, 2015.
DOI: 10.1007/978-3-662-48134-9_7

intrinsic concerns of the robotic systems development. To accommodate such characteristics, the design of robotic systems has evolved from procedural paradigm to object-orientation and, then, to component-orientation [6]. Recently, Service-Oriented Architecture (SOA) [33] has become focus of attention as a promising architectural style for developing robotic systems.

SOA is an architectural style traditionally used in commercial, business systems developed in the industry [1]. It has also been increasingly adopted to develop systems for diverse domains of the academia, such as education [9] and software testing [29]. SOA-based systems are developed by assembling independent, self-contained, and well-defined modules of software called services [32]. Each service shares a set of functionalities that are language-independent and provided through auto-descriptive standard interfaces. Service descriptions can be published in third-party repositories that act as brokers and enable discovery of services by consumers in transparent way. Therefore, SOA promotes the reuse and improves productivity of software systems development [32].

In robotics, SOA has been adopted as a solution to produce more flexible, reconfigurable, and scalable software for robotic systems. The use of SOA is enabling developers to overcome traditional problems of robotics design, such as the integration of heterogeneous hardware devices and reuse of complex algorithms [2]. Several studies reporting on the development of Service-Oriented Robotic Systems (SORS) can be found in the literature and a large number of services are already available for reuse [30]. Most of these services were developed on two well-known environments specially focused on SORS: Robot Operating System (ROS) [36] and Microsoft Robotic Developed Studio (MRDS) [24]. These environments provide functionalities that support creation, execution, and composition of services for different types of robotic systems.

Nevertheless, environments available for the development of SORS lack an important element of SOA: they do not provide an efficient mechanism for publishing and discovering services. Currently, developers of SORS need to manually search the services in repositories containing hundreds of different services. For instance, users have to previously know the name of the services they are going to use in the ROS Wiki[1] repository. Besides that, users of such repository need to follow daily updates in the site to be aware of any new content available. These time-consuming tasks significantly reduce the potential of SOA in providing reuse and hence decrease productivity of SORS development. In this context, a mechanism that enables to catalog and discover services can contribute to the SORS development process, as well as to dissemination of resources useful for the robotics community.

The main objective of this paper is to put forward RoboSeT (Robotics Services Semantic Search Tool), a mechanism that supports cataloging and discovery of services for SORS. Using RoboSeT, robotics services are classified according to a common-sense taxonomy of services for SORS [31] and can be searched using semantic information. These services can be transparently discovered by other developers and integrated into different development environments.

---

[1] http://www.ros.org/browse/list.php.

In this work, we also present a plug-in that integrates ROS with the repository of RoboSeT and enables discovery and deployment of services for SORS directly into projects of such development environment. In order to obtain evidences on the viability of RoboSeT, we designed a robotic system with robust navigation capabilities by reusing ROS services cataloged and discovered in such mechanism. Results indicate that RoboSeT facilitates the discovery of reusable robotics services, which can contribute to a higher productivity during the development of SORS.

The remainder of the paper is organized as follows. Section 2 presents a background on software reuse, robotic systems reuse, and SORS. Section 3 overviews the taxonomy of services on which the repository is based. Section 4 describes RoboSeT, its integration to the development environments, and the plug-in for ROS. Section 5 addresses our case study on the design of a robust mobile robotic system. Section 6 discusses the results, perspectives, and limitations of our work. Section 7 presents the conclusion and future directions of this work.

2   Software Reuse: From Libraries to Services

Software reuse is a key principle of software development that aims at reducing the effort to develop new software by promoting the systematic use of existing solutions. Systematic reuse is recognized as one of the most important approaches to improve productivity and quality [15]. First attempts to systematically incorporate reuse during software development focused on the use of existing subroutines provided as libraries. With the emergence of object-oriented languages, reuse techniques started to adopt classes of objects as main elements of reuse. Object-oriented systems are collections of objects, which encapsulate state, behaviour, and communicate through messages. The whole behaviour of an object-oriented system is determined by the structure of interaction and communication among its objects.

As software systems become larger in both size and complexity, simple reuse of classes and objects evolved to a higher level of abstraction and the importance of design and architecture increased. The adoption of design patters [17], architectural styles [38], and reference architectures [28] during the development of software systems made it possible to reuse not only software design assets but also the knowledge and expertise that lead to such design. Design patterns describe general reusable solutions to commonly occurring problems of software design. Architectural styles shape software systems by enforcing a set of design constraints and architectural decisions to provide predictable, well-known quality properties. In parallel, reference architectures support reuse of design expertise and encompass knowledge of how to structure software systems on specific domains.

Similarly to systems in other domains, there is also a strong move towards the use of software engineering to reduce the effort to develop robotic systems. Several studies focusing on systematic reuse during the development of robotic systems can be found in literature. For instance, Fryer et al. [16] investigate the use of object-orientation to develop modular software for controlling robots. Graves and Czarnecki [18] propose design patterns for developing behaviour-based robotic systems. The systematic literature review described in [12] reports on reference architectures for mobile robotic systems. The work presented in [6] discusses on the use of Component-Based Software Engineering (CBSE) for designing robotic systems as a set of architectural building blocks. In parallel, Model-Driven Engineering (MDE) and Software Product Lines (SPL) techniques have been adopted to support the application of CBSE in robotic systems development. For instance, Iborra et al. [21] associate MDE and CBSE with reference architectures in a process to design robotic systems. The BRICS project [4] uses CBSE and SPL for reducing the development effort of engineering robotic systems. CBSE and SPL are also used as a basis for incorporating certification activity into the design of unmanned aerial vehicles [3]. These works and several others already identified by Schlegel et al. [35] represent important contributions to robotic system development.

More recently, researchers have been investigating the suitability of SOA architectural style for developing robotic systems that are not only reusable, but also more flexible, integrable, and scalable. In a broad, systematic literature review carried out in a previous work [30], we identified 39 studies dedicated to investigate and consolidate the use of SOA in robotics. According to such review, the first attempt to use SOA in robotics was proposed in 2003 by Lee et al. [26], which described an architecture for integrating different robots in a multi-robotic application. Similarly, Ha et al. [19] designed a SOA to support integration among robots and remote sensors in an aware house. With the advent of the first environment focused on the development of SORS, the commercial MRDS, several other systems emerged in literature [7,8]. Currently, ROS development environment is being used as a basis for building a second generation of SORS [25,41]. ROS is an open source environment supported by several research institutes and has already been adopted to design over a thousand of services for SORS. Despite the increasing adoption of SOA in robotics, as well as the support of dedicated tools, there is no mechanism that efficiently enables publication, categorization, and discovery of services for SORS. Unlike services used in commercial, business systems that can be transparently discovered, services for SORS need to be searched manually. Our first measure to mitigate such problem was establishing a taxonomy of types of service to enable the search of services by their functionalities and not simply by their names or textual descriptions. This taxonomy is presented in the following section.

3   A Taxonomy of Services for SORS

To automate the semantic search of services for SORS, it was necessary to organize knowledge about the domain and establish a common vocabulary among stakeholders. Therefore, we proposed a taxonomy [31], which is a form of classification widely accepted in different domains, such as software architecture [10] and robotics [11]. This taxonomy of services is based on the SORS available in the literature [30], a set of reference architectures of robotics [12], and expertise and knowledge of specialists on how to develop robotic systems. It was evaluated by software architects, software engineers, software developers, and research team leaders from six different institutions of five countries, from both academy and industry.

The taxonomy classifies services for SORS into five main groups: (i) Device Driver, (ii) Knowledge, (iii) Task, (iv) Robotic Agent, and (v) Application. Its groups are also divided into several subgroups (types). A brief description of these groups of services and service types is presented as follows. For sake of space, the complete description of all groups and service types, as well as examples, is presented in another work [31].

- Device Driver: encompasses services that control hardware devices, providing their functionalities to other services. Services in this group are responsible for managing the data collection from the environment (i.e., drivers that control sensors) and controlling the interactions of the robot within it (i.e., drivers that control actuators). Sensor drivers are classified as follows: Position, Orientation, Movement, Contact, Distance, Optical, Thermal, and Communication. Actuator drivers are divided into the following service types: Locomotion, Manipulation, and Communication;
- Knowledge: comprises services responsible for gathering, interpreting, storing, and sharing information necessary for performing tasks and controlling the robot as a whole. These services enable the robotic system to learn about characteristics of its environment and objects within it. Knowledge services not only deal with data from sensors, but also with semantic information from a wide range of sources, such as ontologies or machine learning datasets. Services of knowledge group are divided into two types: Internal and external. Internal knowledge services manage information obtained from inside the environment, such as from sensors and back-end servers. External knowledge services manage information obtained from outside the environment, such as from the Web [39];
- Task: encompasses services that provide functionalities considered as the fundamental tasks of robotics. These services enable the robot to perform basic activities, such as moving from one place to another. A service of this group can be implemented according to different behaviours, i.e., a robot can move to another position by either following a wall or keeping the distance between walls. The following service types are encompassed by this group: Mapping (e.g., geometric and grid), Localization (e.g., probabilistic and deterministic), Path Planning (e.g., heuristic search and exhaustive search), Navigation/Control (e.g., reactive, deliberative, and hybrid), Interaction (e.g., with other robots or the environment), Object Manipulation, and Support (e.g., image segmentation and math calculation);
- Robotic Agent: encompasses services that provide high level functionalities to control the robot as a whole (i.e., robot as a service). Services of this group are responsible for coordinating other types of services, such as Task services and Device Driver services. A robotic agent as a service also enables the robot to

be remotely controlled and monitored. Services in these groups are classified as Non-mobile and Mobile (e.g., grounded, aquatic, and aerial); and

– Application: comprises services responsible for managing Robotic Agents in performing more complex activities. These services are particularly orchestrators [34], i.e., they acquire knowledge through the Robotic Agent services, process it, and then request a set of tasks that satisfy a given activity. Services in this groups are divided into the following types: Single Robot, Multi-robot, and Swarm.

This classification has formed the conceptual, initial base for automating cataloging and discovery of services in our mechanism. The next section describes how we developed the service repository and the plug-in for ROS and how these modules interact to enable the reuse of services.

4   Designing RoboSeT

We designed RoboSeT to automate the semantic search for services. This mechanism is composed of two main parts: the on-line service repository and the plug-ins that can be locally integrated into development environments. The service repository enables developers to publish robotics services hosted in different version control systems, such as Git[2] and SVN[3], and describe these services using the taxonomy proposed in the previous section. Each service registered by a service provider is classified according to the type it belongs to and can, therefore, be discovered semantically. Service consumers can search for services they need by using either the web interface provided by RoboSeT or a plug-in installed in their machines. Plug-ins are applications integrated into development environments that access the service repository and allows developers to search and obtain services. Using RoboSeT, services for SORS can be discovered and integrated into local projects transparently, i.e., the service consumer does not need to know where the service is located or who the service provider is in Fig. 1 illustrates the overall organization of the RoboSeT tool. Further details about its development and functionalities are provided as follows. Graphical examples and tutorials on how to use its functionalities are available in the Website[4].

4.1   Services Repository

RoboSeT enables users to store and classify information about robotics services in a repository, as well as search for services to be reused in their robotic systems. Registered service providers can publish and describe their services by using the taxonomy. These services are linked to a control version repository where they are hosted, and the provider describes how they work, license types, versions,

---

[2] http://git-scm.com/.

[3] http://subversion.tigris.org/.

[4] http://www.labes.icmc.usp.br:8595/RegistroServicoWeb/.

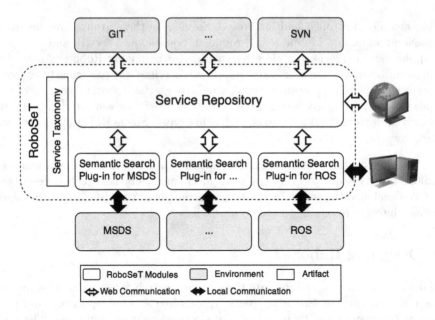

Fig. 1. Overview of RoboSeT

and so forth. Service consumers use the classification available in the taxonomy to search for services that provide the functionalities they need.

For instance, a consumer that needs a service for robotic localization based on a high precision GPS (Global Localization System) can search for a service whose type is "Service/Task/Localization/Non-probabilistic" (for more information about the types of services see [31]). This query would retrieve all services in the repository that provide a functionality of the Task type, related to Localization, and based solely on the information of a sensor, such as a GPS. A less precise search, like "Service/Task/Localization", would also retrieve services of the first query and all other services described as a subtype of Localization, e.g., probabilist localization services.

Figure 2 illustrates the result of a search performed in the RoboSeT service repository. In this screen, service consumers obtain a summary of the services retrieved in the search, such as names, providers, and related service types. Buttons in the right side of the screen can also be used for obtaining further information on a service, accessing its hosting address, or endorsing it. Endorsements are used to recommend a given service and indicate to other potential consumers that such service is a worthwhile choice. In addition to searches using the taxonomy, RoboSeT also provides the following functionalities:

– Account Management: an account is required for the access to the service repository. Three possible types of user are available: consumer, provider, and administrator. Consumers can search for and obtain services in the repository. Providers can obtain services for reuse and also publish their own services in

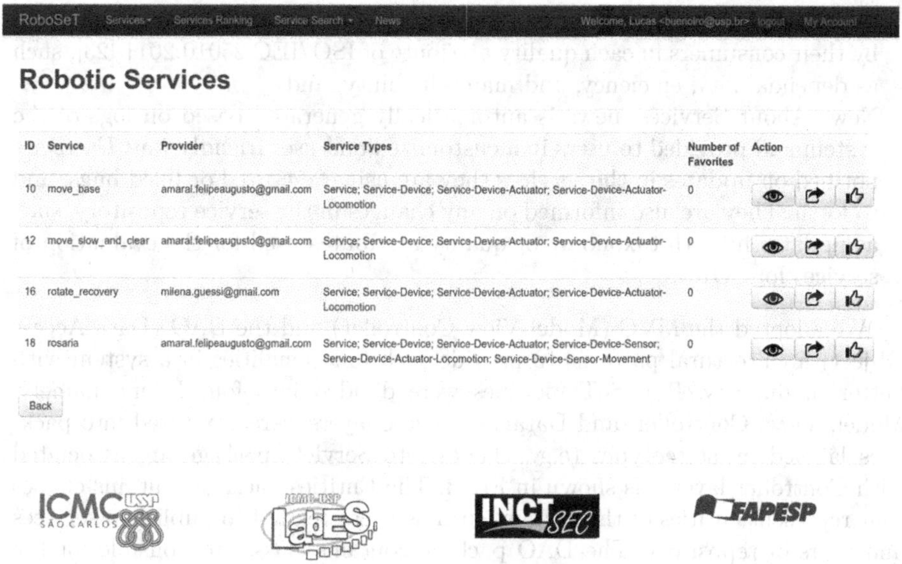

Fig. 2. Result of a search in the service repository

the system. Administrators manage accounts, the elements of the service taxonomy, and other important aspects of the systems. The account management
enables users to edit information and promote their account types from a consumer to a provider. Administrators can also invite consumers and providers
to administrate the service repository;
– Service Management: enables service consumers to get information on services
  they have already obtained, such as configuration instructions, comments from
  other users, and bug reports. Service providers can also manage their published
  services and register new services in the repository;
– Service Ranking: a ranking is provided for the most relevant services available in the repository, therefore, users can find services of better reputation
  and data about their providers. Similarly to the service search functionality,
  additional information on a given service can be obtained and the repository
  where the service is hosted can be accessed;
– Service Search: additionally to the search by type, it is possible to look for
  services using search strings. This type of search complements the semantic
  search and enables users to find services by their names and providers. Services
  are also obtained through searches in parts of the text contained in the service
  description;
– Service Detailing: enables service consumers to obtain all information available
  about a service, such as its full description, service dependencies, number of
  users, number of endorsements, versions, and license of use. Comments made
  by previous consumers and reported bugs are also available as references.
  A complete list of quality attributes is provided to support consumers in

identifying services of higher quality. Services in the repository can be graded by their consumers in each quality attribute of ISO/IEC 25010:2011 [23], such as dependability, efficiency, and maintainability; and

- News About Services: news is automatically generated based on logs of the system and provided to users in a customized and user friendly way. Users are notified on updates in the services they are using, reported or fixed bugs, and so forth. They are also informed on any changes in the service repository, such as updates in both taxonomy or quality attributes used for the evaluation of services for SORS.

We adopted the MVC (Model-View-Controller) and the DAO (Data Access Object) architectural patterns to provide such functionalities in a system with better modularity. RoboSeT modules were divided into four layers, namely: Model, View, Controller, and Database. These layers were organized into packages labeled by stereotypes (e.g., classes into Servlets package are associated with Controller layer), as shown in Fig. 3. The Entities package contains classes that represent entities of the system, such as those related to published services and users of repository. The DAO package contains classes responsible for the persistence of entities in the database. Since we adopted Hibernate[5] framework, XML files for each entity were placed in the Mappings package. The JSP package contains Web pages developed by using the Twitter Bootstrap[6] framework. The Controllers package contains classes responsible for the communication among graphical interface, the entities, and the DAO package. Different servlets were created and placed in the package Servlets for the integration of the graphical interface into the controllers.

4.2   Semantic Search Plug-In

Different plug-ins can be developed to enable communication between the service repository and development environments. A RoboSeT plug-in is a local application that remotely searches services in the repository and integrates the results into the project of a robotic system. Therefore, developers designing a robotic system can create a project in their development environment using the plug-in, search for services necessary for such system, and reuse them. Only services unavailable in the repository and services used to integrate the functionalities of the robotic system have to be implemented. Services used to integrate and coordinate other services are more domain-specific and should be implemented according to the requirements of each project. We have created a plug-in for the ROS development environment to exemplify the functionalities that should be provided by such applications. Although this implementation is specific for ROS, the functionalities can be adapted to any other SORS development environment. The following activities were automated by the plug-in for supporting creation of robotic systems:

---

[5] http://hibernate.org/.

[6] http://getbootstrap.com/.

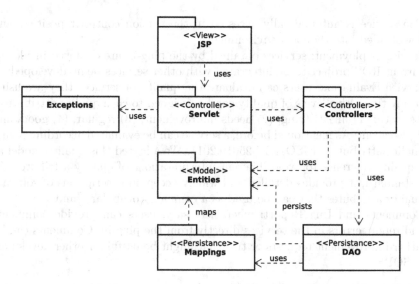

Fig. 3. Packages Diagram of the service repository

- Project Creation: as this plug-in acts as a layer on top of ROS, we have developed a functionality to abstract the creation of projects in such an environment. Therefore, the whole ROS file-system can be built using the plug-in, including the appropriate build and manifest files. The functionality implemented in this plug-in works as a proxy for the respective functionality in ROS (i.e., the roscreate-pkg command);
- Identification of Types of Services: during the design time, developers should identify services that will be used for the creation of a robotic system. They analyze, group, and map the robotic system requirements into the service types of the taxonomy. To support this activity, the last version of the taxonomy available in the repository is obtained every time the plug-in starts, so that developers can get any additional information on a given type of service in their local machines (e.g., parent type, description, and examples);
- Service Search: searches for each type of service identified for the robotic system are performed in the repository by using the plug-in. As a result, all services that have matched the searched types are presented along with their ID, description, provider information, license type, and number of endorsements;
- Service Selection: the search for a given type of service can retrieve more than one service implementation. Therefore, the plug-in enables developers to obtain additional information about services in the repository. The number of recommendations received and score of each quality attribute can help developers to choose the service to be used;
- Service Obtaining: the services that will be used in a robotic system can be obtained by the plug-in. A request using the service ID is sent to the service repository, which answers with the url of the location of the service.

The service is automatically accessed in the version control repository and downloaded into the local environment;

– Service Deployment: services obtained by the plug-in are deployed inside the current ROS project to be integrated with other services being developed;
– Service Evaluation: users can evaluate the quality of services they are using at any time. Five levels of quality can be assigned to each quality attribute of a service: (1) unsatisfying, (2) needs improvement, (3) regular, (4) good, and (5) excellent. As mentioned before, a service can be evaluated according to any quality attributes of ISO/IEC 25010:2011. We adopted this quality model as a quality reference to avoid different interpretations of quality attributes. As a standard, it provides detailed and widely accepted descriptions of software quality attributes that can be used as a common vocabulary; and
– Comments and Bug Report: when necessary, users can provide comments and report errors in the services directly from the plug-in. Comments can be either improvement requests or tips that might be useful for other developers of SORS.

The plug-in we designed for ROS has been implemented in Java and has a command-line user interface. Figure 4 illustrates such an interface being used to obtain information about a probabilistic localization service named *amcl*. We opted for a command-line plug-in to make it more familiar to ROS developers, who already use such type of interface to interact with the development environment. A help command is available to support developers in learning how to use the functionalities available in the plug-in. Currently, the developed plug-in does not support publication of services directly into the service repository. Nevertheless, new services developed in projects that use the plug-in can be published through the Web interface and reused in other projects, thus contributing to the community of robotics.

5   Case Study

In order to illustrate the use of RoboSeT, this section describes the design of a robotic system of robust navigation capability. Robust navigation enables a robotic system to guide the robot through the environment without risk, avoiding collision with humans, objects, and other robots. The design of a robotic system for robust navigation involves coordination of different tasks, such as path planning, motion control, and sensor data processing. Brugalli et al. [5] investigated several development environments to identify existing modules associated with the design of robust navigation functionalities. They realized that modules related to robust navigation typically refer to the same tasks of robotics, but different names are used. These tasks are described as follows:

– Motion Planning: creates a global path between a given starting position and the goal position represented by a sequence of intermediate points in a static environment;

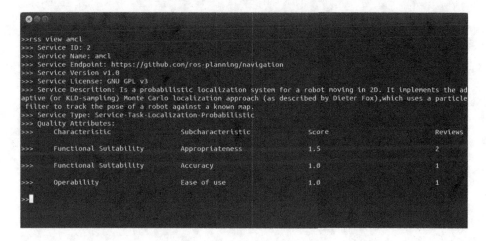

Fig. 4. Interface used to integrate the plug-in with ROS

- Trajectory Generation: defines the velocity of each part of the path. The trajectory is represented as a sequence of planned intermediate positions and associated velocities;
- Obstacle Detection and Representation: represents objects in the environment by using data from different sensors, such as laser rangefinder and cameras. These objects and their respective positions are used to update the map of the environment;
- Obstacle Avoidance: adapts the pre-defined global trajectory to avoid unexpected objects in the path, such as humans or other robots. It enables the robot to navigate in dynamic environments safely;
- Position and Velocity Control: generates instant linear and angular velocity so that the robot can navigate along the computed trajectory. Local navigation is strongly related to the kinematic model used by the robot; and
- Localization: estimates the position of the robot with respect to a global map by using different types of sensors, such as odometer, camera, and laser rangefinder.

In addition to these tasks, functionalities related to the control of sensors and actuators were also considered. Pioneer P3-DX[7] robot was adopted as a base platform in this study. It moves using two-wheel differential drive with rear balancing caster. The two front wheels are independent and can have different speeds if necessary. Each wheel has an encoder sensor that supports the localization task. Moreover, we also used a laser sensor to provide information about objects surrounding the robot. Given these hardware specifications, drivers for the robot and the laser were considered in the design of the robotic system.

The first step in the design of the robotic system was the investigation of services available for reuse. After the creation of an ROS project, each functionality

---

[7] http://www.mobilerobots.com/ResearchRobots/PioneerP3DX.aspx.

Table 1. Functionalities of the robotic system and related service types

Functionality	Service type
Motion planning	Service/Task/Path planning
Trajectory generation	Service/Task/Path planning
Obstacle detection and representation	Service/Task/Mapping
Obstacle avoidance	Service/Task/Path planning
Position and velocity control	Service/Task/Navigation
Localization	Service/Task/Localization
Encoder controller	Service/Device/Sensor/Movement
Differential drive controller	Service/Device/Actuator/Locomotion
Laser controller	Service/Device/Sensor/Distance

necessary for the development of the robotic system was classified according to the service types available in the taxonomy. Table 1 shows the functionalities of the robotic system and the types of services they are associated with.

The search for reusable services was then performed based on the identified types. Each service type was applied to the plug-in developed for ROS so that services available in the service repository could be found. Results of the search were analyzed and the most adequate services for our robotic system were selected. Task service and Device Driver service were the only two groups of the taxonomy necessary for the design of the robotic systems with robust navigation capabilities. However, the design of more complex SORS may result in the use of other groups of service, such as the Knowledge and the Application. Table 2 shows the services identified for the functionalities related to the Task group and the service types associated with them.

Table 2. Functionalities of Task group, service types, and services identified for reuse

Functionality	Task service types	ROS service
Motion planning	Path planning/Heuristic search	NavfnROS, CarrotPlanner
Trajectory generation	Path planning/Heuristic search	TrajectoryPlannerROS, DWAPlannerROS
Obstacle detection and representation	Mapping/Metric/Grid	CostMap2D
Obstacle avoidance	Path planning/Heuristic search	TrajectoryPlannerROS, DWAPlannerROS
Position and velocity control	Navigation	MoveBase
Localization	Localization/Probabilistic	Amcl

The *CostMap2D* service implements a 2D costmap that takes in sensor data from the world and builds a 2D or 3D occupancy grid of the data. *NavfnROS* and *CarrotPlanner* are two complementary implementations of *BaseGlobalPlanner* interface for ROS. *NavfnROS* is an A* [20] path-planner for maps described by occupancy grids. *CarrotPlanner* is a simpler planner that calculates a straight line between the robot position and the goal position and checks collisions along the path. Both path planners are complementary services that can be used to calculate a global path. *TrajectoryPlannerROS* and *DWAPlannerROS* can be used to generate a trajectory for a defined global path. These services produce velocity commands based on the map, the global path, and unexpected objects close to the robot, as well as provide functionalities associated with obstacle avoidance. The localization of the robot can be estimated by the *Amcl* service, which uses Monte Carlo [14] probabilistic method to reduce the error of encoder measurements. Observe that some task services in the repository were able to provide more than one type of functionality. For instance, services *TrajectoryPlannerROS* and *DWAPlannerROS* were associated with both trajectory generation and obstacle avoidance.

We also obtained services for controlling hardware devices used by services of task group. Table 3 shows the services identified for functionalities related to the Device Driver group and the service types associated with them. *RosAria* service provides means for controlling the differential drive and the encoder of Pioneer P3-DX. *SICK Toolbox* service was identified for the control of the SICK[8] laser rangefinder. Similarly to services in task group, *RosAria* provided functionalities in more than one type of service.

Table 3. Functionalities of Device Driver group, service types, and services identified for reuse

Functionality	Device service types	ROS service
Encoder controller	Sensor/Movement	RosAria
Differential drive controller	Actuator/Locomotion	RosAria
Laser controller	Sensor/Distance	SICK toolbox

Figure 5 illustrates the software architecture we designed for the robotic system using the services found in RoboSeT repository. In this architecture, *CostMap2D* builds its map based on information provided by *SICK Toolbox* service. *MoveBase* service orchestrates mapping (*CostMap2D*) service and other services for localization (*Amcl*) and path planning (*NavfnROS, CarrotPlanner, TrajectoryPlannerROS,* and *DWAPlannerROS*) to generate robust navigation commands. These commands are provided to *RosAria* service, which acts as an interface to control the Pioneer P3-DX robot. As the robot moves in the environment, *RosAria* service collects data from the odometer sensor. The odometry information is consumed by *Amcl* service and used to estimate the current localization of the robot.

---

[8] http://www.sick.com/group/EN/home/products/product_portfolio/laser_measure ment_technology.aspx.

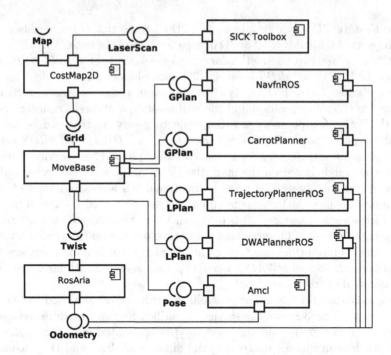

Fig. 5. Software architecture of the robotic system

The navigation system described in the software architecture is similar to the architecture of the 2D Navigation Stack[9] available for ROS. In fact, services identified by the plug-in are part of this ROS stack, but registered in the service repository as independent services. Currently, the services identified for robust navigation are strongly dependent on *MoveBase* to start and, therefore, to work properly. However, a study has already demonstrated these services can work independently after a refactoring process [5].

6   Discussion

The case study in the previous section illustrated how services can be identified, obtained, and reused to develop an SORS. Although the services used in such an example are also available in the ROS Wiki, their localization depends on the developers' previous knowledge. Without the support provided by RoboSeT and the use of the taxonomy, researchers not aware of the existence of such services would need to manually search them among hundreds of other services. RoboSeT also promotes indirect communication among service providers and their service consumers. These characteristics can yield benefits in three different perspectives: service consumer, service provider, and robotic system user.

---

[9] http://wiki.ros.org/navigation.

From the service consumer perspective, RoboSeT can facilitate the discovery of services and, therefore, improve reuse during the development of robotic systems. It is intuitive that services easier to be found are more likely to be reused. However, the reuse of a service does not depend only on its discovery, but on its documentation and suitability to the robotic system under development. RoboSeT provides functionalities that enable consumers to obtain structured information on the services being searched, such as documentation, comments from other users, and quality attributes. These functionalities aim at facilitating the identification of the most suitable service for each robotic system. As a direct consequence of reuse, RoboSeT intends to improve productivity in the development of robotic systems. Although quantitative evidences are still necessary, studies in the literature have already shown reuse improvements positively influence productivity in the development of software systems [27].

As a counterpart, service providers of RoboSeT receive in-use feedback from the robotics community about the services they have published. Services provided to the community are generally executed in several environment configurations and on different robotic platforms, which represents an important corpus of evaluation. Comments, suggestions, bug reports, and quality evaluation of such services are organized in the Web interface of RoboSeT for each service provider. Providers can use the My Services section in the Web interface as a guide to improve the quality of their services. By improving the quality of the service they provide to the community, providers can also improve the overall quality of their own robotic systems.

The collaboration among service providers and service consumers through RoboSeT can also provide benefits from the perspective of robotic systems users. As service providers receive feedback for their services and use it to improve the overall quality of their systems, higher quality robotic systems are made available for end users. Besides, reuse improvements in the development of software systems can reduce costs and result in more affordable systems [27].

Despite the RoboSeT benefits, it is also important highlight limitations of such mechanism. Similarly to other repositories of services for SORS, the success of RoboSeT strongly depends on the cooperation of the robotics community. We are aware that without the adoption of RoboSeT by the community, few services will be available for search, fewer consumers will be interested in searching for them, and weak feedbacks will be offered as counterpart to providers. Therefore, we have designed RoboSeT to be as flexible as possible to stimulate its adoption by the robotics community. The initial version of the taxonomy can be evolved and modified according to the community needs and new quality attributes can be proposed for the evaluation of services. Besides that, we aim at releasing RoboSeT and its plug-in for ROS as open source software to encourage and support the creation of plug-ins for other development environments.

7   Conclusion and Future Work

SOA is an architectural style that can support developers to cope with the design of large, complex robotic systems and, at the same time, provide better reusability and flexibility to such systems. In this perspective, the main contribution of this work is RoboSeT, a mechanism that enables cataloging and discovery of services for robotic systems using semantic information provided by a robotics taxonomy. RoboSeT encompasses two main parts: a repository of services for SORS and plug-ins that integrate development environments into such repository. We describe in this work the structure, main functionalities, and implementation of both parts of RoboSeT. The developed plug-in makes it possible to locally search, obtain, and deploy services directly into ROS projects. Results of our case study indicate that RoboSeT can facilitate the development of robotic systems by supporting the discovery and reuse of services available in the repository. By supporting service reuse, we aim at providing better productivity during the development of robotic systems based on SOA. As future work, we intend to improve RoboSeT by adding new features and creating plug-ins for other development environments. In addition, to contribute to the robotics community, we plan to release RoboSeT as an open source system. Different experiments will also be performed to obtain quantitative evidences about the benefits of using our mechanism.

Acknowledgments. This work is supported by the Brazilian funding agencies CNPq, Capes, and FAPESP (Grant. No.: 2011/06022-0, 2011/23316-8, and 2014/02244-7). It was also supported by National Science and Technology Institute for Critical Embedded Systems – INCT-SEC (Grant N.: 573963/2008-8 and 2008/57870-9).

References

1. Arsanjani, A., Ghosh, S., Allam, A., Abdollah, T., Ganapathy, S., Holley, K.: SOMA: a method for developing service-oriented solutions. IBM Syst. J. **47**(3), 377–396 (2008)
2. Berná-Martínez, J.V., Maciá-Pérez, F., Ramos-Morillo, H., Gilart-Iglesias, V.: Distributed robotic architecture based on smart services. In: Proceedings of the 4th IEEE International Conference on Industrial Informatics (INDIN 2006), pp. 480–485, Singapore, August 2006
3. Braga, R.T.V., Trindade, O., Jr., Branco, K.R.L.J.C., Lee, J.: Incorporating certification in feature modelling of an unmanned aerial vehicle product line. In: Proceedings of the 16th International Software Product Line Conference (SPLC 2012), pp. 249–258, Salvador, Brazil (2012)
4. BRICS. Best practice in robotics. http://www.best-of-robotics.org/. Accessed 10 October 2014
5. Brugali, D., Gherardi, L., Biziak, A., Luzzana, A., Zakharov, A.: A reuse-oriented development process for component-based robotic systems. In: Noda, I., Ando, N., Brugali, D., Kuffner, J.J. (eds.) SIMPAR 2012. LNCS, vol. 7628, pp. 361–374. Springer, Heidelberg (2012)
6. Brugali, D., Scandurra, P.: Component-based robotic engineering (Part I). IEEE Robot. Autom. Mag. **16**(4), 84–96 (2009)
7. Cepeda, J.S., Chaimowicz, L., Soto, R.: Exploring Microsoft robotics studio as a mechanism for service-oriented robotics. In: Proceedings of the 7th Latin American Robotics Symposium and Intelligent Robotic Meeting (LARS 2010), pp. 7–12, São Bernardo do Campo, Brazil, October 2010

8. Cesetti, A., Scotti, C.P., Buo, G.D., Longhi, S.: A service oriented architecture supporting an autonomous mobile robot for industrial applications. In: Proceedings of the 18th Mediterranean Conference on Control Automation (MED 2010), pp. 604–609, Marrakech, Morocco, June 2010

9. Dagger, D., O'Connor, A., Lawless, S., Walsh, E., Wade, V.: Service-oriented e-learning platforms: from monolithic systems to flexible services. IEEE Internet Comput. **11**(3), 28–35 (2007)

10. Koschke, R.: Architecture reconstruction. In: De Lucia, A., Ferrucci, F. (eds.) ISSSE 2006-2008. LNCS, vol. 5413, pp. 140–173. Springer, Heidelberg (2009)

11. Farinelli, A., Iocchi, L., Nardi, D.: Multirobot systems: a classification focused on coordination. IEEE Trans. Syst. Man Cybern. **34**(5), 2015–2028 (2004)

12. Feitosa, D., Nakagawa, E.Y.: An investigation into reference architectures for mobile robotic systems. In Proceedings of the 7th International Conference on Software Engineering Advances (ICSEA 2012), pp. 465–471, Lisbon, Portugal, November 2012

13. Fernandes, L.C., Souza, J.R., Pessin, G., Shinzato, P.Y., Sales, D., Mendes, C., Prado, M., Klaser, R., Magalhães, A.C., Hata, A., Pigatto, D., Branco Jr., K.C., Osorio, F.S., Wolf, D.F.: CaRINA intelligent robotic car: architectural design and applications. J. Syst. Architect. **60**(4), 372–392 (2014)

14. Fishman, G.S.: Monte Carlo: Concepts, Algorithms, and Applications. Springer, New York (1995)

15. Frakes, W.B., Kang, K.: Software reuse research: status and future. IEEE Trans. Softw. Eng. **31**(7), 529–536 (2005)

16. Fryer, J.A., McKee, G.T., Schenker, P.S.: Configuring robots from modules: An object oriented approach. In Proc. of the 8th International Conference on Advanced Robotics (ICAR'97), pp. 907–912, Monterey, USA, July 1997

17. Gamma, E., Helm, R., Johnson, R., Vlissides, J.: Design Patterns: Elements of Reusable Object-oriented Software. Addison-Wesley, Boston (1995)

18. Graves, A., Czarnecki, C.: Design patterns for behavior-based robotics. IEEE Trans. Syst. Man Cybern. Part A Syst. Hum. **30**(1), 36–41 (2000)

19. Ha, Y.-G., Sohn, J.-C., Cho, Y.-J.: Service-oriented integration of networked robots with ubiquitous sensors and devices using the semantic web services technology. In: Proceedings of the 18th IEEE/RSJ International Conference on Intelligent Robots and Systems (IROS 2005), pp. 3947–3952, Alberta, Canada, August 2005

20. Hart, P.E., Nilsson, N.J., Raphael, B.: A formal basis for the heuristic determination of minimum cost paths. IEEE Trans. Syst. Sci. Cybern. Comput. **2**(4), 100–107 (1968)

21. Iborra, A., Caceres, D., Ortiz, F., Franco, J., Palma, P., Alvarez, B.: Design of service robots. IEEE Robot. Autom. Mag. **16**(1), 24–33 (2009)

22. iRobots. iRobot Roomba Vacuum Cleaning Robot. Online, 2014. http://www.irobot.com/us/learn/home/roomba.aspx. Accessed in 10th October 2014

23. ISO/IEC. ISO/IEC 25010:2011 Systems and software engineering - Systems and software Quality Requirements and Evaluation (SQuaRE) - System and software quality models. Standard 25010:2011, International Organization for Standardization (ISO)/International Electrotechnical Commission (IEC) (2011)

24. Jackson, J.: Microsoft robotics studio: a technical introduction. IEEE Robot. Autom. Mag. **14**(4), 82–87 (2007)

25. Koubaa, A.: A service-oriented architecture for virtualizing robots in robot-as-a-service clouds. In: Maehle, E., Römer, K., Karl, W., Tovar, E. (eds.) ARCS 2014. LNCS, vol. 8350, pp. 196–208. Springer, Heidelberg (2014)

26. Lee, K.K., Zhang, P., Xu, Y.: A service-based network architecture for wearable robots. In: Proceedings of the IEEE International Conference on Robotics and Automation (ICRA 2003), pp. 1671–1676, Taipei, Taiwan, September 2003

27. Mohagheghi, P., Conradi, R.: Quality, productivity and economic benefits of software reuse: a review of industrial studies. Empirical Software Eng. **12**(5), 471–516 (2007)

28. Nakagawa, E.Y., Oquendo, F.: RAModel: A reference model for reference architectures. In: Proceedings of the Joint 10th Working IEEE/IFIP Conference on Software Architecture (WICSA 2012) and 6th European Conference on Software Architecture (ECSA 2012), pp. 297–301, Helsinki, Finland, August 2012

29. Oliveira, L.B.R., Nakagawa, E.Y.: A service-oriented reference architecture for software testing tools. In: Crnkovic, I., Gruhn, V., Book, M. (eds.) ECSA 2011. LNCS, vol. 6903, pp. 405–421. Springer, Heidelberg (2011)

30. Oliveira, L.B.R., Osório, F.S., Nakagawa, E.Y.: An investigation into the development of service-oriented robotic systems. In: Proceedings of the 28th ACM/SIGAPP Symposium on Applied Computing (ACM/SAC 2013), pp. 223–226, Coimbra, Portugal, March 2013

31. Oliveira, L.B.R., Osório, F.S., Oquendo, F., Nakagawa, E.Y.: Towards a taxonomy of services for developing service-oriented robotic systems. In: Proceedings of the 26th International Conference on Software Engineering and Knowledge Engineering (SEKE 2014), pp. 344–349, Vancouver, Canada, July 2014

32. Papazoglou, M.P., Heuvel, W.-J.: Service oriented architectures: approaches, technologies and research issues. VLDB J. **16**(3), 389–415 (2007)

33. Papazoglou, M.P., Traverso, P., Dustdar, S., Leymann, F.: Service-oriented computing: a research roadmap. Int. J. Coop. Inf. Syst. **17**(2), 223–255 (2008)

34. Peltz, C.: Web Services Orchestration and Choreography. IEEE Comput. **36**(10), 46–52 (2003)

35. Schlegel, C., Steck, A., Brugali, D., Knoll, A.: Design abstraction and processes in robotics: from code-driven to model-driven engineering. In: Ando, N., Balakirsky, S., Hemker, T., Reggiani, M., von Stryk, O. (eds.) SIMPAR 2010. LNCS, vol. 6472, pp. 324–335. Springer, Heidelberg (2010)

36. Straszheim, T., Gerkey, B., Cousins, S.: The ROS build system. IEEE Robot. Autom. Mag. **18**(2), 18–19 (2011)

37. Takahashi, M., Suzuki, T., Shitamoto, H., Moriguchi, T., Yoshida, K.: Developing a mobile robot for transport applications in the hospital domain. Robot. Auton. Syst. **58**(7), 889–899 (2010)

38. Taylor, R.N., Medvidovic, N., Dashofy, E.M.: Software Architecture: Foundations, Theory, and Practice. Wiley Publishing, New York (2009)

39. Tenorth, M., Klank, U., Pangercic, D., Beetz, M.: Web-enabled robots. IEEE Robot. Autom. Mag. **18**(2), 58–68 (2011)

40. Thrun, S., Montemerlo, M., Dahlkamp, H., Stavens, D., Aron, A., Diebel, J., Fong, P., Gale, J., Halpenny, M., Hoffmann, G., Lau, K., Oakley, C., Palatucci, M., Pratt, V., Stang, P., Strohband, S., Dupont, C., Jendrossek, L.-E., Koelen, C., Markey, C., Rummel, C., van Niekerk, J., Jensen, E., Alessandrini, P., Bradski, G., Davies, B., Ettinger, S., Kaehler, A., Nefian, A., Mahoney, P.: Stanley: the robot that won the DARPA grand challenge. J. Robotic Syst. **23**(9), 661–692 (2006)

41. Waibel, M., Beetz, M., Civera, J., D'Andrea, R., Elfring, J., Galvez-Lopez, D., Haussermann, K., Janssen, R., Montiel, J.M.M., Perzylo, A., Schiessle, B., Tenorth, M., Zweigle, O., van de Molengraft, R.: Roboearth. IEEE Robot. Autom. Mag. **18**(2), 69–82 (2011)

Development and Control of the Lower Limbs
of a Biped Robot

Eduardo Henrique Maciel, Renato Ventura Bayan Henriques,
and Walter Fetter Lages[(✉)]

Federal University of Rio Grande do Sul, Av. Osvaldo Aranha, 103,
Porto Alegre, RS 90035-190, Brazil
eduardo.maciel@ufrgs.br, {rventura,fetter}@ece.ufrgs.br
http://www.ece.ufrgs.br

Abstract. This work presents the development and control of a simplified model of the lower limbs of a biped robot, composed, basically,
of a waist, two femurs, two tibiae and two feet. The mechanical structure has six degrees of freedom and the approximate dimensions of a
human being. The control system uses the computed-torque technique
and was implemented on the Robot Operating System. Contrariwise to
most controllers implemented on the Robot Operating System, here a
multi-input, multi-output controller is proposed. A ROS action server
was used to generate the reference trajectories and the control system
performance was evaluated under step, linear, cubic and quintic polynomial trajectories by using the Gazebo simulator.

Keywords: Biped robot · Robot operating system · Computed torque

1 Introduction

The most used methods for motion on land are wheels, rails other legs [8]. The
motion using legs presents a discontinuous motion, thus being able to overcome
obstacles, slopes, stairs and other irregular structures.

Many research groups are focusing on the development of biped robots [6]
which are able to imitate the motion or even the behavior of human beings [14].

In the beginning of the development of biped robots, the focus was only on
the motion and not on the applicability of those robots in a real environment [10].

The capabilities of a human are different from those of a biped robot. For
example, human beings can move fast while biped robots are slow when compared to the human agility. Structural factors, such as kinematic mapping and
energy consumption make it difficult for a biped robot to achieve a performance
comparable to humans being using the current technology.

E.H. Maciel, R.V.B. Henriques and W.F. Lages—These authors would like to thank
to Coordenação de Aperfeiçoamento de Pessoal de Nível Superior (CAPES) and
Fundação de Apoio à Pesquisa do Estado do Rio Grande do Sul (FAPERGS) for the
financial support.

© Springer-Verlag Berlin Heidelberg 2015
F.S. Osório et al. (Eds.): LARS/SBR/Robocontrol 2014, CCIS 507, pp. 133–152, 2015.
DOI: 10.1007/978-3-662-48134-9_8

In recent years, the Robot Operating System (ROS) [9] has emerged as a dominant platform for research in robotics and there are already some biped robots using ROS such as the Tulip [13] and the NAO [5]. However, most robots using ROS employ a simple control structure based on independent PID controllers on each joint. Nonetheless, robots are nonlinear multi-input, multi-output (MIMO) plants, which, in general require nonlinear MIMO controllers.

Here, a biped robot based on the human structure and using ROS is proposed. Contrariwise to most robots using ROS, a MIMO nonlinear controller based on computed torque is implemented.

2 Mechanical Structure

Figure 1 shows the methodology used to develop the robot, named Orbit.

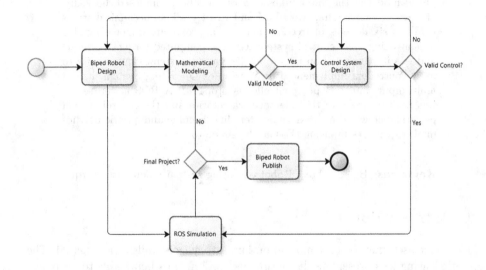

Fig. 1. Development flow.

Figure 2 presents the evolution of the proposed prototype.

The design follows a simplified model of the inferior members of the human body, composed of a hib, two femurs, two tibiae and two feet. The inferior members of humans have a total of 30 degrees of freedom (DoF) in each leg [9]. A biped robot should have at least 8 DoF in order to be a good approximation of the human body [3]. However, the Orbit robot uses a simpler kinematic approximation, with 6 DoF but with dimensions similar to those a human being, as shown in Fig. 3.

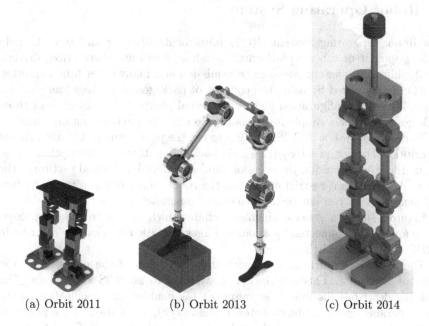

(a) Orbit 2011   (b) Orbit 2013   (c) Orbit 2014

Fig. 2. Evolution of the Orbit prototype.

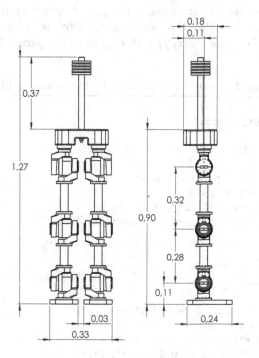

Fig. 3. Dimensions of the proposed robot (m).

3   Robot Operating System

The Robot Operating System (ROS) implements libraries and tools to help in development of robotic platforms, including, hardware abstraction, drivers, specific libraries, viewers, message transmission and many other functionalities.

ROS is organized by using the concept of packages. A package can contain, nodes, libraries, configuration files and external plugins. The objective of those packages is to offer a simple functionality, so that the package can be reused.

To describe a robot in ROS, a way is to use the package named Unified Robot Description Format (URDF) [12]. This package enables the description of the kinematics, the dynamics, the collision model, material, color and texture of the robot. An important restriction is that the robots must follow a tree structure and hence URDF can not be used to describe parallel robots.

Figure 4 shows a generic kinematic chain which uses a tree-like topology. There are 4 links connected by 3 joints. This kinematic chain can be describe in URDF as shown in Listing 1.

The robot tag starts a block with the description of the name, links and joints of the robot. This description is available to all ROS subsystems. The link tag describes the link. The inertial tag enables the specification of the inertia parameters of the link: center of mass (xyz), orientation of the principal axis (rpy) and mass (mass) of the link. I the example shown in Fig. 4 there are 4 links named link1 to link4 and 3 joints. Joints are described by the joint tag, which includes the specification of the parent (parent) and child (child) links. The joint enables also, the naming of the joint, select its type, specify its position (xyz) and orientation(rpy) with respect to the parent link, and moving axis.

Listing 1. URDF for the kinematic chain shown in Fig. 4.

```xml
<?xml version="1.0"?>
<robot name="robot_generic">

  <link name="link1">
    <inertial>
      <origin xyz="0 0 0" rpy="0 0 0"/>
      <mass value="1.0" />
      <inertia ixx="1.0" ixy="0.0" ixz="0.0"
               iyy="1.0" iyz="0.0" izz="1.0"/>
    </inertial>
  </link>

  <link name="link2">
    <inertial>
      <origin xyz="0 0 0" rpy="0 0 0"/>
      <mass value="1.0" />
      <inertia ixx="1.0" ixy="0.0" ixz="0.0"
               iyy="1.0" iyz="0.0" izz="1.0"/>
    </inertial>
```

```
    </link>

    <link name="link3">
      <inertial>
        <origin xyz="0 0 0" rpy="0 0 0"/>
        <mass value="1.0" />
        <inertia ixx="1.0" ixy="0.0" ixz="0.0"
                 iyy="1.0" iyz="0.0" izz="1.0"/>
      </inertial>
    </link>

    <link name="link4">
      <inertial>
        <origin xyz="0 0 0" rpy="0 0 0"/>
        <mass value="1.0" />
        <inertia ixx="1.0" ixy="0.0" ixz="0.0"
                 iyy="1.0" iyz="0.0" izz="1.0"/>
      </inertial>
    </link>

    <joint name="joint1" type="continuous">
      <parent link="link1"/>
      <child link="link2"/>
      <origin xyz="5 3 0" rpy="0 0 0" />
      <axis xyz="-0.9 0.15 0" />
    </joint>

    <joint name="joint2" type="continuous">
      <parent link="link1"/>
      <child link="link3"/>
      <origin xyz="-2 5 0" rpy="0 0 1.57" />
      <axis xyz="-0.707 0.707 0" />
    </joint>

    <joint name="joint3" type="continuous">
      <parent link="link3"/>
      <child link="link4"/>
      <origin xyz="5 0 0" rpy="0 0 -1.57" />
      <axis xyz="0.707 -0.707 0" />
    </joint>

</robot>
```

The simulation of a robot described in URDF can be done using the Gazebo 3D simulator [7].

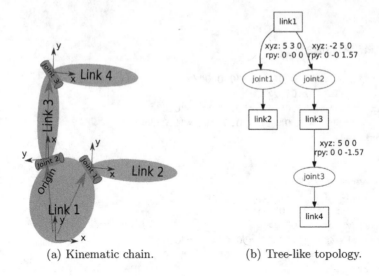

(a) Kinematic chain.   (b) Tree-like topology.

Fig. 4. Generic kinematic model.

3.1 OROCOS Kinematics and Dynamics Library

The computations required by the kinematic and dynamic models of a robot can be done by using a packages named OROCOS Kinematics and Dynamics Library (KDL) [1].

For the implementation of the controller for the Orbit robot, the `Chain` class was used. This class abstracts a kinematic chain and is used by the `ChainIdSolver_RNE` class, which implements the well-known Newton-Euler algorithm [2].

The dynamic model of the robot is described by [4]:

$$\tau = D(q)\ddot{q} + H(q,\dot{q}) + G(q) \tag{1}$$

where: q: Joint position;
$D(q)$: Inertia matrix;
$H(q,\dot{q})$: Vector of centrifugal and Coriolis forces;
$G(q)$: Vector of gravitational forces;
τ: Joint torques.

3.2 Control System

The control system developed for the Orbit robot uses the computed torque technique [4], whose structure is shown in Fig. 5. Note that there is an abuse with respect to the usual semantics of a block diagram. The variables are represented in time domain and while the continuous lines denote inputs which are multiplied by the block gain, the dashed lines denote inputs which are just need by the block computation.

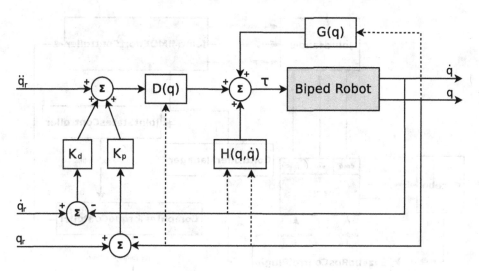

Fig. 5. Block diagram of the computed torque control.

The computed torque control uses the dynamic model of the robot to implement a feedback linearization. Then, a PD controller is used to control the resulting linear system. The computed torque control law is given by:

$$\tau = D_n(q)[\ddot{q}_r + K_d(\dot{q}_r - \dot{q}) + K_p(q_r - q)] + H_n(q, \dot{q}) + G_n(q) \qquad (2)$$

where: q_r is the position reference, K_p is the proportional gain matrix, K_d is the differential gain matrix, $D_n(q)$ is the nominal inertia matrix, $H_n(q, \dot{q})$ is the nominal vector of centrifugal and Coriolis forces and $G_n(q)$ is the nominal vector of gravitational forces.

Note that to compute the computed torque control law (2), it is possible to use the classical form of the Newton-Euler iteration (1) by letting:

$$\ddot{q} = \ddot{q}_r + K_d(\dot{q}_r - \ddot{q}) + K_p(q_r - q) \qquad (3)$$

If there is not model mismatch, then $D(q) = D_n(q), H(q, \dot{q}) = H_n(q, \dot{q}), G(q) = G_n(q)$, and it is possible to obtain:

$$\ddot{e} + K_d\dot{e} + K_pe = 0 \qquad (4)$$

where $e = q_r - q$.

Expression (4) shows that by choosing the matrices K_p and K_d in a diagonal form, it is possible to obtain a decoupled closed-loop system, where the behavior of each joint error is given by a second order differential equation. The natural frequency ω_n and the damping coefficient ξ_n of each equation are determined by choosing the gain matrices: $K_p = \text{diag}\left(\omega_n^2\right)$ and $K_d = \text{diag}(2\xi\omega_n)$. By choosing $\xi = 0.7$ and $\omega_n = 100\pi$ rad/s: $K_p = \text{diag}(98696)$ and $K_d = \text{diag}(628.319)$.

Figure 6 shows a diagram of the control signal flow in ROS.

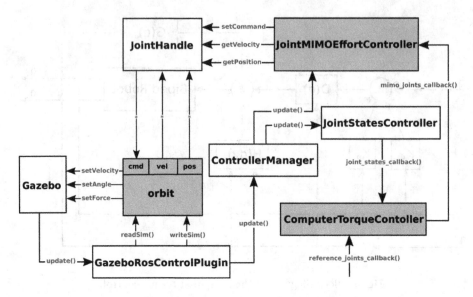

Fig. 6. Control signal flow in ROS.

The `ControllerManager` block is responsible for loading the controller through a plugin, implemented by the `GazeboROSControlPlugin` block, which connects a hardware interface between Gazebo and ROS. The `DefaultRobotHWSim` (orbit) block is the hardware interface, which in the case of a simulation implements a generic interface to Gazebo. The `computerTorqueController` block is the implementation of the computed torque controller and sends a vector of efforts (`mimo_efforts`) to the `JointMIMOEffortController` block. This block is just a bypass, with its output reflecting its inputs values, using a MIMO structure and making it possible to apply the control signal to all joints simultaneously. This is need because the default controllers existing in ROS are all single input, single output (SISO) controllers. The `JointHandle` block is used to interface to sensors and actuators. The dotted lines means that the respective variables are accessed directly through pointers instead of having its values returned by functions.

3.3   Trajectory Generation

Trajectory generation in ROS is usually done through an action server. An action server is a ROS communication mechanism for tasks requiring a long time for execution, such as a trajectory. A service requested though an action server can be canceled, preempted and send status and feedback information to its client. Figure 7 shows the connection between an action client and an action server. The client requests service though a topic called `goal` and can cancel the execution of the requested service through the `cancel` topic. The action server signal the full execution of the service through the `result` topic and send intermediate status and feedback information through the `status` and `feedback` topics, respectively.

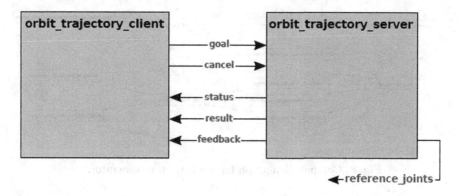

Fig. 7. Messages flow in the Orbit robot trajectory generator.

The trajectory generator action server receives trajectory via points and generates trajectory points at the appropriate rate and publishes them for the joint controller use. More specifically, the use of the topics is:

goal: used to receive trajectory via points;

cancel: used to receive the service cancellation command;

status: used to notify the client about the action server state such as Pending, Active, Recalling, Preempting, Rejected, Succeeded, Aborted, Recalled or Preempted;

feedback: used to send periodic, partial information about the execution of a goal;

result: used to signal the conclusion of a goal.

The trajectory generation action server implemented in this work uses the KDL package, more precisely, the KDL::VelocityProfile_Spline class to generate the trajectory. The orbit_trajectory_client node provides the via points for the desired trajectory. Based on the data available on those via points, the trajectory generator uses the proper interpolation. If the via points specify only position, a linear interpolation is used, if position and velocities are specified, a cubic interpolation is used, while a quintic interpolation is used when position, velocity and acceleration at each via point is specified.

Figure 8 shows the ROS computation graph of the whole system, including the computed torque controller and the trajectory generator. The orbit_trajectory_client node send the via points through the /orbit/joint_trajectory_action/goal topic to the orbit_trajectory_server node, which generates the trajectory points sent through the /orbit/ComputedTorqueController/reference_joints topic to the /computed_torque_controller node, which implements the joint controller.

4   Results

In this section, simulations of the proposed computed torque control implementation in ROS are shown. The simulations actuate the left leg of the Orbit robot.

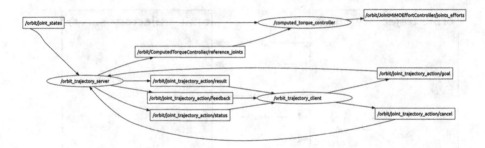

Fig. 8. Computation graph for the trajectory generator.

Four cases are considered for the reference: step without saturating control, step with saturating control, linear interpolation trajectory and quintic interpolation trajectory. Linear and quintic interpolation trajectories with saturating control are not considered because the torque values are small and do not cause saturation, hence the results with or without saturation would be the same. Figure 9 shows the ROS computation graph used to simulate the control system.

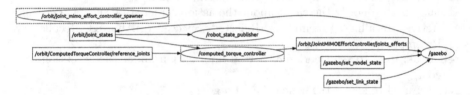

Fig. 9. Computation graph for the Orbit robot.

The /robot_state_publisher node publishes the poses of the links. The /orbit/joint_states topic is published by the /gazebo node, and informs the position and velocity of each joint. The /computed_torque_controller node implements the computed torque controller, while the JointMIMOEffort Controller node controller, which implements the MIMO interface, is not represented in this diagram because it is not a ROS node, but a plugin loaded by the /orbit/joint_mimo_effort_controller_spawner node. Figure 10 shows a picture of animation of the Orbit robot simulated in Gazebo.

4.1   Step Reference Without Saturation

Figure 11 shows the step response for a position step of 0.1 rad applied in the joint 1 of the leg of the robot.

Figure 12 shows the input torque applied to joint 1. There is a peak of 1058 Nm associated to the position overshoot shown in Fig. 11. It is important to note that those values are for the joint axis and not for the actuator axis since reductions were not included in the model.

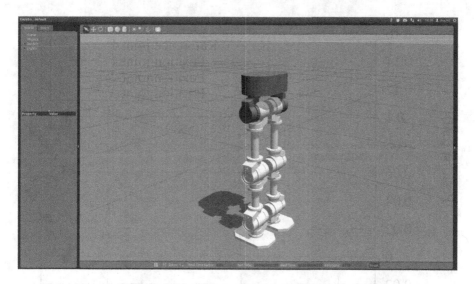

Fig. 10. Orbit robot simulated in Gazebo.

The peaks shown in Figs. 11 and 12 are intrinsic to feedback linearization controllers, such as the computed torque controller, which are known to generate large effort signals for step references. This problem is mitigated in robotics by not applying a step input directly to the joints, but using a trajectory generator to smooth the reference applied to the joint controller. Furthermore, as the model used to compute the control law was implemented by using the ChainIdSolver_RNE from KDL and the simulation performed by Gazebo is based on the ODE library [11], it is possible that some model mismatch remains.

Figure 13 shows the input torque applied to joints 2 and 3. There is a peak of 430 Nm (joint 2) and 50 Nm (joint 3), associated to the position overshoot shown in Fig. 11. It is important to note that those values are for the joint axis and not for the actuator axis since a reduction was not included in the model.

4.2   Step Reference with Saturating Control

As shown in Sect. 4.1, the torque required to follow a step reference is very high and in an actual robot would lead to actuator saturation. In this section the simulation is repeated but now considering that actuators have their torques limited to 20.7 Nm, which is the nominal torque for the Schunk PRL 80 actuator. The step reference applied to joint 1 has an amplitude of 0.1 rad.

Figure 14 shows the reference and positions for joint 1, 2 and 3. There is an limitation on the rising rate, which is forced by the saturation of the actuator. Then there is as small overshoot and the steady state error is close to zero.

Figure 15 shows the torque applied to joint 1. Note that there is a saturation at 20.7 Nm between 1 s and approximately 1.2 s.

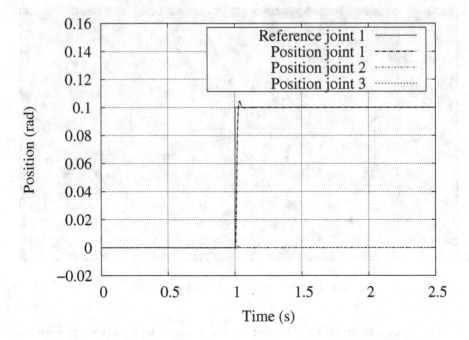

Fig. 11. Reference for joint 1 and positions of joints 1, 2 and 3.

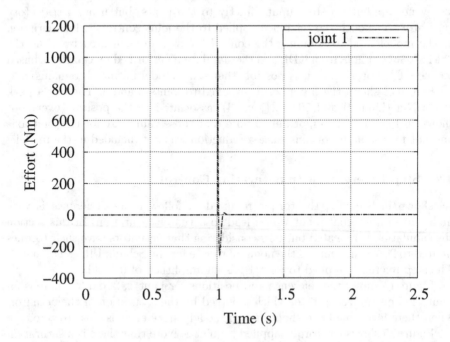

Fig. 12. Effort applied to joint 1.

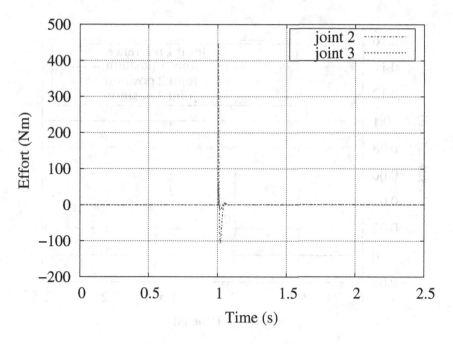

Fig. 13. Efforts applied to joints 2 and 3.

Figure 16 shows the torque on joints 2 and 3. Those torques are generated by the controller as compensating forces to keep the knee joint (joint 2) and the foot joint (joint 3) at their desired position. It is possible to note from Fig. 14 that those joints move about 0.07 rad. That motion is larger than in the case without saturation because the torques on joints 2 and 3 saturate as well.

5 Linear Interpolation Trajectory

To reduce the torque required to move the joint a smooth trajectory based on quintic polynomial interpolation was used. Then, position, velocity and acceleration references are feed to the computed torque controller (see Fig. 5), which tends to produce a smoother trajectory and lower torque requirements. The reference and position for joint can be seen in Fig. 17, where its possible to note that the joint position follows the reference with a very small error.

The torque required is much smaller than the required for the step reference. Figure 18 shows that due the smoother reference, the torque applied to joint 1 is reduced with peaks of 4.24 Nm at the inflection points at 1 s and 2 s.

Torques on joints 2 and 3 are also significantly reduced when compared to the values required for the step reference, as shown in Fig. 19.

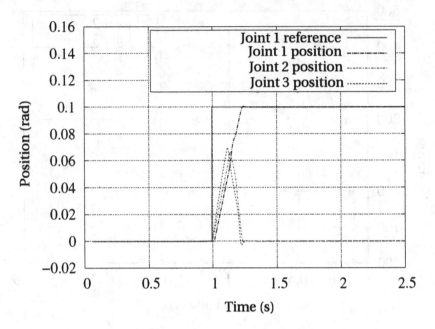

Fig. 14. Reference for joint 1 and positions of joints 1, 2 and 3 with saturating control.

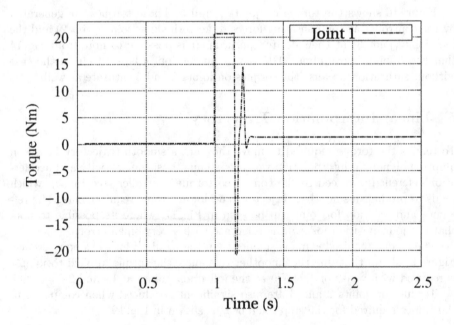

Fig. 15. Effort applied to joint 1 with saturating control.

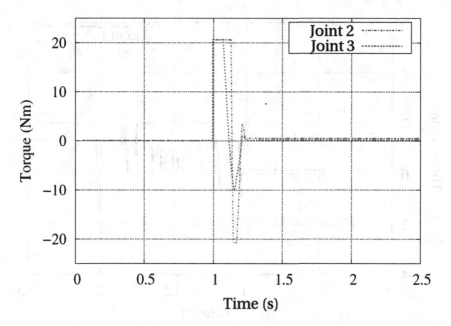

Fig. 16. Efforts on joints 2 and 3 with saturating control.

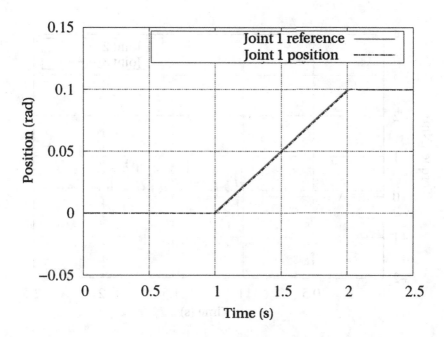

Fig. 17. Reference and position for joint 1.

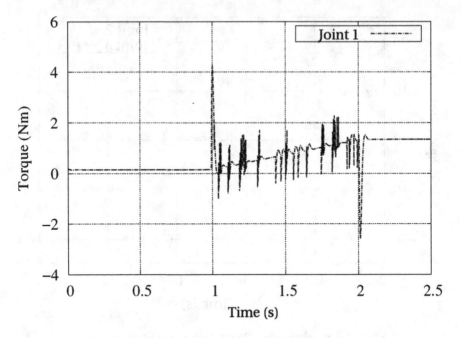

Fig. 18. Effort applied to joint 1.

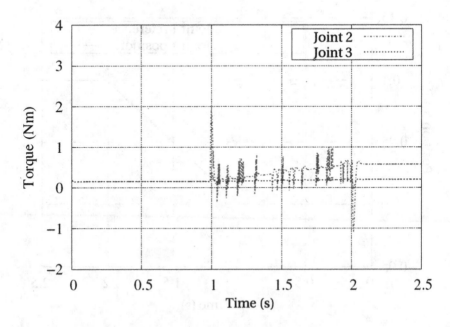

Fig. 19. Effort applied to joints 2 and 3.

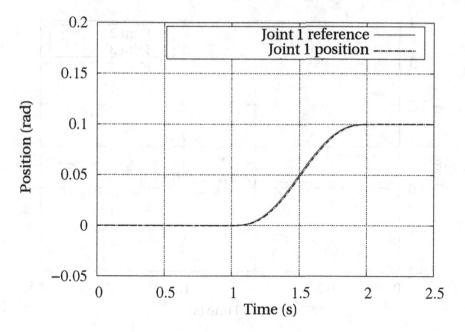

Fig. 20. Reference and position for joint 1.

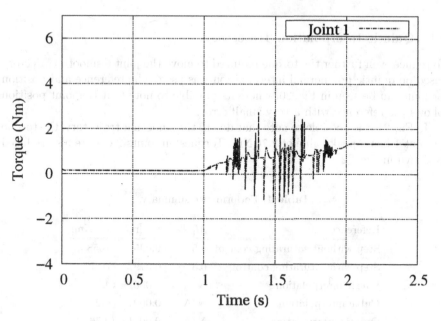

Fig. 21. Torque applied on joint 1.

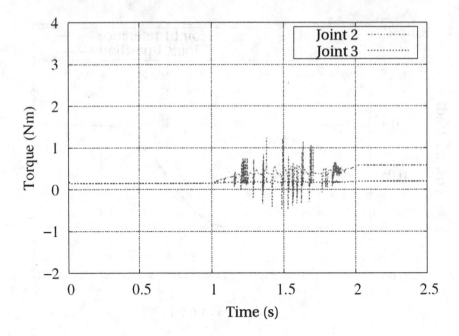

Fig. 22. Torques on joints 2 and 3.

5.1   Quintic Interpolation Trajectory

To reduce even further the torque required to move the joint a smooth trajectory based on quintic polynomial interpolation was used. The reference and position for joint can be seen in Fig. 20, where its possible to note that the joint position follows the reference with a very small error.

In Fig. 21 it is possible to note that due to the smoother trajectory, the torque on joint 1 has a peak value of 2.76 Nm. Torques on joints 2 e 3 are also reduced as shown in Fig. 22.

Table 1. Performance summary.

Reference	M_p [%]	ϵ_{ss} [rad]	τ_p [Nm]
Step without saturating control	4.5	0.0955	1058
Step with saturating control	0.3	0.0997	20.7
Linear interpolation	N/A	0.0001	4.24
Cubic interpolation	N/A	0.0001	2.20
Quintic interpolation	N/A	0.0001	2.76

Table 1 summarizes the results for the computed torque controller. The over-shoot (M_p), steady state error (ϵ_{ss}) and the peak torque (τ_p) for each reference trajectory are shown. The curves for the cubic interpolation trajectories are not shown in previous sections due to space limitations. It can be verified that the tracking error is small, but for the step reference, the required torque is very high. That is a characteristic of the computed torque controller, which is not adequate for step references.

6   Conclusion

This work presented the development of a simplified model of the lower members of a biped robot with six degrees o freedom. The use of ROS reduced the implementation time due to reuse of components such as the `joint_states_publisher` and the `robot_state_publisher`. However, there is a lack of documentation on how to write controllers for ROS, in special for general nonlinear and/or MIMO controllers and this work intents to fill a part of this gap in the literature. Most controllers implemented in ROS use a SISO architecture with a PID control law. Contrariwise, here a MIMO, no linear controller based on the computed torque controller was implemented.

The performance of the controller, evaluated with step, linear, cubic and quintic polynomial trajectories, was adequate for linear, cubic and quintic reference trajectories, with steady state error under 0.0001 rad and torque well under saturating limits, while the step reference trajectory caused saturation of the controller output and three orders of magnitude larger errors.

After some improvements in its documentation, the package developed in this work will be made available to ROS users.

References

1. Bruyninckx, H.: Open robot control software: the OROCOS project. In: Proceedings of the IEEE International Conference on Robotics and Automation (ICRA), pp. 2523–2528 (2001)
2. Featherstone, R.: Robot Dynamics Algorithms. Kluwer international series in engineering and computer science: Robotics. Springer, New York (2008)
3. Fred, R. Sias, J., Zheng, Y.F.: How many degrees-of-freedom does a biped need. In: Proceedings of the IEEE International Workshop on Intelligent Robtots and System, California, USA, pp. 297–302 (1990)
4. Fu, K.S., Gonzalez, R.C., Lee, C.S.G.: Robotics Control, Sensing, Vision and Intelligence, 2nd edn. Mcgraw-Hill Book Company, New York (1987)
5. Gouaillier, D., Hugel, V., Blazevic, P., Kilner, C., Monceaux, J., Lafourcade, P., Marnier, B., Serre, J., Maisonnier, B.: Mechatronic design of NAO humanoid. In: Proceedings of the IEEE International Conference on Robotics and Automation (ICRA), Kobe, Japan, pp. 769–774 (2009)
6. Hasehawa, Y., Arakawa, T., Fukuda, F.: Trajectory generation for bipedal locomotion robots. Mechatronics $10(1–2)$, 67–89 (2000)
7. Koenig, N., Howard, A.: Design and use paradigms for gazebo, an open-source multi-robot simulator. In: Proceedings of the IEEE/RSJ International Conference on Intelligent Robots and Systems, pp. 2149–2154 (2004)

8. Lum, H.K., Zribi, M., Soh, Y.C.: Planning and control of a biped robot. Int. J. Eng. Sci. **37**(10), 1319–1349 (1999)

9. Quigley, M., Conley, K., Gerkey, B.P., Faust, J., Foote, T., Leibs, J., Wheeler, R., Ng, A.Y.: ROS: an open-source robot operating system. In: Proceedings of the ICRA Workshop on Open Source Software. IEEE Press, Kobe (2009)

10. Riezenman, M.J.: Robots stand on own two feet. In: IEEE Spectrum, vol. 39, pp. 24–25 (2002)

11. Smith, R.: Open dynamics engine. <http://www.ode.org> (2005)

12. Sucan, I.: Wiki of the unified robot description format (URDF), February 2009. <http://wiki.ros.org/urdf> [Online; acessado em 07 February 2014]

13. Van Zutven, P.W.M., Assman, T.M., Caarls, J., Cilli, C., Boshoven, T.P.M., Ilhan, E., Baelemans, J.A.J., Heck, D.J.F., Spoelstra, M.P.A., Nijmeijer, H.: Tech united eindhoven robocup adult size humanoid team description 2013. In: Proceedings of the 17th Annual RoboCup International Symposium (2013)

14. de Waard, M., Inja, M., Visser, A.: Analysis of flat terrain for the atlas robot. In: Proceedings of the 3rd Joint Conference of AI & Robotics and 5th RoboCup Iran Open International Symposium, vol. 3, pp. 1–6 (2013)

Adaptive Path Planning for Multiple Vehicles with Bounded Curvature

Douglas G. Macharet[✉] and Mario F.M. Campos

Computer Vision and Robotics Laboratory, Computer Science Department,
Universidade Federal de Minas Gerais, Belo Horizonte, MG, Brazil
{doug,mario}@dcc.ufmg.br

Abstract. In this paper we introduce the k-Dynamic Dubins TSP with Neighborhoods (k-DDTSPN), the problem consisting of planning efficient paths among a set of target regions dynamically selected in the environment for multiple robots with bounded curvature (Dubins vehicle). We propose a decentralized auction-based technique, which uses a greedy constructive strategy to dynamically calculate the cost of insertion of the new region to each path and selects the one with the minimum impact on the length. We provide a formal analysis of the proposed technique, presenting an upper bound for the length of the longest tour. Several trials were executed in a simulated environment, allowing for a statistical investigation of the results.

Keywords: Dynamic vehicle routing problem · Dubins vehicle · Traveling salesman problem with neighborhoods

1 Introduction

Finding feasible paths for mobile agents that are either length or time optimized has been the goal of several research fields. In this context, the Traveling Salesman Problem (TSP) remains as one of the most studied problems. However, for several real-world scenarios the mathematical formulation of the TSP may be either insufficient or too simplistic to be useful.

The TSP has been generalized in several ways. In the Dubins TSP (DTSP), the travel path must conform to a minimum turning radius ρ (known as a nonholonomic constraint) at all points. The TSP with Neighborhoods (TSPN) considers each city as a region instead of a point, and to visit a city, the salesman must reach any point inside that region. The k-TSP (k-TSP) employs k salesmen that start and end at a single city, and the cities must be visited once by one of the salesmen. Others generalizations consider combinations of the previously mentioned problems, such as the Dubins TSP with Neighborhoods (DTSPN) and the k-Dubins TSP with Neighborhoods (k-DTSPN).

Howerver, even tackling the aforementioned problems together, current literature usually considers static instances, i.e., the vehicles are dispatched to follow an immutable, previously planned path. Therefore, actual methodologies do not

© Springer-Verlag Berlin Heidelberg 2015
F.S. Osório et al. (Eds.): LARS/SBR/Robocontrol 2014, CCIS 507, pp. 153–168, 2015.
DOI: 10.1007/978-3-662-48134-9_9

take into account the intrinsically dynamic nature of many different issues that may arise. For example, in a Wireless Sensor Network (WSN) new nodes (or those awakening from sleep states) must be attended by the vehicles as soon as possible. In other words, the path (actually its untraveled portion) should be reshaped to cover new regions of interest that are randomly created over time, after the vehicle has departed.

In the present paper we introduce the k-Dynamic Dubins TSP with Neighborhoods (k-DDTSPN), where the vehicles' paths may be modified in real-time (with the robot in motion) to account for new target regions. We propose a decentralized auction-based algorithm to solve this problem and provide an empirical competitive analysis of our results [12].

Figure 1 illustrates the problem addressed here, allowing for a better visualization of the key issues described previously. It is possible to observe the initial distribution of some regions on the environment, followed by the paths considering these already known regions. Next, after all vehicles have started the navigation, and with the insertion of new regions, the paths might be adapted. Therefore, the main objective is to visit all regions with the minimum time possible.

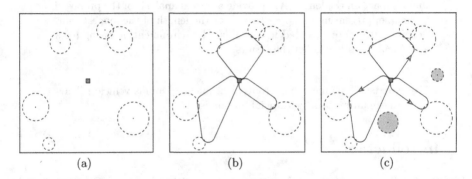

(a)   (b)   (c)

Fig. 1. Example of the dynamic routing problem with nonholonomic vehicles to visit a set of target regions. (a) Initial distribution of the regions (dashed circles), where the central square represents the departure/return point. (b) Initial set of routes through all previously known regions. (c) The vehicles (yellow triangles) already executing the routes when new regions (shown in gray) are added to the environment (Color figure online).

The main contribution of this paper is a decentralized auction-based path planning algorithm for multiple vehicles with bounded curvature to visit regions that are dynamically selected in the environment. To the best of our knowledge, this work is the first to address the dynamic version of the k-DTSPN [16].

The remainder of this paper is structured as follows. A review of the literature is presented in Sect. 2; in Sect. 3, initially we provide the problem formalization, next we discuss the proposed methodology and present a formal analysis regarding time and length complexity; numerical results for different scenarios and statistical analysis are shown in Sect. 4. Finally, in Sect. 5 we draw the conclusions and discuss avenues for future investigation.

2 Related Work

Several shortest path algorithms for vehicles with no constraints can be found in the literature. The Traveling Salesman Problem (TSP), for example, is a fundamental optimization problem and has been widely studied [1].

The challenge of generating a minimum length path through a set of waypoints for a single vehicle, subject to minimum curvature constraints and making use of Dubins curves [9], was initially introduced in [21]. This problem was named DTSP and was further studied in [13,14,25].

The TSPN was initially introduced in [2], where each city to be visited is represented as a geographic region, referred to as the neighborhood of the city. The TSPN is often used to model problems related to the generation of tours to collect data from Wireless Sensor Networks [5,28].

Recently, the constraints imposed by the DTSP and the TSPN began to be considered as part of the same problem, which will be referred here as the DTSPN. In [11,18] a sampling based approach is used, while in [15] a simple three-step evolutionary algorithm was presented.

The k-TSP aims to generate paths to k salesmen departing from a given city and returning to it, after each one of all cities have been visited by a single salesman [7,27]. The generation of paths for multiple Dubins vehicles has been the focus of a great amount of research, specially for Unmanned Aerial Vehicles (UAVs) [10,19]. However, in most works the problem is not modeled with a single start/end point (i.e. a base) for all vehicles, in contrast to the constraints imposed by the classical Vehicle Routing Problem (VRP).

The TSPN has also been approached considering the use of multiple vehicles [3,26]. However, in both works the possible constraints of the vehicle are not considered by the methodologies, resulting in paths that may be unfeasible by a real vehicle. The extension to consider multiple Dubins vehicles (i.e. k-DTSPN) was first introduced in [16], where two approaches were proposed, an heuristic based on classical techniques on the literature and a memetic algorithm.

Finally, the last issue to be considered is the dynamic nature posed by the problem. More specifically, we refer to scenarios where not all information on the locations to be visited is available when the paths are initially planned and the vehicles are already en route. Most of the works dealing with the dynamic problem mantains the vehicles in a constant pattern [20] or divide the environment, making each vehicle responsible for a subregion [10]. These approaches lead to a high energy consumption.

3 Methodology

3.1 Theoretical Formalization

Let us consider the scenario where a team of k robots must visit a set of regions of interest, such as nodes of a wireless network or targets for visual inspection (i.e., environmental surveillance). Let $\mathcal{H} = \{\mathcal{H}_0, \mathcal{H}_1, \ldots, \mathcal{H}_N\}$, where $\mathcal{H}_i \subset \mathbb{R}^2$, be a set of $N+1$ closed regions representing the neighborhood of each node i. The key to the underlying problem is to guarantee that every region $\mathcal{H}_i$ is visited by at least one robot. We call $\mathcal{H}_0$ the *base area*, where all robots are initially located and to which all must return at the end of the mission.

For simplicity reasons[1], we consider that each region $\mathcal{H}_i$ is circular and centered at coordinates $\mathbf{n}_i = (x_i, y_i)$. Each region can be formally defined as:

$$\mathcal{H}_i = \{\mathbf{p} \in \mathbb{R}^2 : \|\mathbf{p} - \mathbf{n}_i\| \leq r_i\},$$

where r_i is the radius of the i-th node neighborhood.

We model each robot on the team as a classical Dubins vehicle [9], constrained to a predefined maximum curvature (κ) and unable to move backwards. As far as the underlying physics of the system is concerned, the curvature may be defined as a quantity directly proportional to the lateral acceleration of the vehicle. The value of κ is then inversely proportional to the minimum radius of curvature (ρ) of the curve the vehicle is capable of executing. We use the notation $\mathbf{q} = \langle \mathbf{p}, \psi \rangle$, where $\mathbf{q} \in \text{SE}(2)$, to represent a configuration that a robot must eventually reach (*waypoint*). A waypoint is always placed inside some region $\mathcal{H}_i$, i.e., $\mathbf{q} \in \bigcup_{i=1}^{N} \mathcal{H}_i$. When a robot assumes a configuration $\mathbf{q}$, we consider that the corresponding region $\mathcal{H}_i$ was *visited* by that robot. The entire set of waypoints (excluding the base) will be referenced as $\mathcal{Q} = \{\mathbf{q}_1, \ldots, \mathbf{q}_P\}$.

Now, let $\mathcal{T} = \{\tau_1, \tau_2, \ldots, \tau_k\}$ be the set of tours τ_j assigned to each robot j, where each tour by definition begins and ends at the waypoint lying on the base area. Formally:

$$\tau_j = \langle \mathbf{q}_{\text{base}}^{(j)}, \mathbf{q}_1^{(j)}, \mathbf{q}_2^{(j)}, \ldots, \mathbf{q}_{\text{base}}^{(j)} \rangle,$$

where the waypoints $\mathbf{q}_c^{(j)}$ are in one-to-one correspondence with the set $\mathcal{Q}$, i.e.:

$$\mathbf{q}_c^{(j)} \in \mathcal{Q} \qquad \text{subject to}$$
$$\mathbf{q}_c^{(j)} \neq \mathbf{q}_{c'}^{(j')} \qquad \forall c \neq c' \vee j \neq j'$$

and the base waypoints $\mathbf{q}_{\text{base}}^{(j)}$ are all inside the base region, $\mathcal{H}_0$. For simplicity reasons, we define each tour τ_j as a sequence $\Sigma_j = \langle 0, a, b, \ldots, 0 \rangle$ of waypoint (configuration) indexes from the set $\mathcal{Q}$.

Before tackling the dynamic part of this article, let us first provide some definitions for the particular initial scenario, where a set of known regions was already inserted in the environment (i.e. k-DTSPN). In this case, we must optimize the Dubins circuit length as

$$\underset{\mathcal{T}}{\text{minimize}} \ \mathcal{X}(\mathcal{Q}), \tag{1}$$

having $\mathcal{X} : \text{SE}(2)^P \to \mathbb{R}_0^+$, where

---

[1] This is not a restriction of the method – just a convenience to keep reasoning, implementation, and results visualization simple. The methodology proposed in this paper covers continuous, convex regions in general.

$$\mathcal{X}(\mathcal{Q}) = \max_{j} \left[\mathcal{L}_\rho^j(\mathcal{Q}_{\Sigma_j}) \right], \ j = 1, \dots, k, \tag{2}$$

is the Dubins circuit length of the longest tour in $\mathcal{T}$, calculated as

$$\mathcal{L}_\rho^j(\mathcal{Q}_{\Sigma_j}) = \sum \mathcal{D}_\rho(\mathbf{q}_c^{(j)}, \mathbf{q}_{c+1}^{(j)}) \qquad \forall \mathbf{q}_c^{(j)} \in \tau_j, \tag{3}$$

and $\mathcal{D}_\rho : \mathrm{SE}(2) \times \mathrm{SE}(2) \to \mathbb{R}_0^+$ is the length of the shortest Dubins path with minimum radius of curvature ρ between two configurations of a tour.

Therefore, the k-Dynamic Dubins TSP with Neighborhoods (k-DDTSPN) can be defined as: given an unbounded number of new regions of interest being selected in the environment, the problem of serving a new region is the problem of creating a new waypoint sequence for a certain tour over a starting waypoint sequence originally solved for the k-DTSPN.

3.2 Decentralized Auction-Based Path Planning

In a static scenario (i.e. k-DTSPN), one can assume that the calculation of the mission is performed initially and then allocated to each of the vehicles (remaining the same throughout the navigation). However, in a dynamic scenario (i.e. k-DDTSPN), with the selection of a new region in the environment, it is necessary to make a decision during the execution of the mission, i.e., which vehicle will be responsible for visiting the region. Thus, the initial set of routes must be adapted, demanding some sort of coordination between the vehicles.

Therefore, the methodology works as follows: whenever a new demand arrives to the routing system, we use a greedy constructive distributed strategy to compute the cost of insertion of this region to each path, and select the one with the minimum impact on the length. This approach is similar to the classical Push-forward Insertion Heuristic (PFIH) [24]. Recalling that the main objective is to minimize the total time of visit, which is directly related to the length of the longest tour (we assume that all vehicles travel with a constant and equal speed). Figure 2 presents an overall flowchart of the execution.

An approach widely used for solving the problem of coordinating multiple agents is based on economic market-based models, more specifically the auction mechanism [8]. In an auction, a set of items is offered by an auctioneer and the

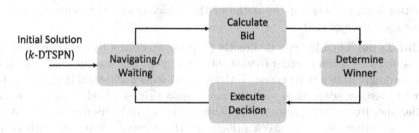

Fig. 2. Methodology flowchart.

participants can make bids according to the intention of obtaining such items. Then after all the bids have been collected, it is up to the auctioneer to determine the winner of each item based on some specific metric.

However, one of the main problems of a classical auction is the use of a centralized entity for the determination of winners. Thus, if a problem occurs with this particular agent, the functioning of the entire system would be compromised. Considering this problem, several studies have proposed extensions to the auction method enabling to use it in a distributed and decentralized manner by removing the need for a central auctioneer [4, 17, 29].

In this paper we use similar concepts to the aforementioned works. When a new region of interest is selected, each vehicle calculates a value for the bid and sends a *broadcast* for all other vehicles on the environment. After receiving all bids, each vehicle executes an internal auction and determines the winner. The winning vehicle must then modify their route in order to visit the new region. We assume a perfect communication network between vehicles.

In order to ensure a completely decentralized method, a key step is the choice of the information that will compose the bid. This information should be sufficient for all vehicles participating in the auction to always make the same decision about the winning bid. Furthermore, it is important to consider the use of a small number of fields, reducing the size of the message and making it easier (and faster) to be sent. Thus, we define that a given bid **b** is a tuple consisting of the following information:

$$\mathbf{b} = \langle \text{cost, bid type, tiebreaker field, vehicle id} \rangle,$$

where

- **Cost**: Represents the cost for the vehicle to visit the new region. The cost is directly related to the impact on the path's length. If the path does not need to be modified, the bid will have zero cost. If the previously calculated path needs to be changed, the cost associated with the bid will be the length of the path still to be traveled considering the required change, given by

$$\hat{\mathcal{L}}_\rho^{\text{rem}} = \hat{\mathcal{L}}_\rho - \mathcal{L}_\rho^{\text{vehicle}}, \tag{4}$$

where $\hat{\mathcal{L}}_\rho$ represents the new path length if the change was made and $\mathcal{L}_\rho^{\text{vehicle}}$ is the distance already traveled by the vehicle in the path. Considering the remaining distance to be traveled, the algorithm will be able to maintain a better balance between the paths of the vehicles, and therefore, optimizing the total time of visit.

- **Bid Type**: The bid type is directly mapped according to the type of action that must be taken in order to visit the new region. The actions are determined accordingly to two basic cases: (i) the path remains unchanged (Fig. 3); (ii) the path must be adapted to visit the new region (Fig. 4). Each type receives an identifier from those presented in Table 1, which will be used primarily as one of the tiebreakers. It is given priority to those cases where the path is not changed, e.g., types 0 through 2.

Table 1. Bid types.

Identifier	Description
0	Trivial case, new region encompasses the vehicle's current position
1	Waypoint already within the reach of the new region
2	New region has intersection with active part of the path
3	Vehicle must change the current movement to visit the region
4	Active part of the path must be modified to reach the region

– **Tiebreaker Field**: Parameter used for the tiebreaker if the former fields (cost and bid type) are unable to guarantee the uniqueness of the winning bid. This field will be set according to the bid type, being:
  - **Type 0**: Determined as the total number of waypoints (active and not active) in the current path of the vehicle, represented by $|\mathcal{Q}_{\text{vehicle}}|$.
  - **Type 1**: Determined as the number of regions already associated to a given waypoint $\mathbf{q}_p$ which is within the reach of the new region, represented as $|\mathcal{H}_{\mathbf{q}_p}|$, where

$$\mathcal{H}_{\mathbf{q}_p} = \{\mathcal{H}_i \in \mathcal{H}_{\mathbf{q}_p} : \mathbf{q}_p \in \mathcal{H}_i, \ \forall \ \mathcal{H}_i \in \mathcal{H}\}. \tag{5}$$

  - **Type 2**: Determined as the distance from the current vehicle position until the intersection with the new region, following the current path of the vehicle, represented by the variable L.
  - **Type 3** and **Type 4**: Determined as the total number of active points in the current path of the vehicle, represented by $|\mathcal{Q}_{\text{vehicle}}^{\text{active}}|$.

  In all cases priority is given to the bidder who has the tie-breaking field with the lowest value. In the cases where there is no need to change the path, the criteria were chosen so that it is possible to consider a future task execution time once the vehicle has reached the waypoint.
– **Vehicle id**: Unique identifier for each vehicle defined as $\mathcal{V}_{\text{id}}$, used to distinguish each one from the others in the group. Will be used if a tie persists in the auction. In this case, it may be considered that any of the vehicles that made these conflicted bids can be the winner, without compromising the effectiveness of the method.

Algorithm 1 presents the steps each vehicle must execute in order to determine the bid that will be held. The algorithm is based on a greedy strategy, verifying sequentially which type (accordingly to Table 1) applies to the specific current scenario of insertion of a new region.

Finally, Algorithm 2 presents the proposed method for determining the winning bid of the auction. The method takes as input the set $\mathcal{B} = \{\mathbf{b}_1, \mathbf{b}_2, \ldots, \mathbf{b}_k\}$, consisting of all bid of all vehicles. Locally, in a decentralized manner, each vehicle goes through the set and the winner is selected considering the fields of the bids sequentially.

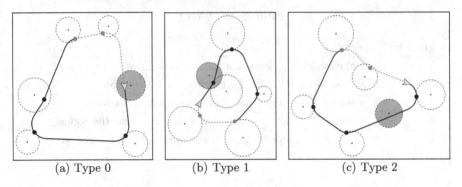

(a) Type 0   (b) Type 1   (c) Type 2

Fig. 3. Examples illustrating the cases where the path is not changed with the insertion of a new region. The yellow triangle represents the vehicle and the dark gray region is the last one inserted. The light gray dashed part of the path has already been traversed, and the black part represents the active part (yet to be traveled) (Color figure online).

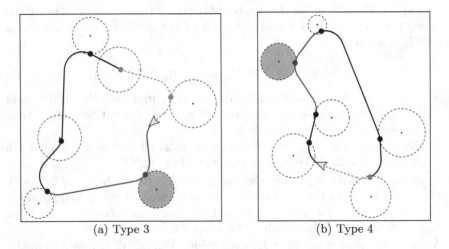

(a) Type 3   (b) Type 4

Fig. 4. Examples illustrating the cases where the path must be dynamically modified in order to visit the new region. The blue part of the path represents a part that did not previously exist before the insertion of the new region (dark gray circle) (Color figure online).

The fields that compose a bid were chosen to prevent the existence of conflicts (draws). Therefore, it is guaranteed that, in a decentralized manner, all vehicles will determine the same winning bid for the auction.

3.3   Complexity Analysis

In this section we present the analysis of the computational complexity of the proposed methodology, which is based on a decentralized auction algorithm.

Algorithm 1. CreateBid($\mathcal{H}_{\text{new}}$)

1: **if** Type 0 **then**
2:      **return** b $= \langle 0,\ 0,\ |\mathcal{Q}_{\text{vehicle}}|,\ \mathcal{V}_{\text{id}} \rangle$
3: **else if** Type 1 **then**
4:      **return** b $= \langle 0,\ 1, |\mathcal{H}_{\mathbf{q}_p}|,\ \mathcal{V}_{\text{id}} \rangle$
5: **else if** Type 2 **then**
6:      **return** b $= \langle 0,\ 2, L,\ \mathcal{V}_{\text{id}} \rangle$
7: **else if** Type 3 produces better result than Type 4 **then**
8:      **return** b $= \langle \hat{\mathcal{L}}_\rho^{\text{rem}},\ 3,\ |\mathcal{Q}_{\text{vehicle}}^{\text{active}}|,\ \mathcal{V}_{\text{id}} \rangle$
9: **else**
10:      **return** b $= \langle \hat{\mathcal{L}}_\rho^{\text{rem}},\ 4,\ |\mathcal{Q}_{\text{vehicle}}^{\text{active}}|,\ \mathcal{V}_{\text{id}} \rangle$
11: **end if**

Algorithm 2. DetermineWinningBid($\mathcal{B}$)

1: $\mathcal{B}^* \leftarrow$ Select bids in $\mathcal{B}$ with the lowest cost
2: **if** $|\mathcal{B}^*| == 1$ **then**
3:      **return** Single element of $\mathcal{B}^*$
4: **else**
5:      $\mathcal{B}^* \leftarrow$ Select bids in $\mathcal{B}$ with the smallest type identifier
6:      **if** $|\mathcal{B}^*| == 1$ **then**
7:          **return** Single element of $\mathcal{B}^*$
8:      **else**
9:          $\mathcal{B}^* \leftarrow$ Select bids in $\mathcal{B}$ according to the tiebreaker field
10:          **if** $|\mathcal{B}^*| == 1$ **then**
11:              **return** Single element of $\mathcal{B}^*$
12:          **else**
13:              **return** b $\in \mathcal{B}^*$ with the smallest vehicle identifier
14:          **end if**
15:      **end if**
16: **end if**

Initially, we consider the asymptotic behavior relative to the runtime of the algorithm, then the upper limit for the path length (longest route) is discussed.
    The technique is divided in two main steps, as follows:

- **Bid Calculation:** This step evaluates all possible cases in order to calculate the bid cost and type. Therefore, all P waypoints are traversed and in a greedly manner it is determined if the path must be changed or not. Since, $P \leq N$ (considering the existance of intersections between the regions), in the worst case, a robot will take $O(n)$ to calculate the bid, where n is the number of regions and only one robot must attend all regions.
- **Winner Selection:** This step consists of running through the entire set of bids to determine which one has the lowest cost. Therefore, also having a linear cost $O(m)$, where m is the number of bids made, which is directly proportional to the number of vehicles being used.

Therefore, the overall computational cost of the methodology is $O(n)+O(m)$, accordingly to the number of regions already selected in the environment (n) and the number of vehicles being used to execute the mission (m).

For the sake of simplicity, in this work we model the inclusion rate of new regions as a homogeneous spatio-temporal Poisson process, with constant $\lambda > 0$ that represents an estimate of the amount of new regions created in a given time unit. The cumulative distribution function of a Poisson process can be represented by the exponential distribution:

$$F(x) = 1 - e^{-\lambda x}, \qquad x \geq 0. \tag{6}$$

Winning bids with types identifiers between 0 and 2, i.e., trivial case, waypoint already in range and intersection with active part, do not result in a change in the path, and thus have no impact on the final length of the longest route. Bids with types 3 and 4, i.e., change current movement or change active part of the path, will be considered accordingly to the worst case scenario, where all new regions are placed in the same route – a fact that might not occur due to the strategy used to better balance the distribution of regions between vehicles.

Therefore, it can be assumed that the approximate average length of the longest route in a instant of time t is obtained by

$$\mathcal{X}^t \lesssim \mathcal{X}^0 + (\lambda t)(2D^{\mathcal{X}}_{\max} k\rho\pi), \tag{7}$$

where $\mathcal{X}^0$ is the initial length of the longest route for the static case (i.e. k-DTSPN) and λt is the expected average number of new regions in the time interval $(0,t]$ according to the rate λ of the Poisson process used. The value $D^{\mathcal{X}}_{\max}$ is defined as

$$D^{\mathcal{X}}_{\max} = \max_{\forall i,j \,\mid\, \mathbf{p}_i,\mathbf{p}_j \,\in\, \mathcal{X}} \|\mathbf{p}_i - \mathbf{p}_j\|, \tag{8}$$

and corresponds to the maximum Euclidean distance between two waypoints that belong to the longest route.

Recalling that accordingly to Theorem 3.4 from [22], the upper bound of the length of a Dubins curve connecting two configurations is given by

$$\mathcal{D}_\rho(\mathbf{q}_i, \mathbf{q}_j) \leq \|\mathbf{p}_i - \mathbf{p}_j\| + k\rho\pi, \tag{9}$$

where $k \in [2.657, 2.658]$ and ρ is the minimum turning radius of the vehicle.

Finally, the number of messages sent by each vehicle along the execution is directly proportional to the number of inserted regions, i.e., λt, and the number of messages received is $(k-1)(\lambda t)$. Therefore, the total number of messages exchanged in the network will be $k(\lambda t)$.

4   Numerical Evaluation

In this section we describe our simulations and the corresponding statistical analysis. All Euclidean Traveling Salesman Problem (ETSP) problems instances were solved to optimality using the well-known TSP solver *Concorde* [6]. The initial solutions to the static problem (k-DTSPN) were obtained using the Memetic Algorithm proposed in [16].

Initially, the images shown in Fig. 5 present an example execution of the methodology over time for a given instance. In this example, we used an environment with dimensions 3000 m × 3000 m containing, initially, 20 regions randomly

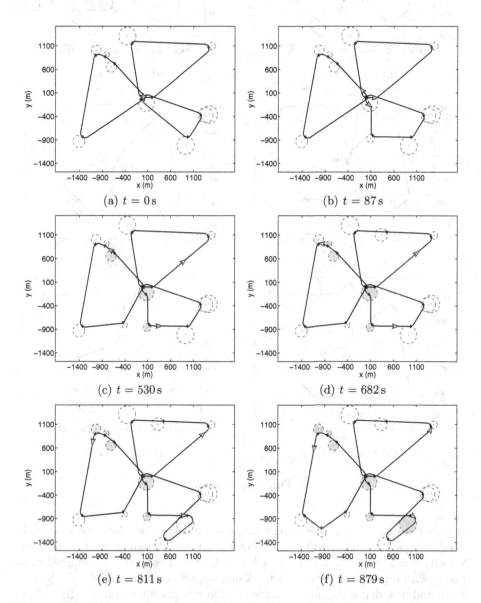

Fig. 5. Example of the methodology execution over time for a given instance. The regions highlighted (green) represent the ones already visited. The yellow triangles represent the position of the vehicles at that time (Color figure online).

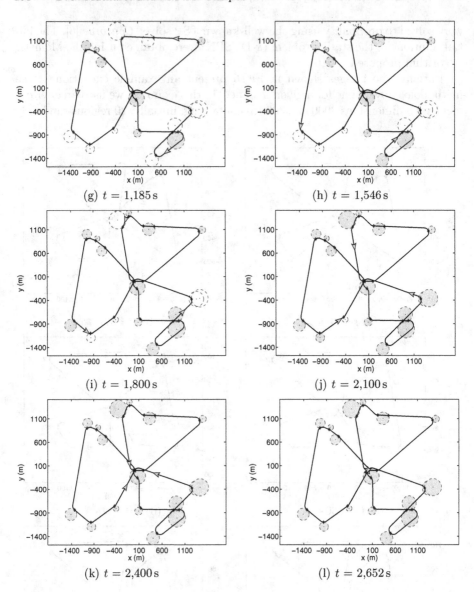

(g) $t = 1{,}185\,\mathrm{s}$

(h) $t = 1{,}546\,\mathrm{s}$

(i) $t = 1{,}800\,\mathrm{s}$

(j) $t = 2{,}100\,\mathrm{s}$

(k) $t = 2{,}400\,\mathrm{s}$

(l) $t = 2{,}652\,\mathrm{s}$

Fig. 5. (*continued*)

distributed uniformly. It was determined the use of at most three vehicles, each one having a minimum turning radius of $\rho = 100\,\mathrm{m}$ and moving with a constant velocity $\nu = 2\,\mathrm{m/s}$. The radius of each circular region was also determined randomly within the range $[50\,\mathrm{m}, 200\,\mathrm{m}]$. A new region insertion rate of $\lambda = \frac{1}{180}$ was used, and new demands must be added in the execution interval $(0\,\mathrm{s}; 1600\,\mathrm{s})$.

The variable used as the cost of the bid (length of the remaining path after a possible modification) produces an important effect which is a better load balance between all robots. This is evidenced in the fact that, despite the significant difference of the paths in the mission start, by the end, the robots return to the base almost at the same time. The load balance allows to reduce the impact on the length of the longest tour, and therefore helping to minimize the total time of visit.

The most widely accepted approach in the literature to measure the performance of Online Algorithms (i.e., those concerning instances partially known at the beginning and gradually increased) is the *Competitive Analysis* [12]. This approach was firstly introduced in [23] and presents a way to evaluate the performance of such algorithms based on the competitive ratio criterion.

The competitive ratio of an algorithm is defined as the ratio between the worst result obtained by the online algorithm (upper bound) and the optimal result obtained by an offline method (lower bound). Formally:

$$\mathbf{cr}_A = \sup_I \frac{z(A, I)}{z^*(I)}, \tag{10}$$

where $z(A, I)$ is the cost of the result found by the online algorithm A for an instance I, and z^* is the cost of the optimal result found by an offline algorithm with prior knowledge for any instance I. In our context, "cost" means the length of the longest Dubins tour. Since neither upper and lower bounds are formally defined for this problem, we carried out an empirical competitive analysis.

Therefore, we have executed 300 experiments in an environment with dimensions $4000\,\text{m} \times 4000\,\text{m}$, and initially containing 10 circular regions placed according to an uniform random distribution. The radius of each circular region was also chosen randomly from the interval $[50\,\text{m}, 250\,\text{m}]$. It was determined the use of at most four vehicles, each one with a minimum turning radius of $\rho = 100\,\text{m}$ and moving with constant speed $\nu = 2\,\text{m/s}$. New regions were inserted with a rate of $\lambda = \frac{1}{120}$, and regions were scheduled to be inserted within the interval of $(0\,\text{s}; 3600\,\text{s}]$. Since, to the best of our knowledge, no optimal offline algorithm currently exists for the k-DTSPN, the comparison analysis was made against the Memetic Algorithm presented in [16].

After the execution of the experiments, the largest ratio between the cost obtained by the online algorithm and the cost obtained by the offline algorithm was $\mathbf{c} \approx 1.56$. Figure 6 shows a histogram of all values of ratio found, allowing for a better comprehension of the general behavior of the algorithm.

As can be seen, the general behavior of the algorithm is better than that determined from the competitive analysis (which represents the worst case scenario), with a considerably lower average ratio value than the competitive ratio. On average, it was obtained a ratio of 1.17 (with a standard deviation of 0.12). It was performed an analysis using the T-test hypothesis test, where we verified the following hypothesis:

$$H_0 : \frac{\text{Cost}_{online}}{\text{Cost}_{offline}} = 1 \quad \text{vs.} \quad H_1 : \frac{\text{Cost}_{online}}{\text{Cost}_{offline}} > 1, \tag{11}$$

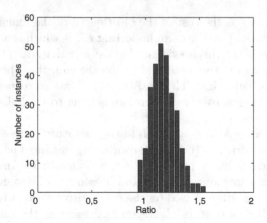

Fig. 6. Competitive ratio histogram for results obtained by the online algorithm (proposed methodology) compared to an offline method (Memetic Algorithm [16]).

where the null hypothesis is the case where both algorithms possess the same performance. The result reports with statistical significance that the null hypothesis was rejected with $t(299) = 163.68$ and $p = 0$, and the ratio lies in the interval $(1.16, 1.19)$ with a 95 % confidence level.

As expected, the need to dynamically modify the path accordingly to previously unknown information will impact the overall performance (length) of the mission. However, the model used in the methodology is sufficiently robust and can handle efficiently this problem. The better load balance is shown in the fact that in most of the cases the length of the longest tour will be increased by less than 20 %, which is a competitive value.

5   Conclusion and Future Work

In this work we have introduced the k-Dynamic Dubins TSP with Neighborhoods (k-DDTSPN), which consists of dynamically planning efficient paths among regions for multiple vehicles with bounded curvature.

We proposed a decentralized auction-based technique, which uses a greedy constructive strategy to dynamically compute the cost of insertion of the new region to each path and selects the one with the minimum impact on the length.

The performance of the methodology was evaluated using the technique of competitive analysis, which verifies the ratio between the results found by an online algorithm and the optimal result obtained by an offline algorithm. We executed an empirical analysis, since the formal upper and lower bounds for the k-DDTSPN and k-DTSPN, respectively, are not known. The ratio found in the worst case was 1.56, and we used the Memetic Algorithm [16] as the offline algorithm. However, the algorithm showed a better outcome for the average case, 1.17. As can be seen, the average impact on the final outcome (length of the longest route) is reasonably small, specially due to the better load balancing among the vehicles obtained by the methodology.

Future directions include the extension of the proposed methodology to groups of heterogeneous robots (i.e., with different curvature constraints and velocities) and to environments containing obstacles, a scenario that best represents real world cases. We also intend to study possible techniques for generating smoother variations of acceleration profiles, e.g., the use of other types of curves such as clothoids.

Acknowledgments. This work was developed with the support of the Conselho Nacional de Desenvolvimento Científico e Tecnológico (CNPq), Coordenação de Aperfeiçoamento de Pessoal de Nível Superior (CAPES) and Fundação de Amparo à Pesquisa do Estado de Minas Gerais (FAPEMIG).

References

1. Applegate, D.L., Bixby, R.E., Chvatal, V., Cook, W.J.: The Traveling Salesman Problem: A Computational Study (Princeton Series in Applied Mathematics). Princeton University Press, Princeton (2007)
2. Arkin, E.M., Hassin, R.: Approximation algorithms for the geometric covering salesman problem. Discrete Appl. Math. **55**, 197–218 (1994)
3. Bhadauria, D., Tekdas, O., Isler, V.: Robotic data mules for collecting data over sparse sensor fields. J. Field Robot. **28**(3), 388–404 (2011)
4. Choi, H.L., Brunet, L., How, J.: Consensus-based decentralized auctions for robust task allocation. IEEE Trans. Robot. **25**(4), 912–926 (2009)
5. Comarela, G., Gonçalves, K., Pappa, G.L., Almeida, J., Almeida, V.: Robot routing in sparse wireless sensor networks with continuous ant colony optimization. In: Proceedings of the 13th Annual Conference Companion on Genetic and Evolutionary Computation (GECCO' 2011), pp. 599–606. ACM, New York (2011)
6. Concorde TSP Solver (2013). http://www.tsp.gatech.edu/concorde/index.html. Accessed 17-10-2013
7. Dantzig, G.B., Ramser, J.H.: The truck dispatching problem. Manage. Sci. **6**(1), 80–91 (1959)
8. Dias, M.B., Zlot, R., Kalra, N., Stentz, A.: Market-based multirobot coordination: a survey and analysis. Proc. IEEE **94**(7), 1257–1270 (2006)
9. Dubins, L.E.: On curves of minimal length with a constraint on average curvature, and with prescribed initial and terminal positions and tangents. Am. J. Math. **79**(3), 497–516 (1957)
10. Enright, J.J., Savla, K., Frazzoli, E., Bullo, F.: Stochastic and dynamic routing problems for multiple UAVs. AIAA J. Guidance, Control, Dyn. 32(4), 1152–1166 (2009)
11. Isaacs, J.T., Klein, D.J., Hespanha, J.P.: Algorithms for the traveling salesman problem with neighborhoods involving a dubins vehicle. In: Proceedings of the IEE American Control Conference (ACC' 2011), pp. 1704–1709 (2011)
12. Larsen, A., Madsen, O.B., Solomon, M.M.: Recent developments in dynamic vehicle routing systems. In: Golden, B., Raghavan, S., Wasil, E., Sharda, R., Voß, S. (eds.) The Vehicle Routing Problem: Latest Advances and New Challenges, Operations Research/Computer Science Interfaces Series, vol. 43, pp. 199–218. Springer, US (2008)

13. Le Ny, J., Frazzoli, E., Feron, E.: The curvature-constrained traveling salesman problem for high point densities. In: Proceedings of the 46th IEEE Conference on Decision and Control (CDC' 2007), pp. 5985–5990 (2007)

14. Ma, X., Castañón, D.A.: Receding horizon planning for dubins traveling salesman problems. In: Proceedings of the 45th IEEE Conference on Decision and Control (CDC' 2006), pp. 5453–5458 (2006)

15. Macharet, D.G., Alves Neto, A., da Camara Neto, V.F., Campos, M.F.M.: An evolutionary approach for the Dubins' traveling salesman problem with neighborhoods. In: Proceedings of the 21th Genetic and Evolutionary Computation Conference (2012)

16. Macharet, D.G., Alves Neto, A., da Camara Neto, V.F., Campos, M.F.M.: Efficient target visiting path planning for multiple vehicles with bounded curvature. In: Proceedings of the IEEE/RSJ International Conference on Intelligent Robots and Systems (IROS), pp. 3830–3836 (2013)

17. Michael, N., Zavlanos, M., Kumar, V., Pappas, G.: Distributed multi-robot task assignment and formation control. In: Proceedings of the IEEE International Conference on Robotics and Automation (ICRA' 2008), pp. 128–133 (2008)

18. Obermeyer, K.J., Oberlin, P., Darbha, S.: Sampling-based roadmap methods for a visual reconnaissance UAV. In: Proceedings of the AIAA Conference on Guidance, Navigation and Control, Toronto, ON, Canada (2010)

19. Rathinam, S., Sengupta, R., Darbha, S.: A resource allocation algorithm for multivehicle systems with nonholonomic constraints. IEEE Trans. Autom. Sci. Eng. 4(1), 98–104 (2007)

20. Savla, K., Bullo, F., Frazzoli, E.: On traveling salesperson problems for Dubins' vehicle: stochastic and dynamic environments. In: Proceedings of the 44th IEEE Conference on Decision and Control and European Control Conference (CDC-ECC' 2005), pp. 4530–4535 (2005)

21. Savla, K., Frazzoli, E., Bullo, F.: On the point-to-point and traveling salesperson problems for Dubins' vehicle. In: Proceedings of the IEE American Control Conference (ACC' 2005), vol. 2, pp. 786–791 (2005)

22. Savla, K., Frazzoli, E., Bullo, F.: Traveling salesperson problems for the Dubins vehicle. IEEE Trans. Autom. Control 53(6), 1378–1391 (2008)

23. Sleator, D.D., Tarjan, R.E.: Amortized efficiency of list update and paging rules. Commun. ACM 28(2), 202–208 (1985)

24. Solomon, M.M.: Algorithms for the vehicle routing and scheduling problems with time window constraints. Oper. Res. 35(2), 254–265 (1987). http://dx.doi.org/10.1287/opre.35.2.254

25. Tang, Z., Özgüner, Ü.: Motion planning for multitarget surveillance with mobile sensor agents. IEEE Trans. Robot. 21(5), 898–908 (2005)

26. Tekdas, O., Isler, V., Lim, J., Terzis, A.: Using mobile robots to harvest data from sensor fields. IEEE Wireless Commun. 16(1), 22–28 (2009)

27. Toth, P., Vigo, D. (eds.): The Vehicle Routing Problem. Society for Industrial and Applied Mathematics, Philadelphia (2001)

28. Yuan, B., Orlowska, M., Sadiq, S.: On the optimal robot routing problem in wireless sensor networks. IEEE Trans. Knowl. Data Eng. 19(9), 1252–1261 (2007)

29. Zavlanos, M., Spesivtsev, L., Pappas, G.: A distributed auction algorithm for the assignment problem. In: Proceedings of the 47th IEEE Conference on Decision and Control (CDC' 2008), pp. 1212–1217 (2008)

Author Index

Printed in the United States
By Bookmasters